FROM THE PAGES OF PROJECT SUPERPOWERS ™

BLACK TERROR ®

VOLUME THREE

STORY ALEX ROSS & PHIL HESTER

SCRIPT PHIL HESTER

ART WAGNER REIS (ISSUES 10-11) & JACK HERBERT (ISSUES 12-14)

COLORS IVAN NUNES

LETTERS SIMON BOWLAND

COVERS & ART DIRECTION ALEX ROSS

CONTRIBUTING EDITOR JOSEPH RYBANDT

COLLECTION DESIGN JASON ULLMEYER

SPECIAL THANKS TO T.J. ROSS & BRIAN HOFACKER

THIS VOLUME COLLECTS ISSUES 10-14 OF BLACK TERROR.

First Printing   ISBN-10: 1-60690-234-2   ISBN-13: 978-1-60690-234-9   10 9 8 7 6 5 4 3 2 1

ENTERTAINMENT

WWW.DYNAMITE.NET

NICK BARRUCCI   •   PRESIDENT
JUAN COLLADO   •   CHIEF OPERATING OFFICER
JOSEPH RYBANDT   •   EDITOR
JOSH JOHNSON   •   CREATIVE DIRECTOR
RICH YOUNG   •   DIR. BUSINESS MANAGEMENT
JASON ULLMEYER   •   SENIOR DESIGNER
JOSH GREEN   •   TRAFFIC COORDINATOR
CHRIS CANIANO   •   PRODUCTION ASSISTANT

For information regarding press, media rights, foreign rights, licensing, promotions, and advertising e-mail:
marketing@dynamite.net

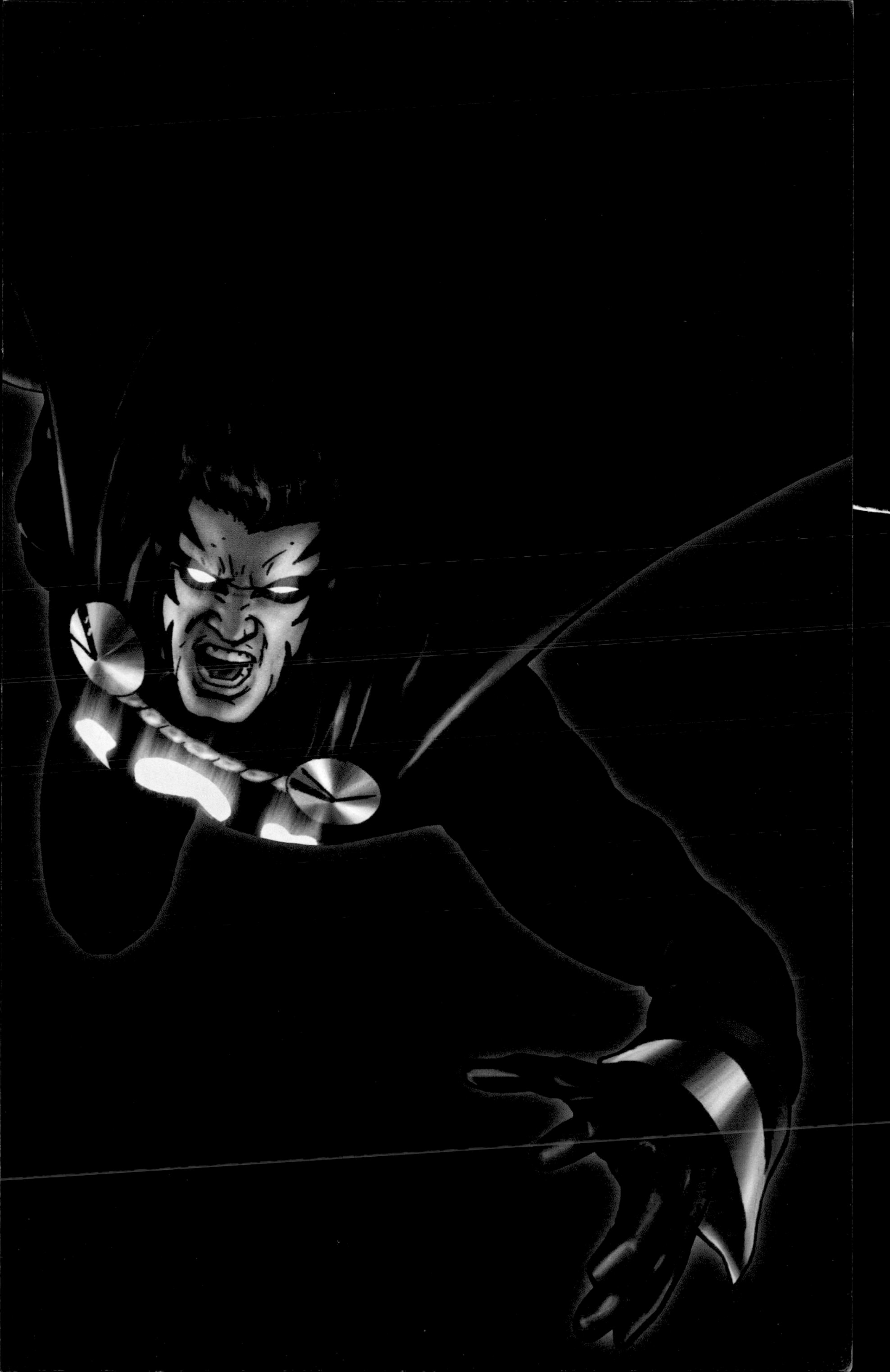

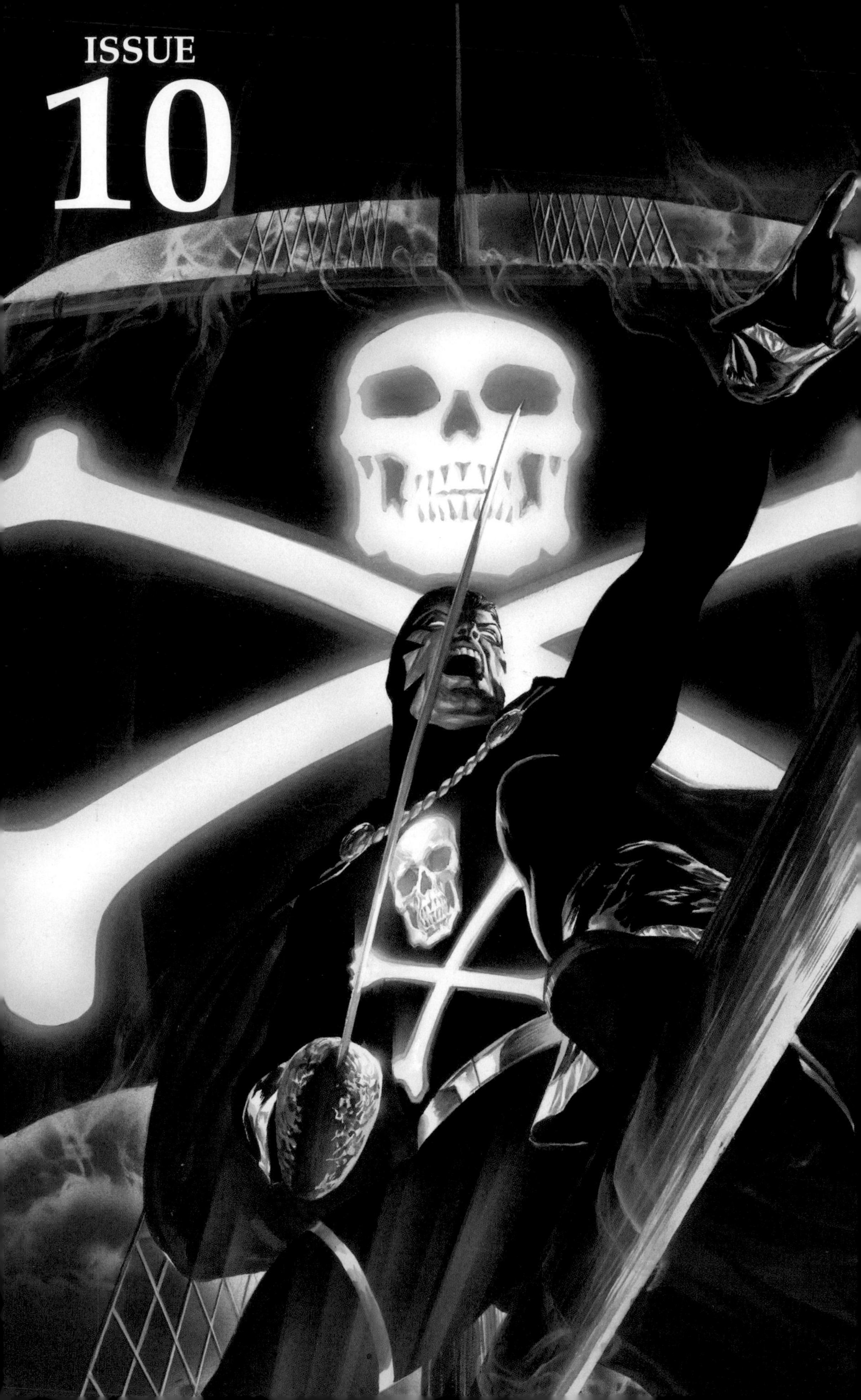
ISSUE
10

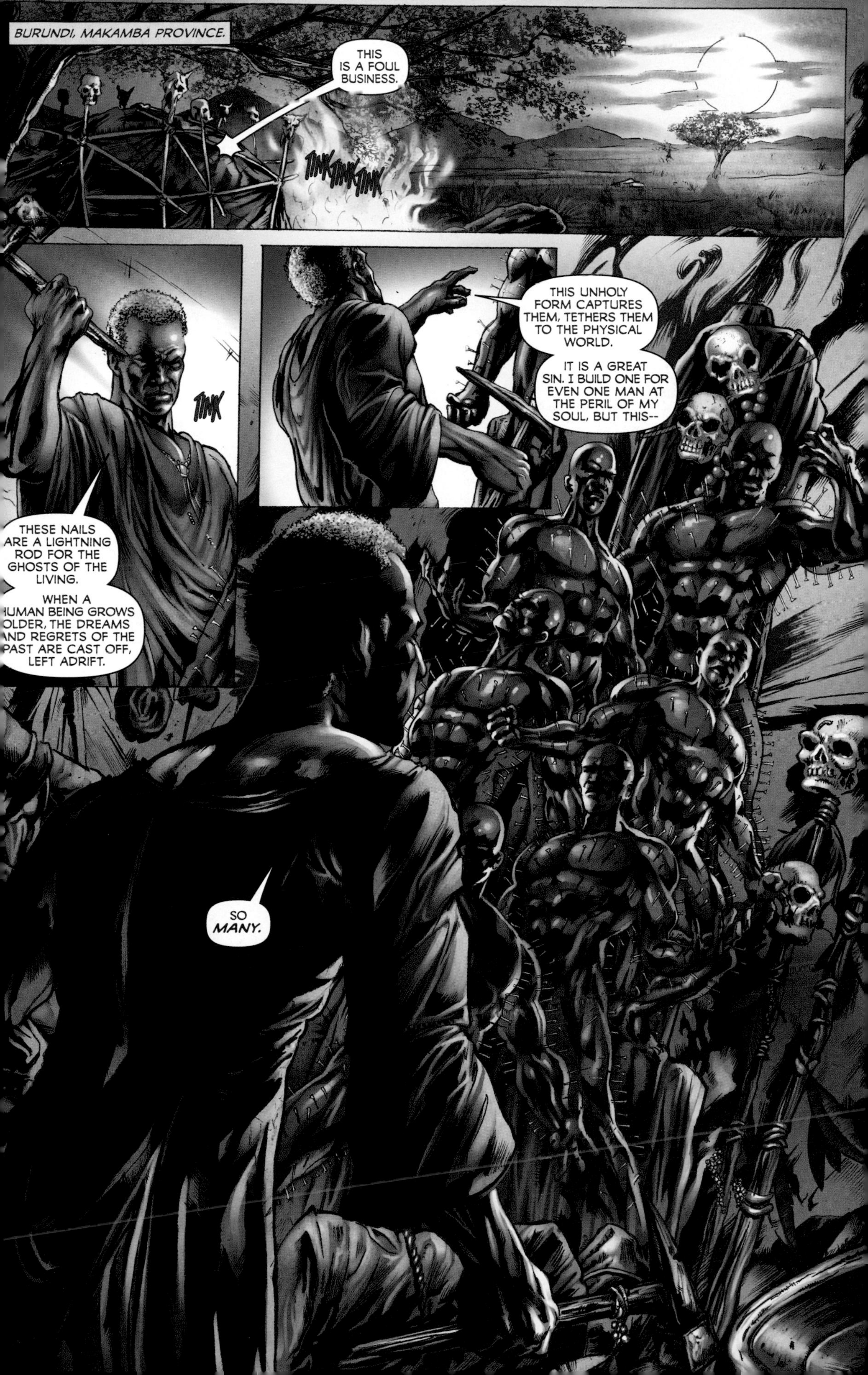
BURUNDI, MAKAMBA PROVINCE.
THIS IS A FOUL BUSINESS.
TINK TINK TINK
TINK
THESE NAILS ARE A LIGHTNING ROD FOR THE GHOSTS OF THE LIVING.
WHEN A HUMAN BEING GROWS OLDER, THE DREAMS AND REGRETS OF THE PAST ARE CAST OFF, LEFT ADRIFT.
THIS UNHOLY FORM CAPTURES THEM, TETHERS THEM TO THE PHYSICAL WORLD.
IT IS A GREAT SIN. I BUILD ONE FOR EVEN ONE MAN AT THE PERIL OF MY SOUL, BUT THIS--
SO MANY.

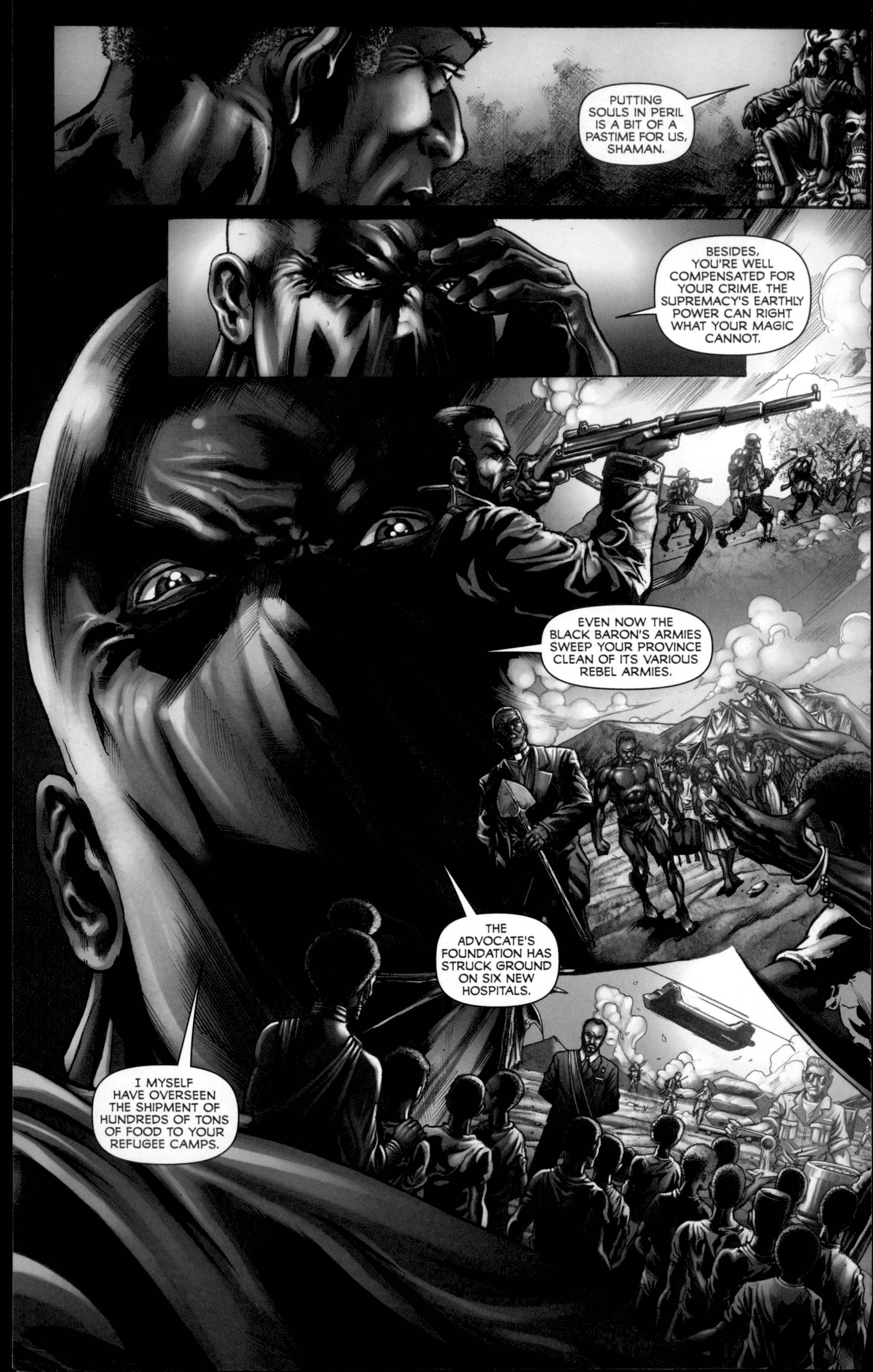
PUTTING SOULS IN PERIL IS A BIT OF A PASTIME FOR US, SHAMAN.
BESIDES, YOU'RE WELL COMPENSATED FOR YOUR CRIME. THE SUPREMACY'S EARTHLY POWER CAN RIGHT WHAT YOUR MAGIC CANNOT.
EVEN NOW THE BLACK BARON'S ARMIES SWEEP YOUR PROVINCE CLEAN OF ITS VARIOUS REBEL ARMIES.
THE ADVOCATE'S FOUNDATION HAS STRUCK GROUND ON SIX NEW HOSPITALS.
I MYSELF HAVE OVERSEEN THE SHIPMENT OF HUNDREDS OF TONS OF FOOD TO YOUR REFUGEE CAMPS.

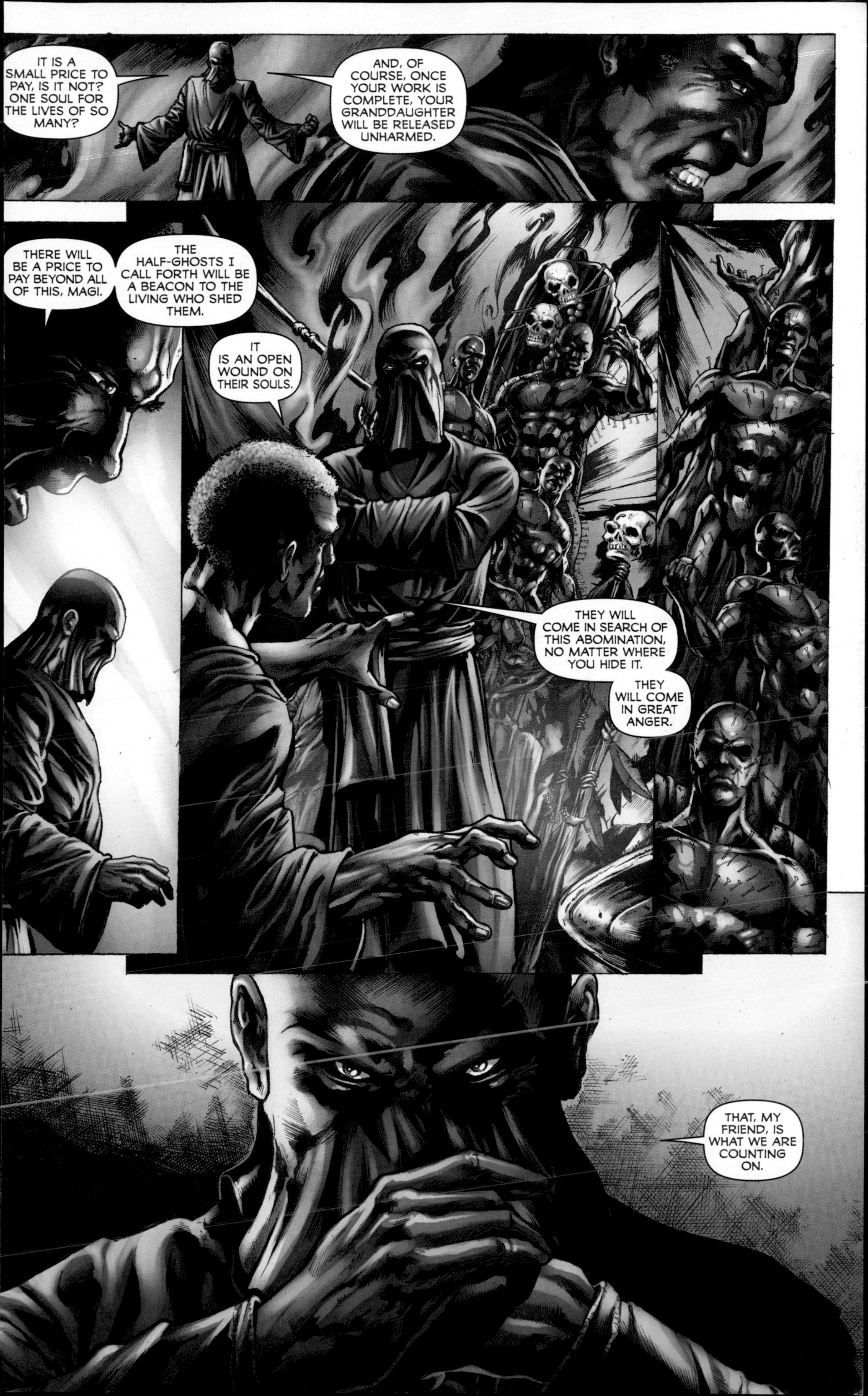
IT IS A SMALL PRICE TO PAY, IS IT NOT? ONE SOUL FOR THE LIVES OF SO MANY?
AND, OF COURSE, ONCE YOUR WORK IS COMPLETE, YOUR GRANDDAUGHTER WILL BE RELEASED UNHARMED.
THERE WILL BE A PRICE TO PAY BEYOND ALL OF THIS, MAGI.
THE HALF-GHOSTS I CALL FORTH WILL BE A BEACON TO THE LIVING WHO SHED THEM.
IT IS AN OPEN WOUND ON THEIR SOULS.
THEY WILL COME IN SEARCH OF THIS ABOMINATION, NO MATTER WHERE YOU HIDE IT.
THEY WILL COME IN GREAT ANGER.
THAT, MY FRIEND, IS WHAT WE ARE COUNTING ON.

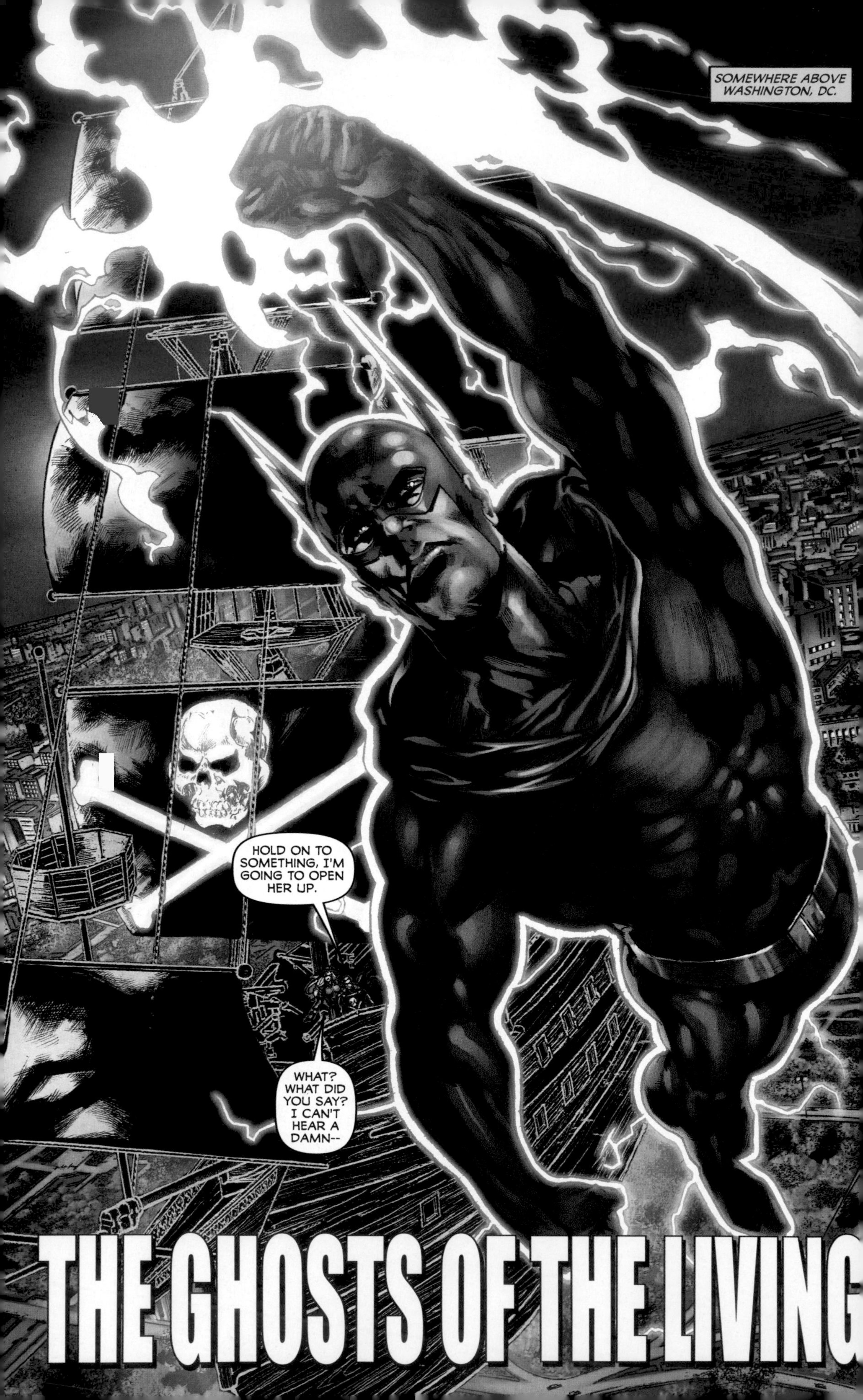
SOMEWHERE ABOVE WASHINGTON, DC.
HOLD ON TO SOMETHING, I'M GOING TO OPEN HER UP.
WHAT? WHAT DID YOU SAY? I CAN'T HEAR A DAMN--
THE GHOSTS OF THE LIVING

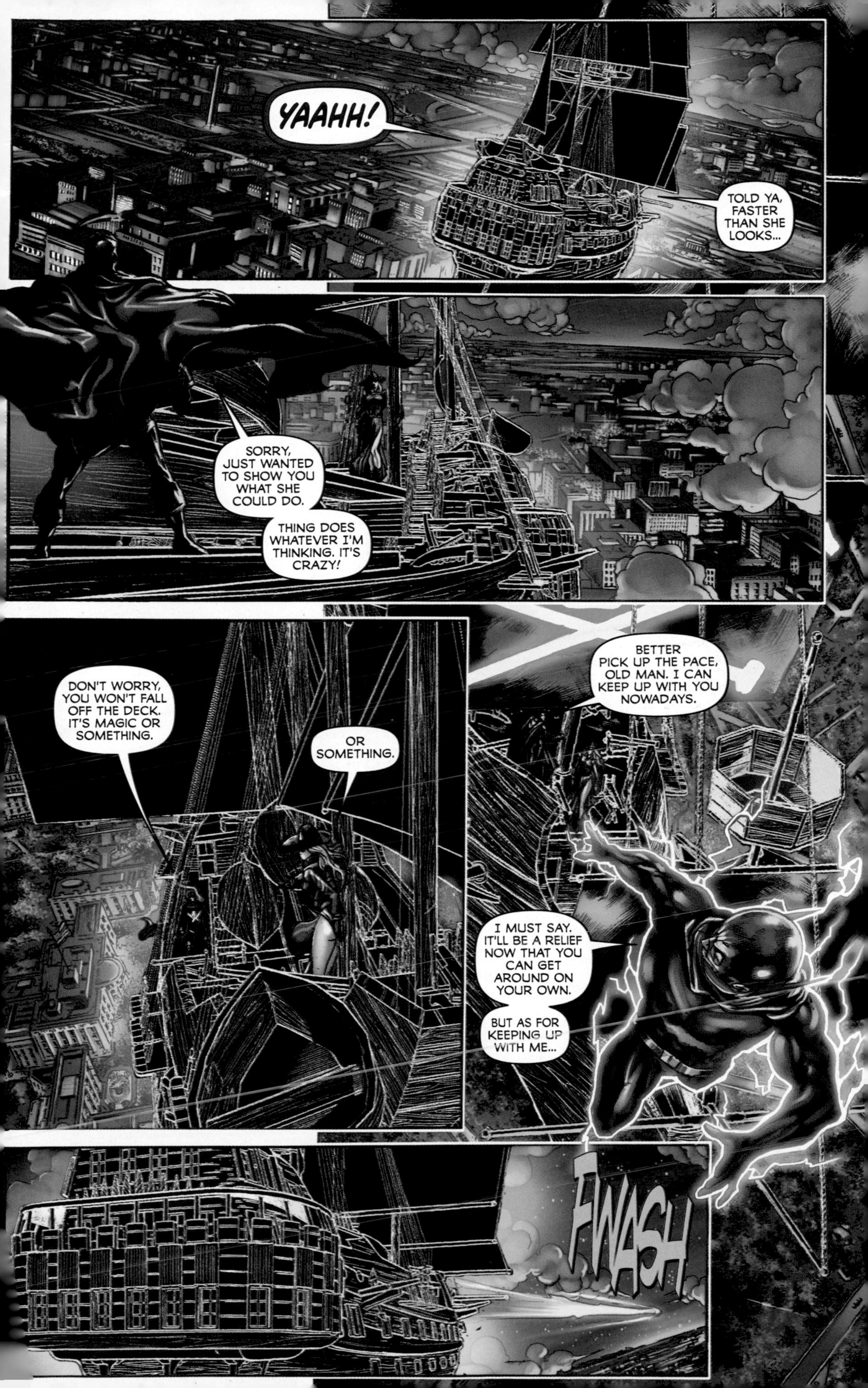
YAAHH!
TOLD YA, FASTER THAN SHE LOOKS...
SORRY, JUST WANTED TO SHOW YOU WHAT SHE COULD DO.
THING DOES WHATEVER I'M THINKING. IT'S CRAZY!
DON'T WORRY, YOU WON'T FALL OFF THE DECK. IT'S MAGIC OR SOMETHING.
OR SOMETHING.
BETTER PICK UP THE PACE, OLD MAN. I CAN KEEP UP WITH YOU NOWADAYS.
I MUST SAY. IT'LL BE A RELIEF NOW THAT YOU CAN GET AROUND ON YOUR OWN.
BUT AS FOR KEEPING UP WITH ME...
FWASH

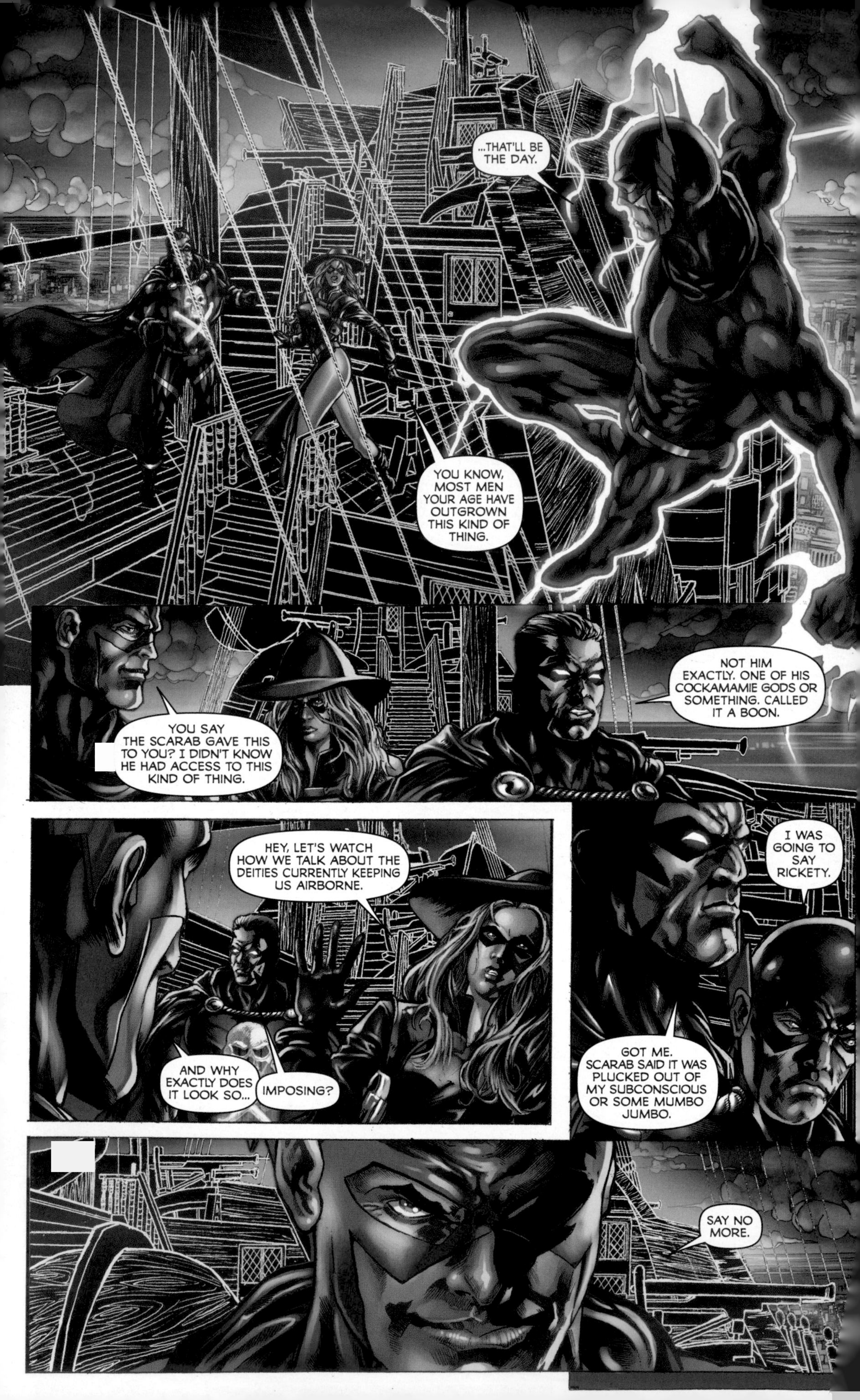
YOU KNOW, MOST MEN YOUR AGE HAVE OUTGROWN THIS KIND OF THING.
...THAT'LL BE THE DAY.
YOU SAY THE SCARAB GAVE THIS TO YOU? I DIDN'T KNOW HE HAD ACCESS TO THIS KIND OF THING.
NOT HIM EXACTLY. ONE OF HIS COCKAMAMIE GODS OR SOMETHING. CALLED IT A BOON.
AND WHY EXACTLY DOES IT LOOK SO...
IMPOSING?
HEY, LET'S WATCH HOW WE TALK ABOUT THE DEITIES CURRENTLY KEEPING US AIRBORNE.
I WAS GOING TO SAY RICKETY.
GOT ME. SCARAB SAID IT WAS PLUCKED OUT OF MY SUBCONSCIOUS OR SOME MUMBO JUMBO.
SAY NO MORE.

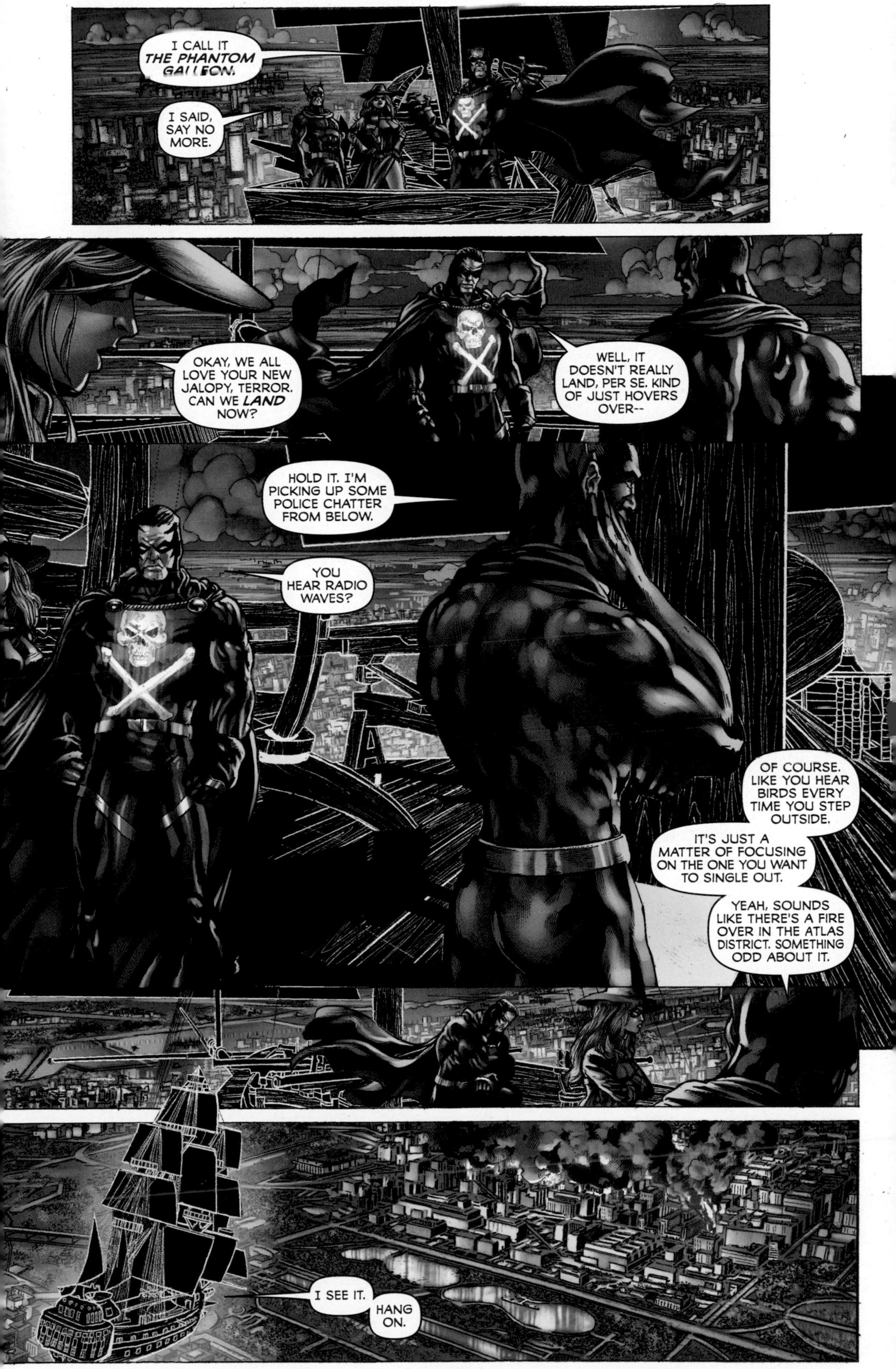
I CALL IT THE PHANTOM GALLEON.
I SAID, SAY NO MORE.
OKAY, WE ALL LOVE YOUR NEW JALOPY, TERROR. CAN WE LAND NOW?
WELL, IT DOESN'T REALLY LAND, PER SE. KIND OF JUST HOVERS OVER--
HOLD IT. I'M PICKING UP SOME POLICE CHATTER FROM BELOW.
YOU HEAR RADIO WAVES?
OF COURSE. LIKE YOU HEAR BIRDS EVERY TIME YOU STEP OUTSIDE.
IT'S JUST A MATTER OF FOCUSING ON THE ONE YOU WANT TO SINGLE OUT.
YEAH, SOUNDS LIKE THERE'S A FIRE OVER IN THE ATLAS DISTRICT. SOMETHING ODD ABOUT IT.
I SEE IT.
HANG ON.

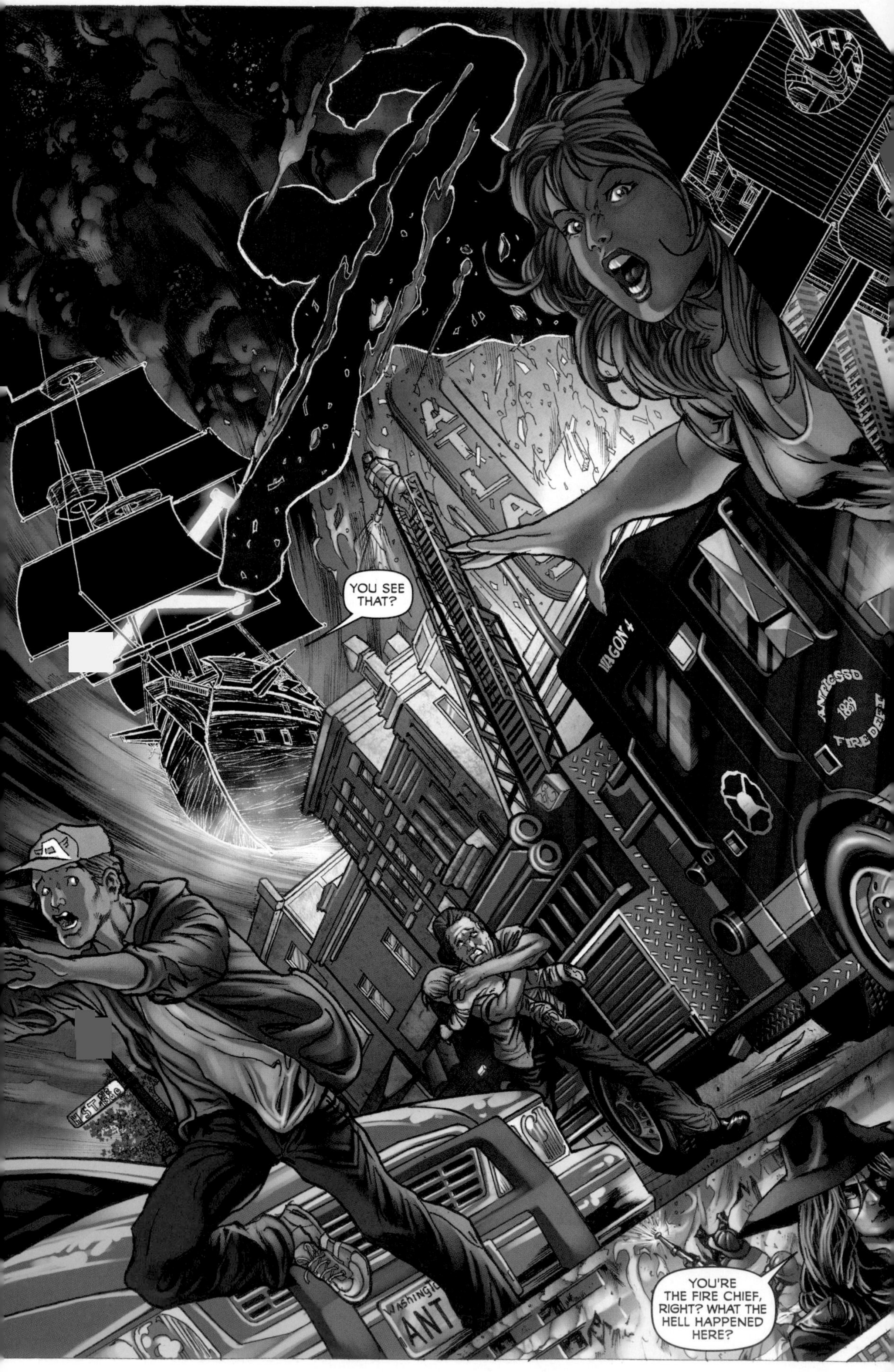
YOU SEE THAT?
YOU'RE THE FIRE CHIEF, RIGHT? WHAT THE HELL HAPPENED HERE?

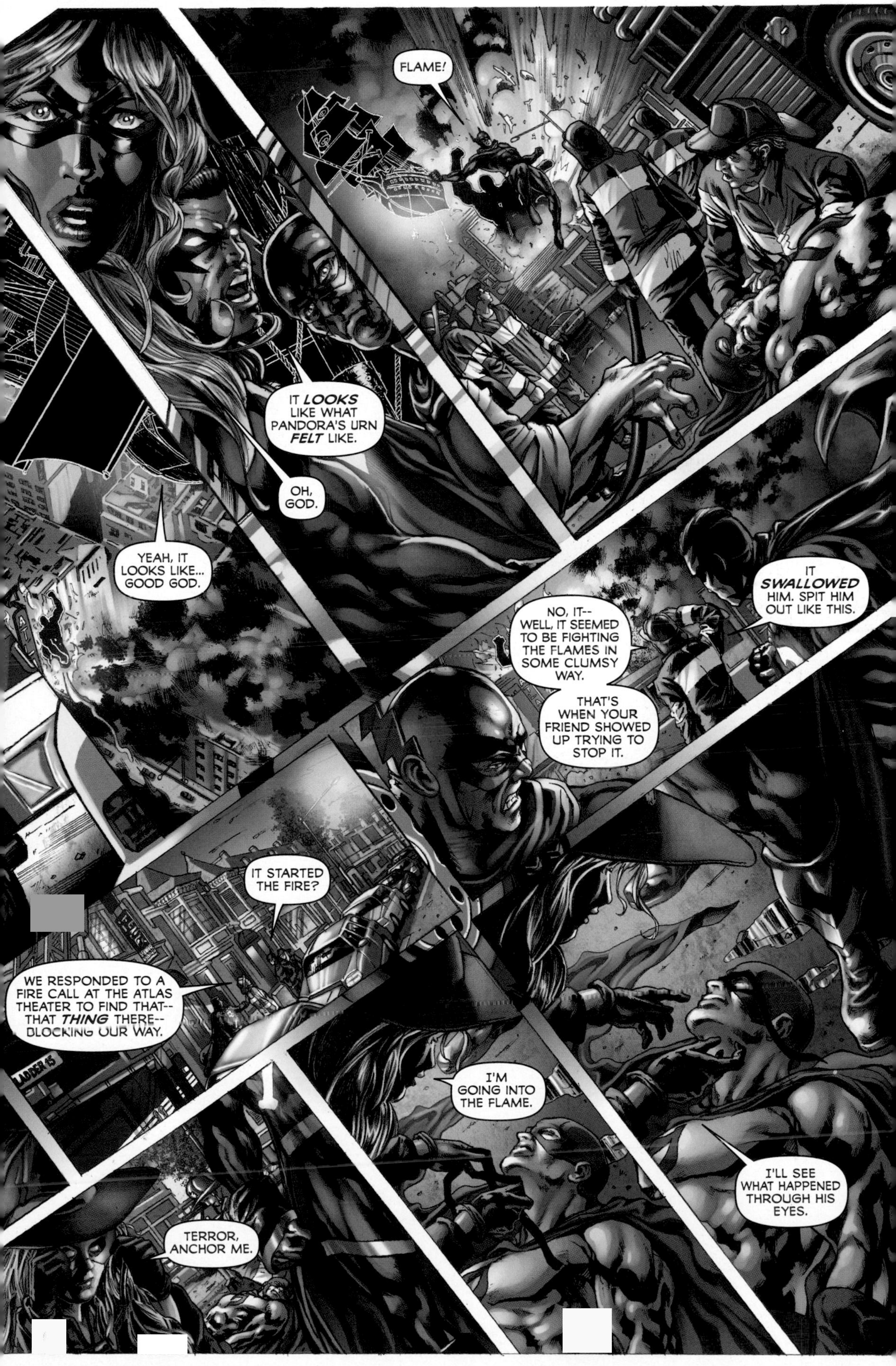
FLAME!
IT LOOKS LIKE WHAT PANDORA'S URN FELT LIKE.
OH, GOD.
YEAH, IT LOOKS LIKE... GOOD GOD.
WE RESPONDED TO A FIRE CALL AT THE ATLAS THEATER TO FIND THAT-- THAT THING THERE-- BLOCKING OUR WAY.
IT STARTED THE FIRE?
NO, IT-- WELL, IT SEEMED TO BE FIGHTING THE FLAMES IN SOME CLUMSY WAY.
THAT'S WHEN YOUR FRIEND SHOWED UP TRYING TO STOP IT.
IT SWALLOWED HIM. SPIT HIM OUT LIKE THIS.
LADDER 45
TERROR, ANCHOR ME.
I'M GOING INTO THE FLAME.
I'LL SEE WHAT HAPPENED THROUGH HIS EYES.

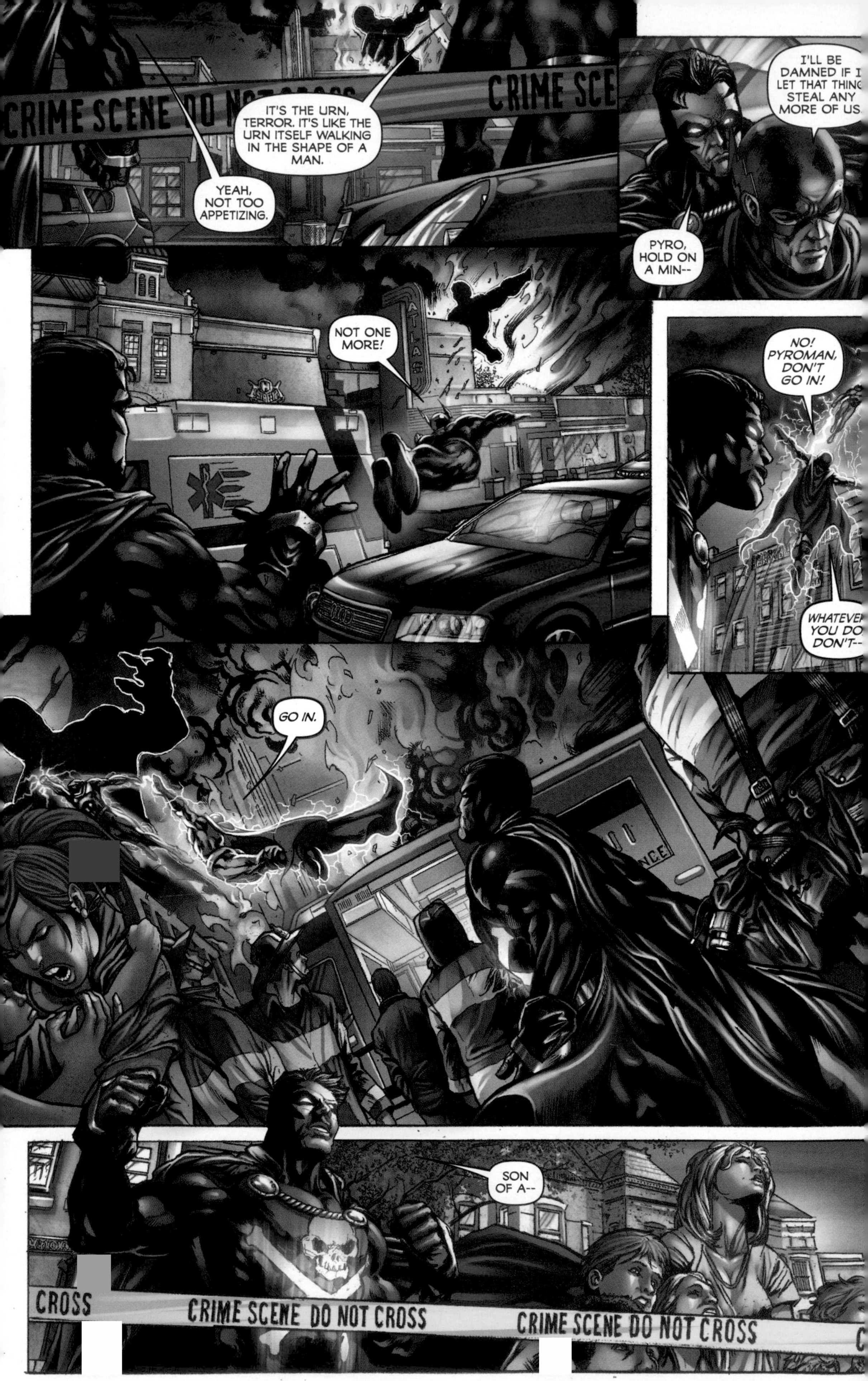
CRIME SCENE DO NO
IT'S THE URN, TERROR. IT'S LIKE THE URN ITSELF WALKING IN THE SHAPE OF A MAN.
YEAH, NOT TOO APPETIZING.
CRIME SCE
I'LL BE DAMNED IF I LET THAT THING STEAL ANY MORE OF US.
PYRO, HOLD ON A MIN--
NOT ONE MORE!
ATLAS
NO! PYROMAN, DON'T GO IN!
WHATEVE YOU DO DON'T--
GO IN.
SON OF A--
CROSS
CRIME SCENE DO NOT CROSS
CRIME SCENE DO NOT CROSS

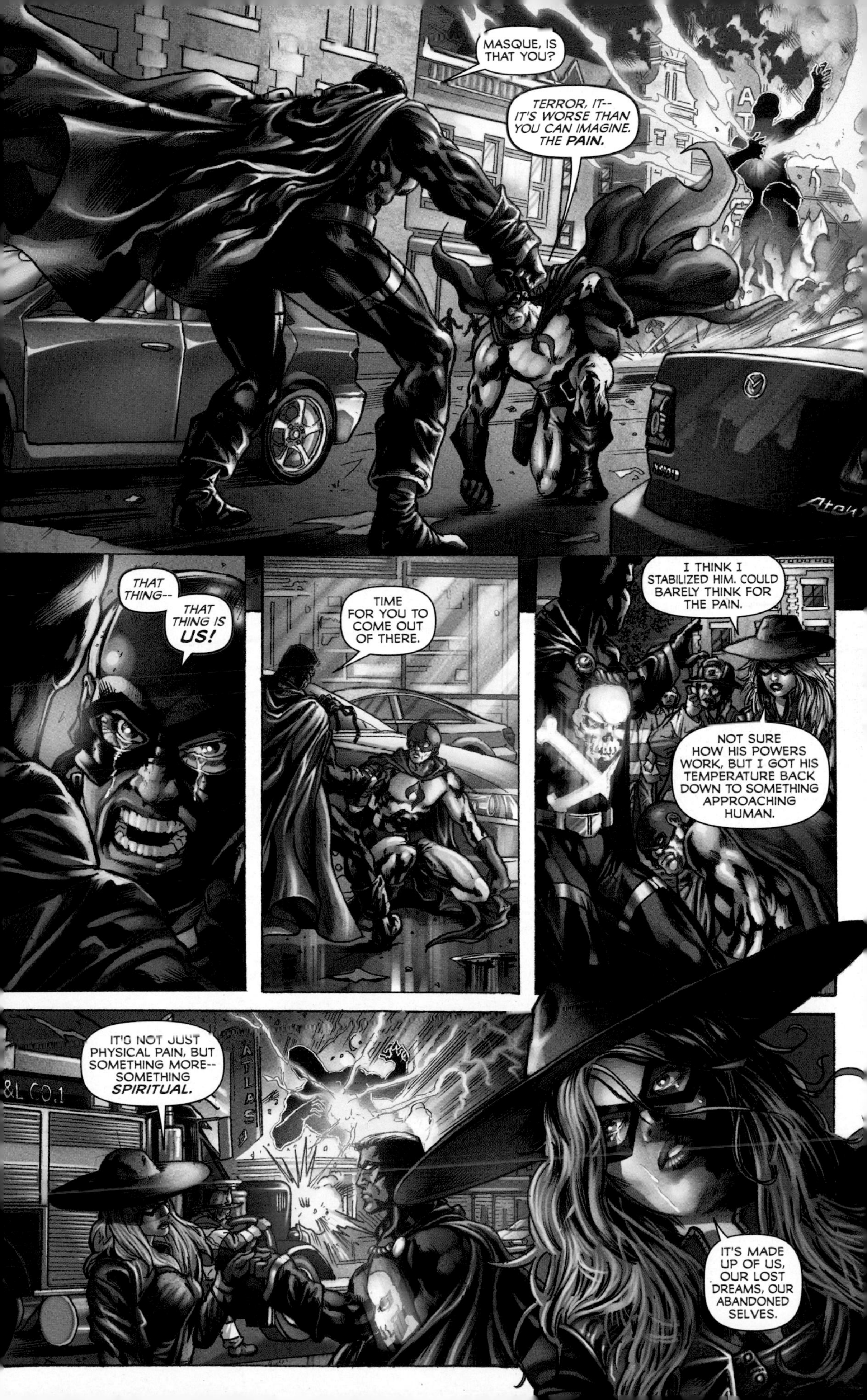
MASQUE, IS THAT YOU?
TERROR, IT-- IT'S WORSE THAN YOU CAN IMAGINE. THE PAIN.
THAT THING-- THAT THING IS US!
TIME FOR YOU TO COME OUT OF THERE.
I THINK I STABILIZED HIM. COULD BARELY THINK FOR THE PAIN.
NOT SURE HOW HIS POWERS WORK, BUT I GOT HIS TEMPERATURE BACK DOWN TO SOMETHING APPROACHING HUMAN.
IT'S NOT JUST PHYSICAL PAIN, BUT SOMETHING MORE-- SOMETHING SPIRITUAL.
ATLAS
&L CO.1
IT'S MADE UP OF US, OUR LOST DREAMS, OUR ABANDONED SELVES.

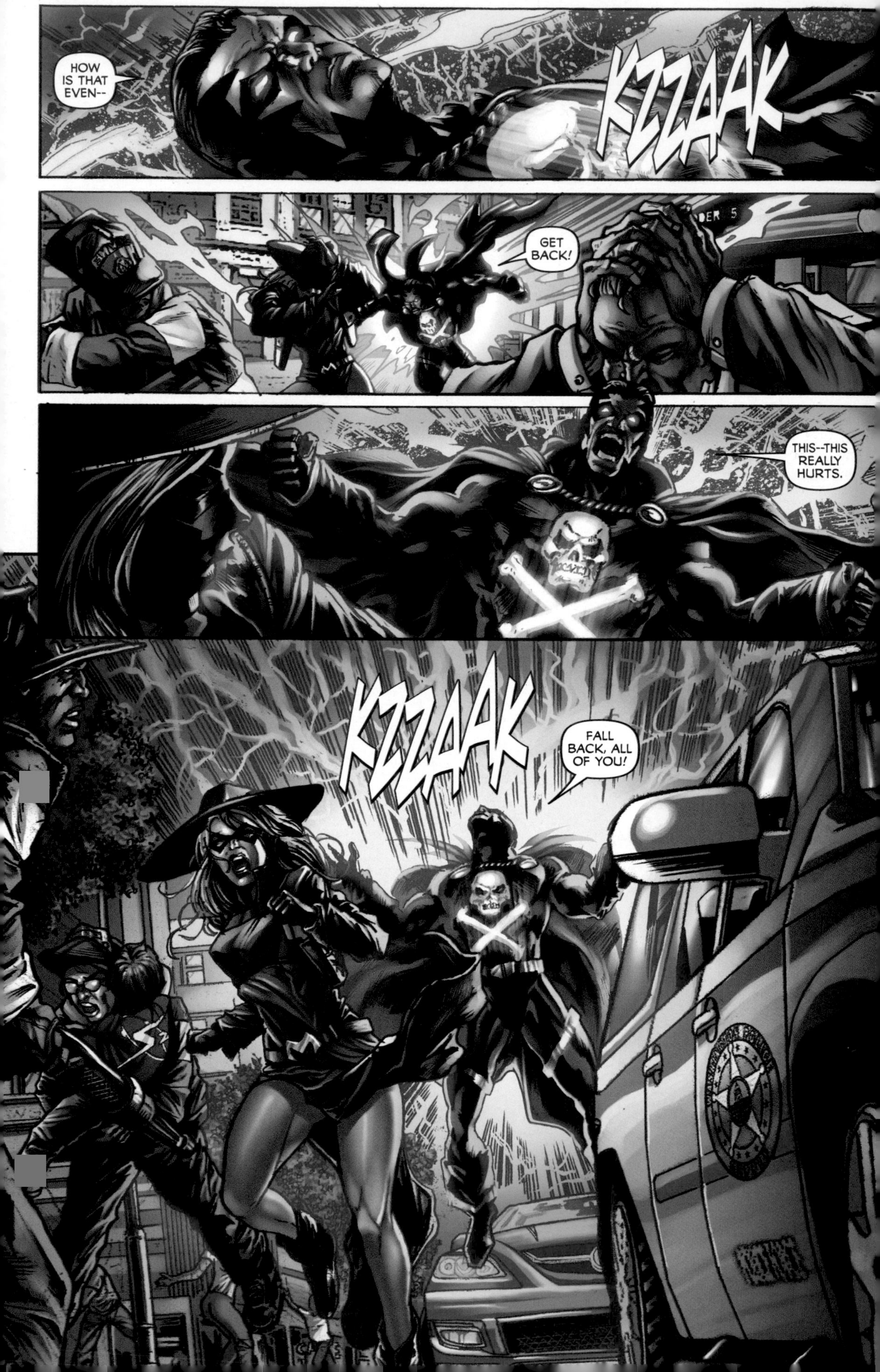
HOW IS THAT EVEN--
KZZAAK
GET BACK!
THIS--THIS REALLY HURTS.
KZZAAK
FALL BACK, ALL OF YOU!

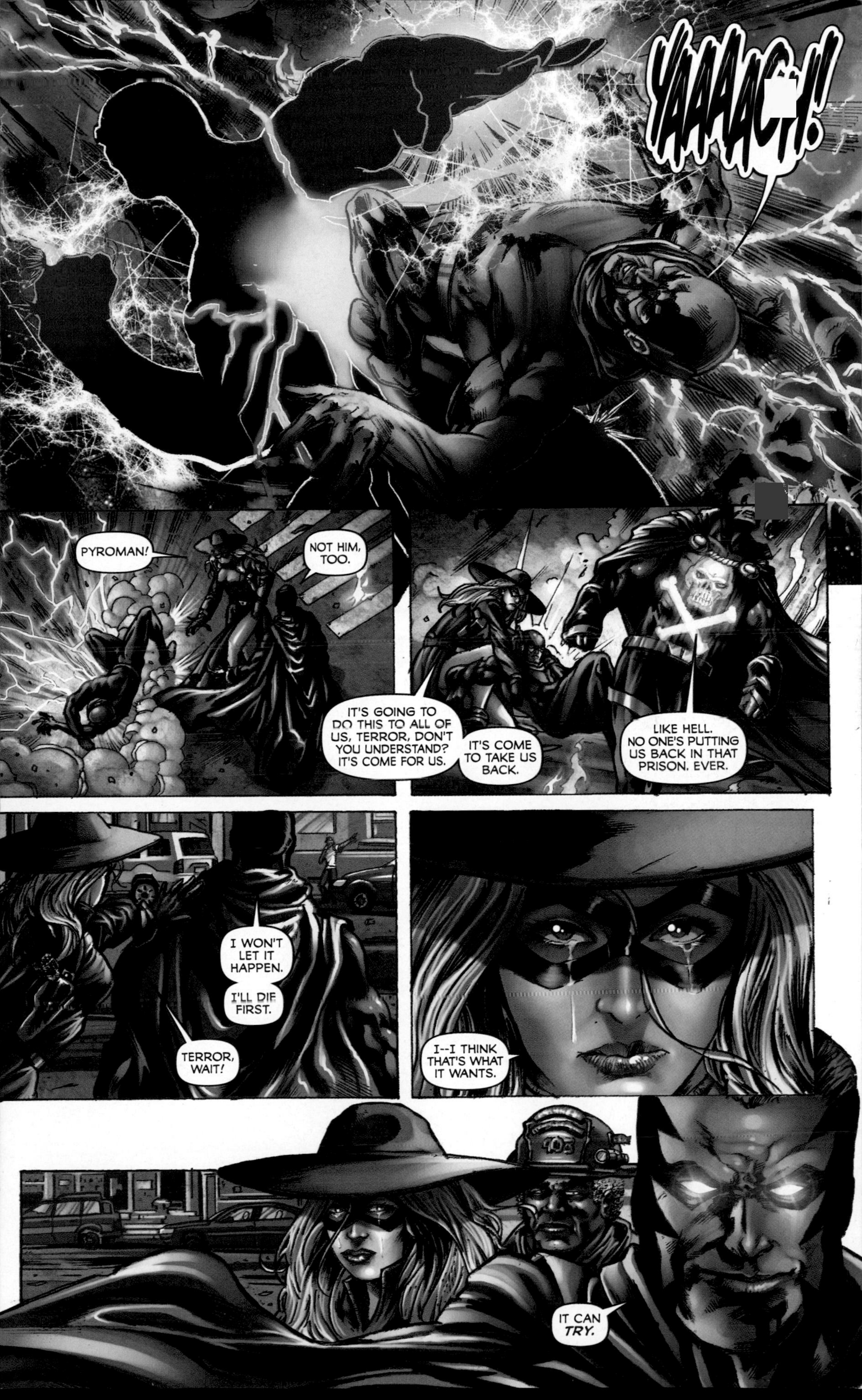
PYROMAN!
NOT HIM, TOO.
IT'S GOING TO DO THIS TO ALL OF US, TERROR, DON'T YOU UNDERSTAND? IT'S COME FOR US.
IT'S COME TO TAKE US BACK.
LIKE HELL. NO ONE'S PUTTING US BACK IN THAT PRISON. EVER.
I WON'T LET IT HAPPEN.
I'LL DIE FIRST.
TERROR, WAIT!
I--I THINK THAT'S WHAT IT WANTS.
IT CAN TRY.

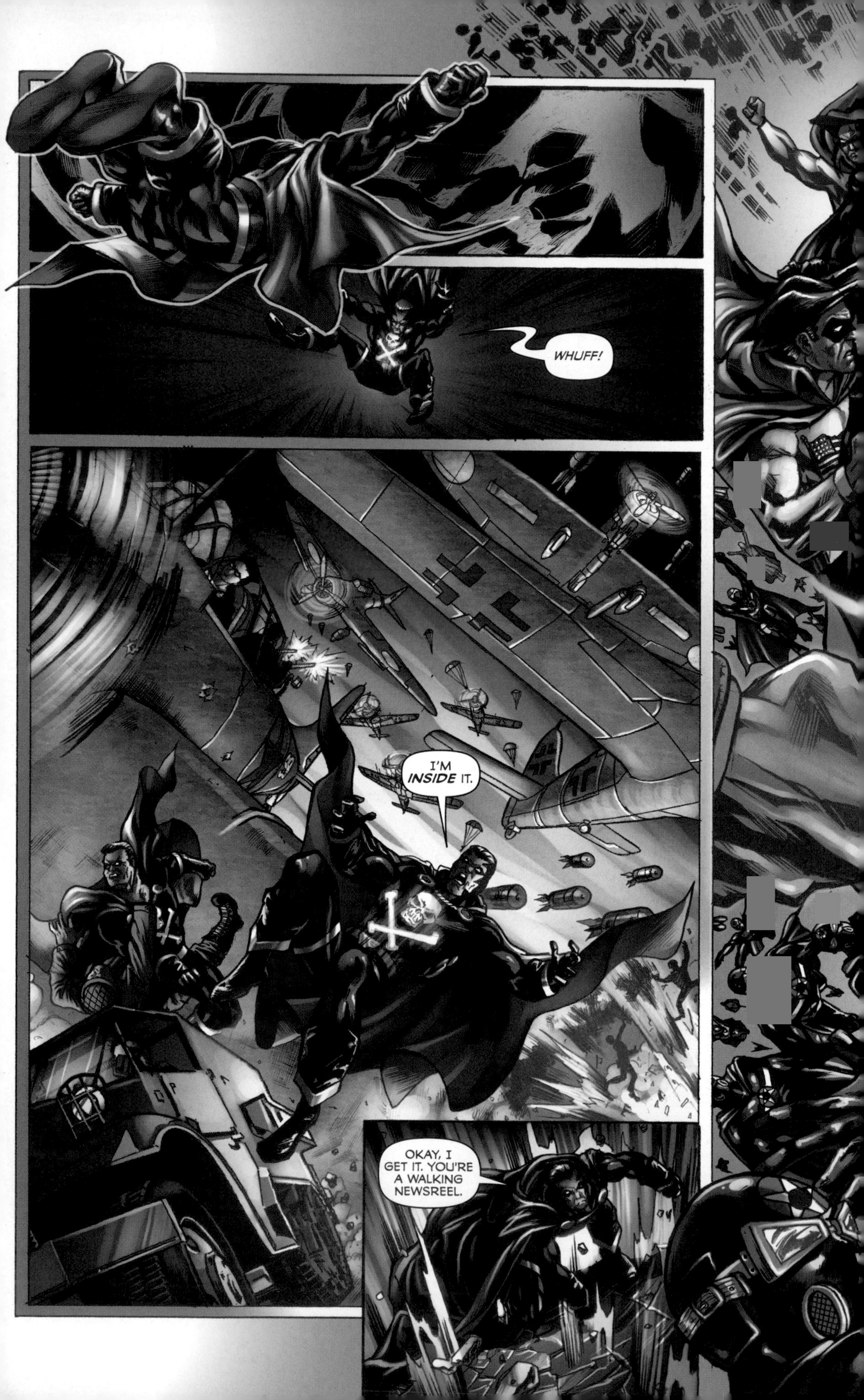
WHUFF!
I'M *INSIDE* IT.
OKAY, I GET IT. YOU'RE A WALKING NEWSREEL.

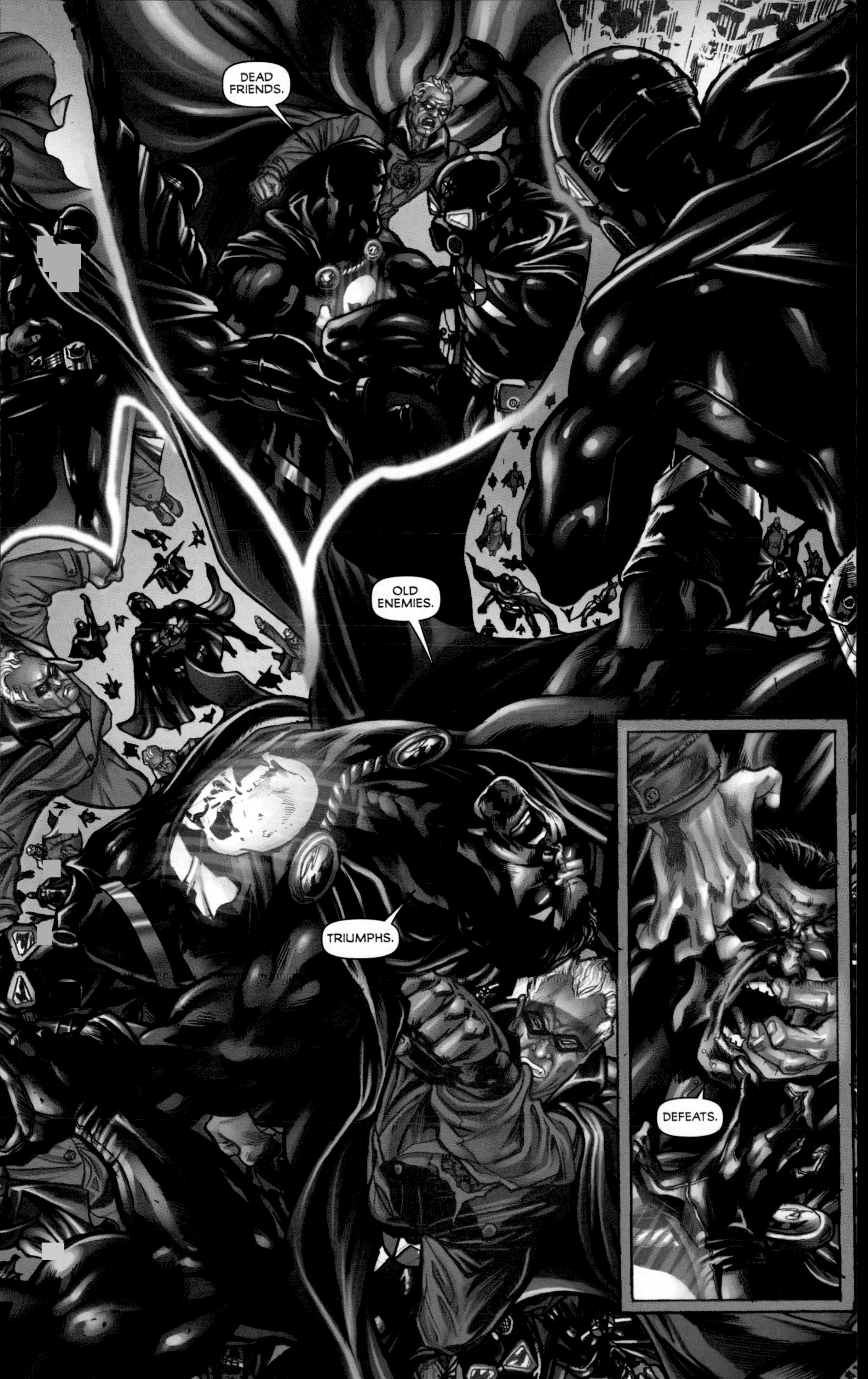
DEAD FRIENDS.
OLD ENEMIES.
TRIUMPHS.
DEFEATS.

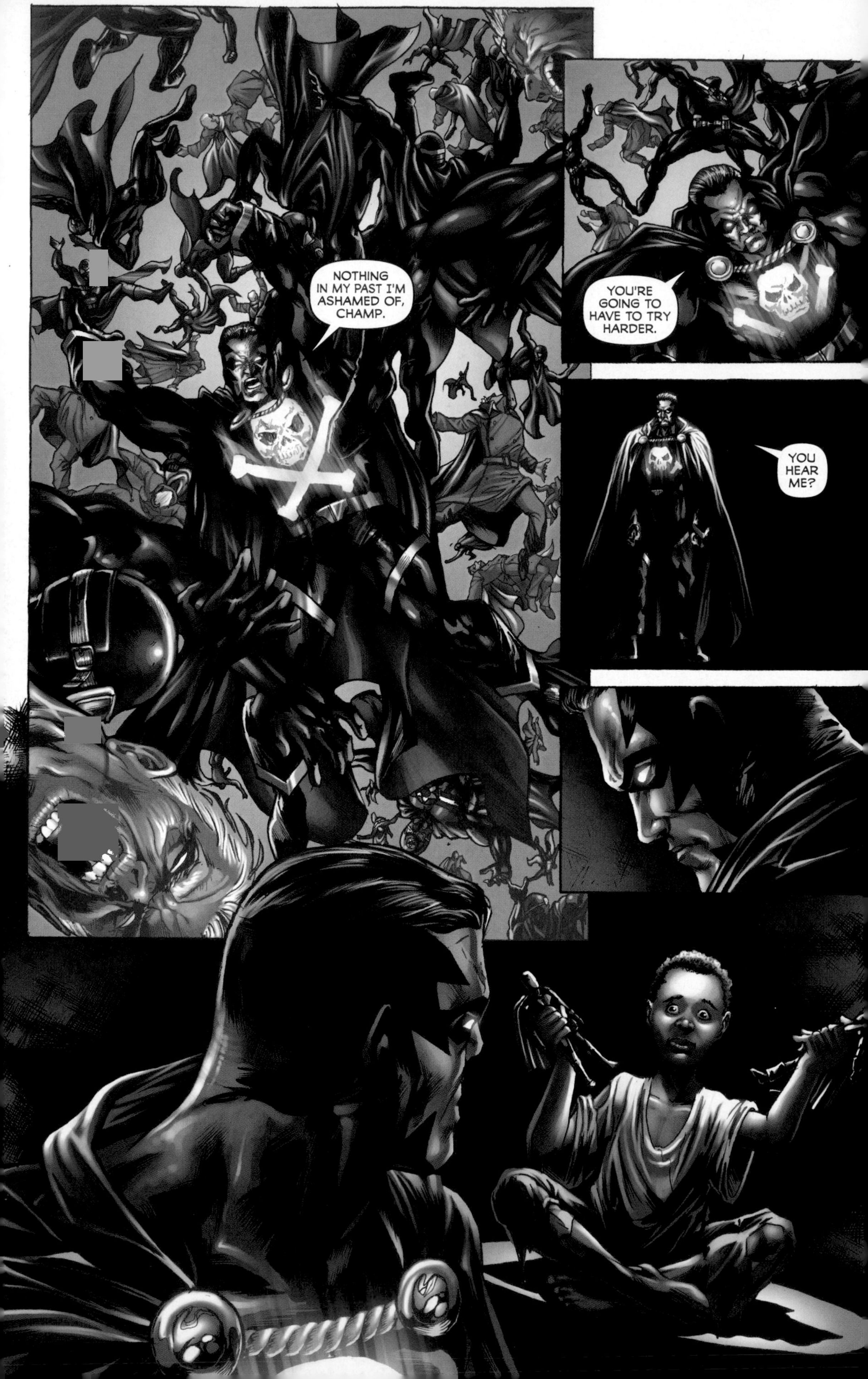
NOTHING IN MY PAST I'M ASHAMED OF, CHAMP.
YOU'RE GOING TO HAVE TO TRY HARDER.
YOU HEAR ME?

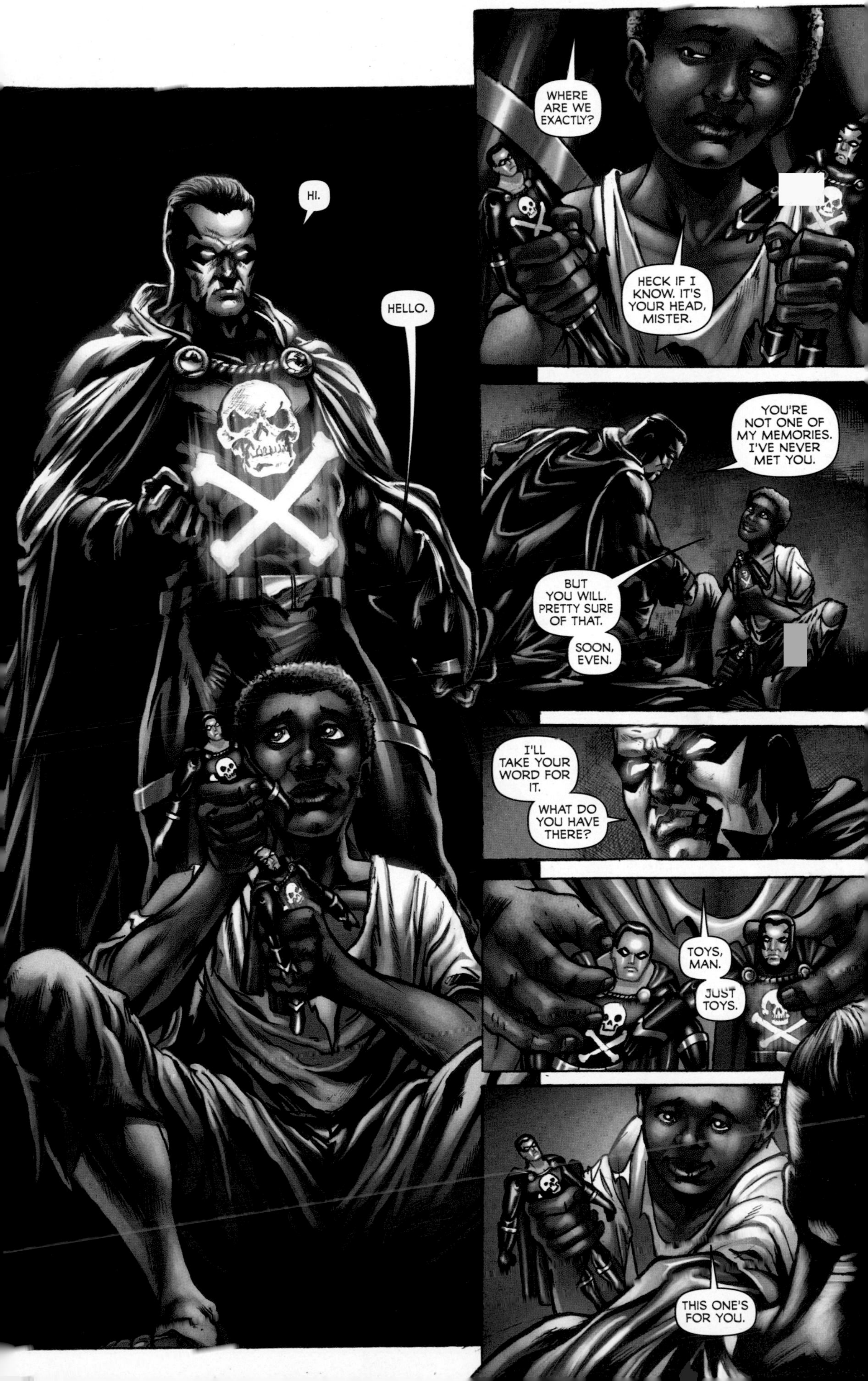
HI.
HELLO.
WHERE ARE WE EXACTLY?
HECK IF I KNOW. IT'S YOUR HEAD, MISTER.
YOU'RE NOT ONE OF MY MEMORIES. I'VE NEVER MET YOU.
BUT YOU WILL. PRETTY SURE OF THAT.
SOON, EVEN.
I'LL TAKE YOUR WORD FOR IT.
WHAT DO YOU HAVE THERE?
TOYS, MAN.
JUST TOYS.
THIS ONE'S FOR YOU.

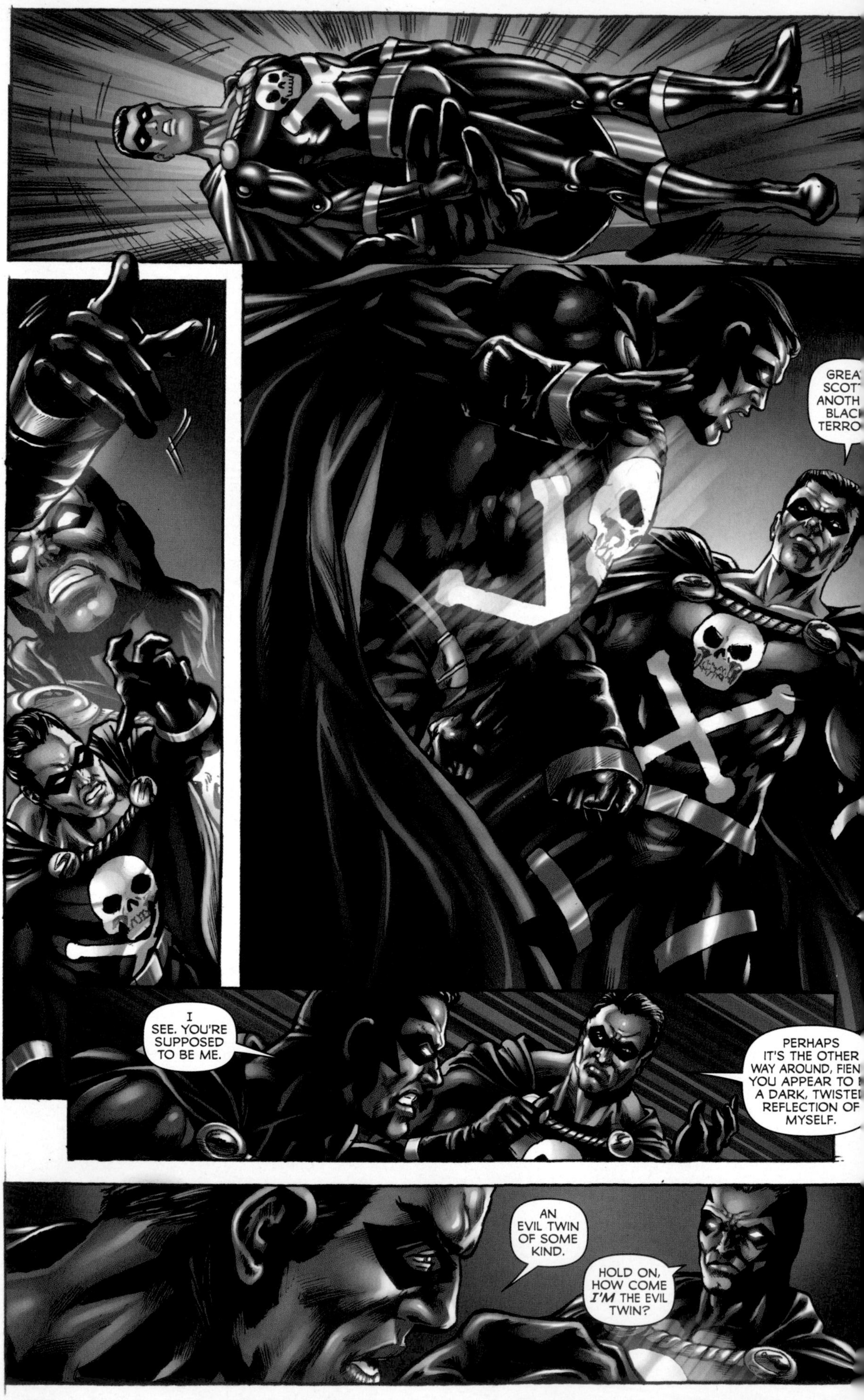
GREA
SCOTT
ANOTH
BLAC
TERRO
I SEE. YOU'RE SUPPOSED TO BE ME.
PERHAPS IT'S THE OTHER WAY AROUND, FIEN YOU APPEAR TO A DARK, TWISTE REFLECTION OF MYSELF.
AN EVIL TWIN OF SOME KIND.
HOLD ON, HOW COME *I'M* THE EVIL TWIN?

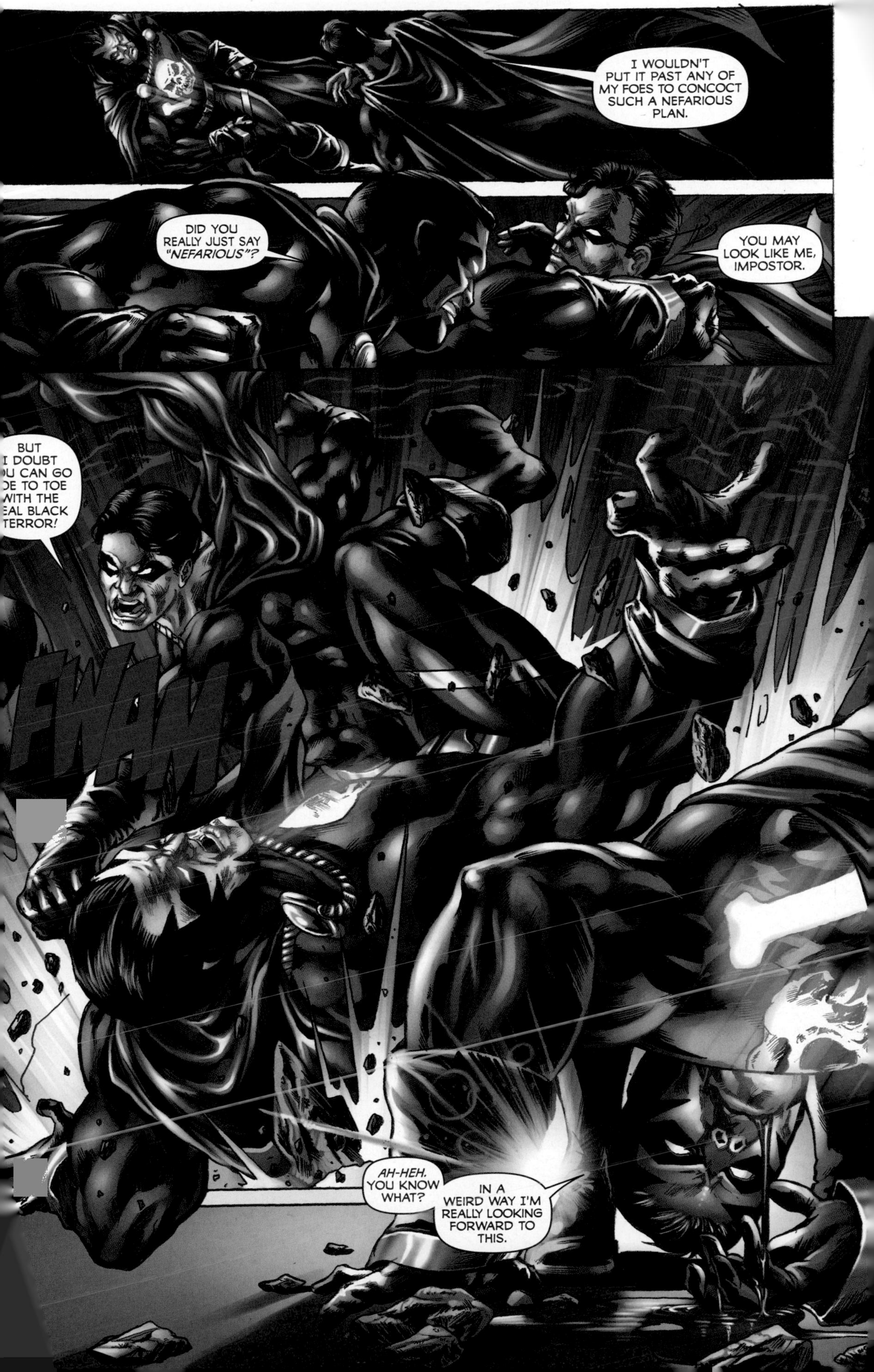
I WOULDN'T PUT IT PAST ANY OF MY FOES TO CONCOCT SUCH A NEFARIOUS PLAN.
DID YOU REALLY JUST SAY "*NEFARIOUS*"?
YOU MAY LOOK LIKE ME, IMPOSTOR.
BUT I DOUBT OU CAN GO DE TO TOE WITH THE EAL BLACK TERROR!
FWAM
AH-HEH. YOU KNOW WHAT?
IN A WEIRD WAY I'M REALLY LOOKING FORWARD TO THIS.

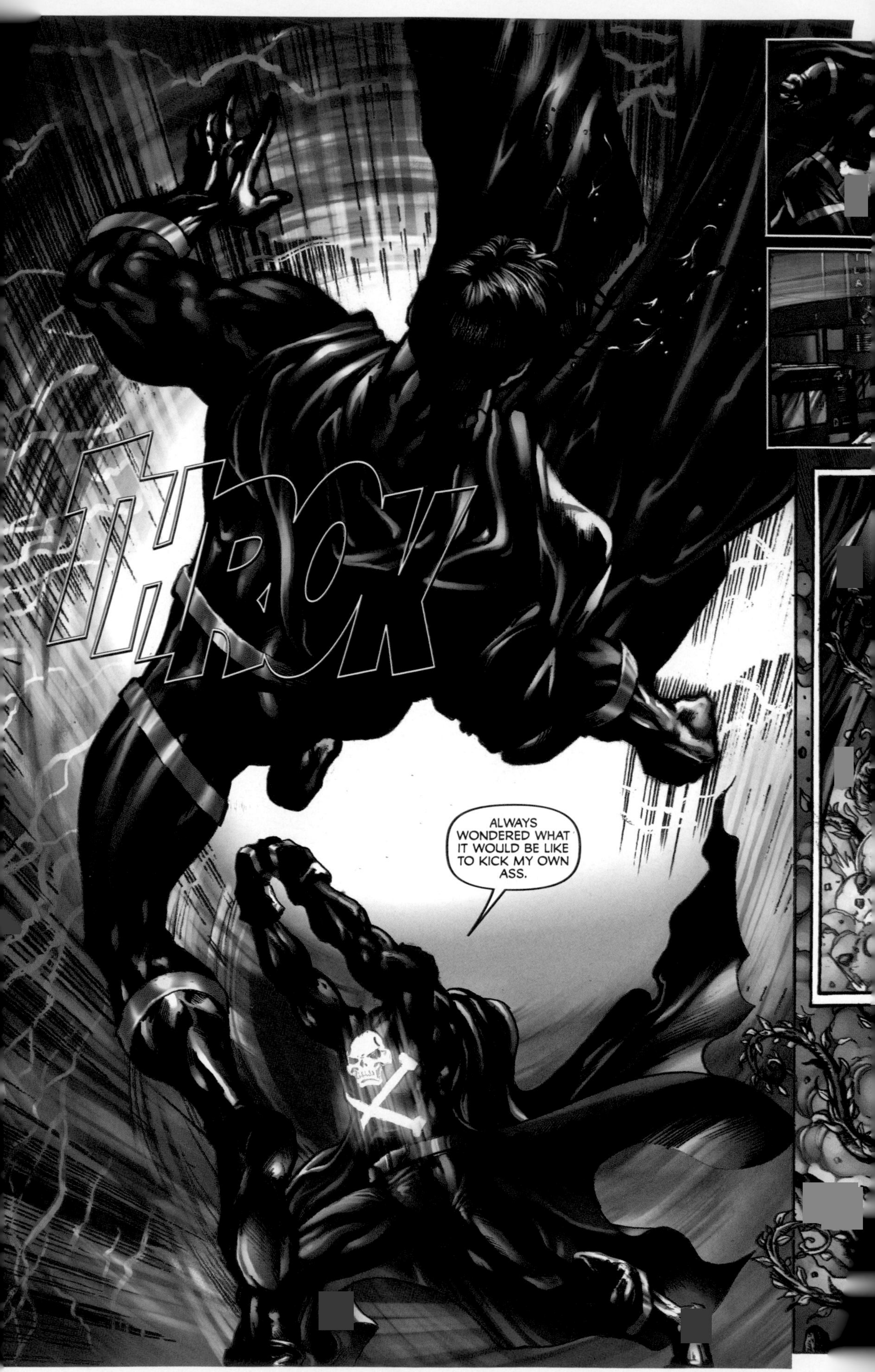
THACK
ALWAYS WONDERED WHAT IT WOULD BE LIKE TO KICK MY OWN ASS.

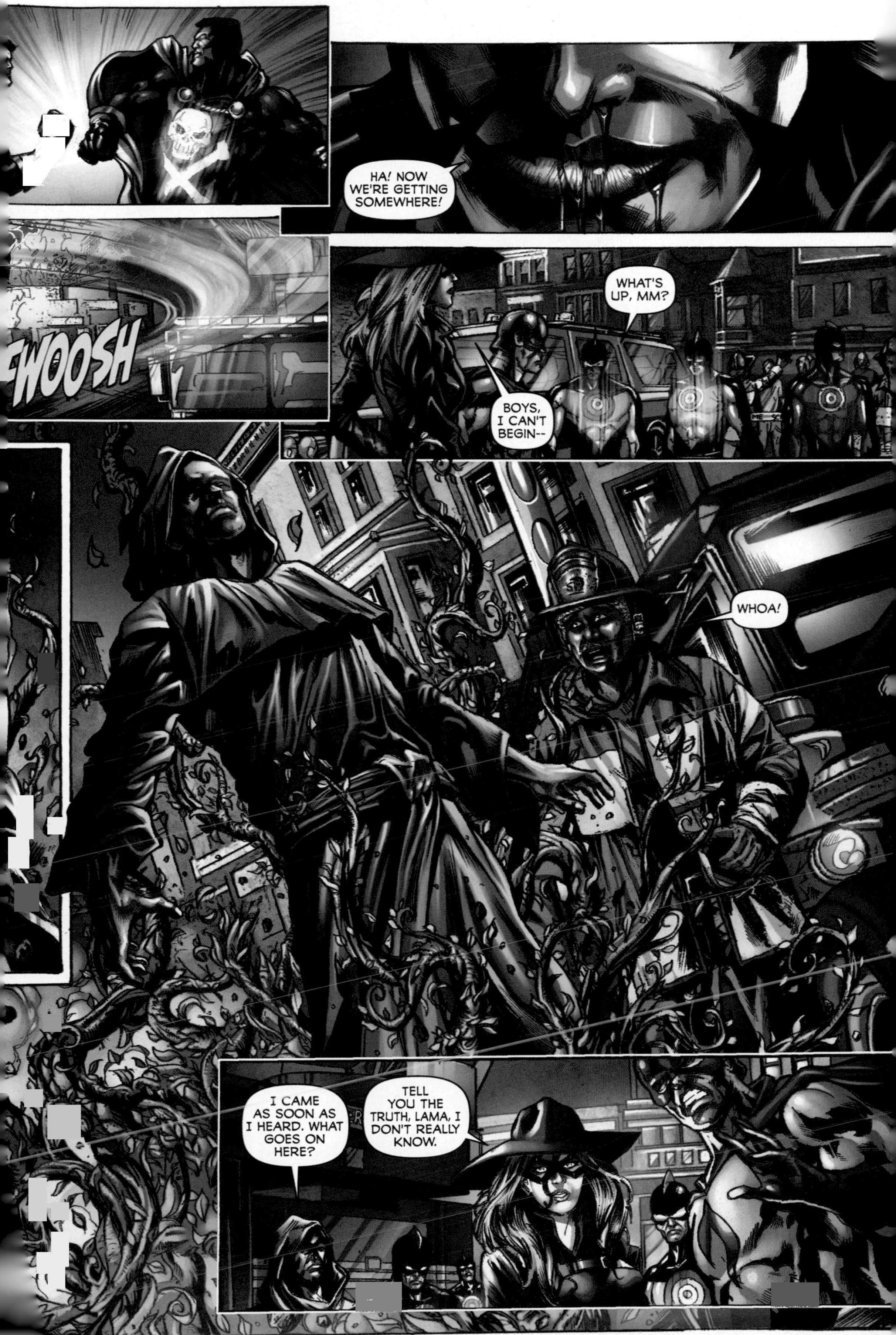
HA! NOW WE'RE GETTING SOMEWHERE!
FWOOSH
WHAT'S UP, MM?
BOYS, I CAN'T BEGIN--
WHOA!
I CAME AS SOON AS I HEARD. WHAT GOES ON HERE?
TELL YOU THE TRUTH, LAMA, I DON'T REALLY KNOW.

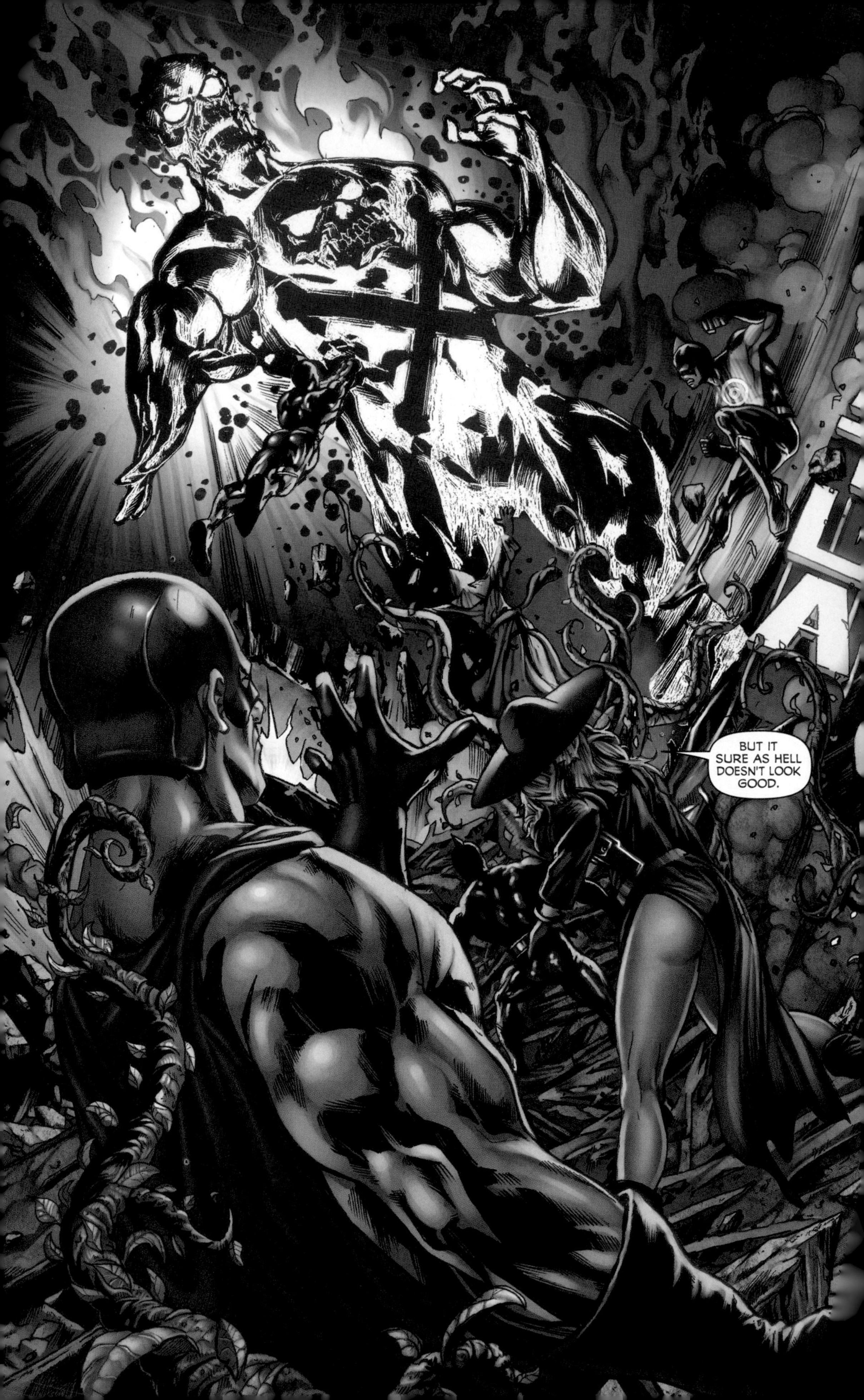
BUT IT SURE AS HELL DOESN'T LOOK GOOD.

ISSUE 11

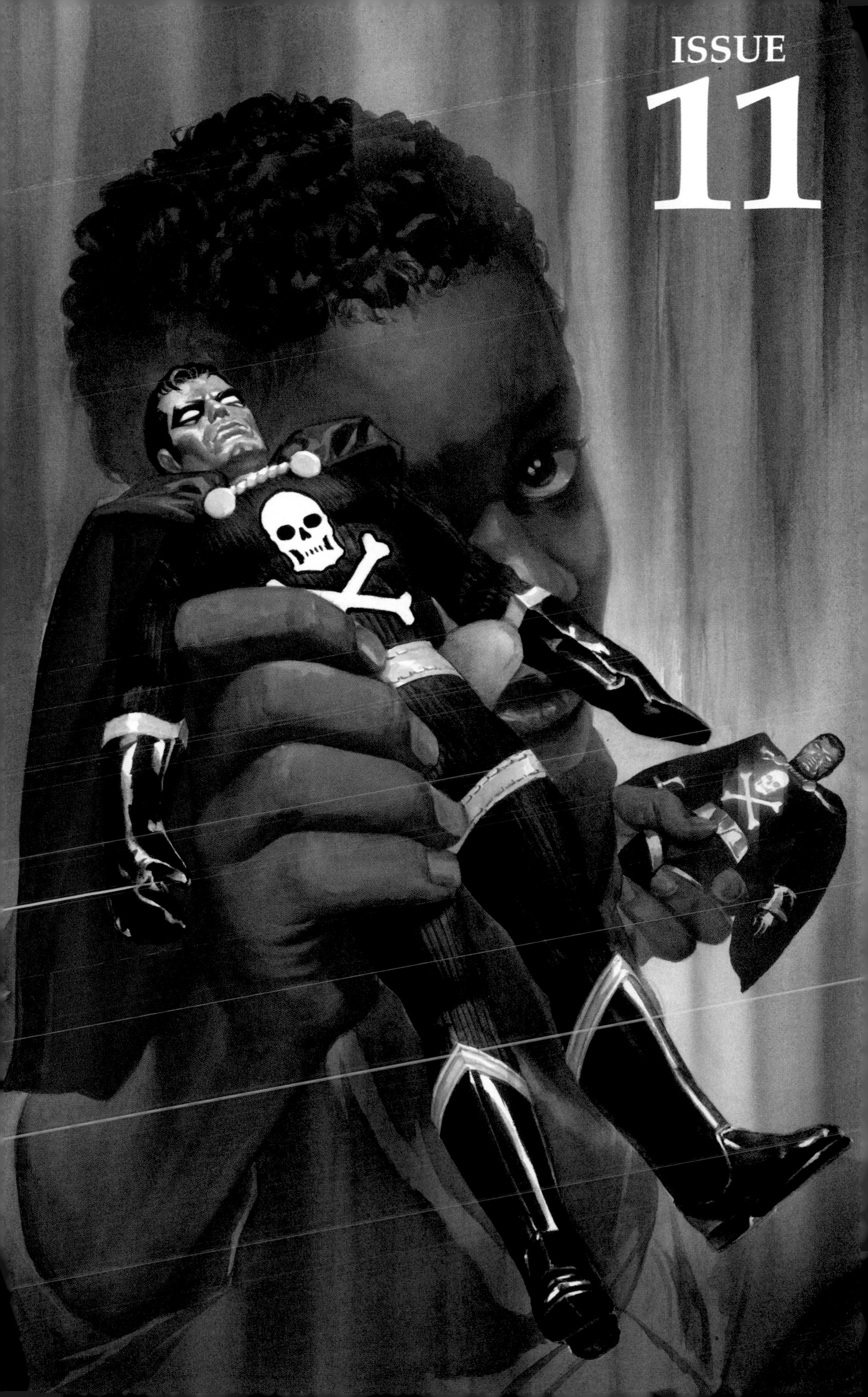

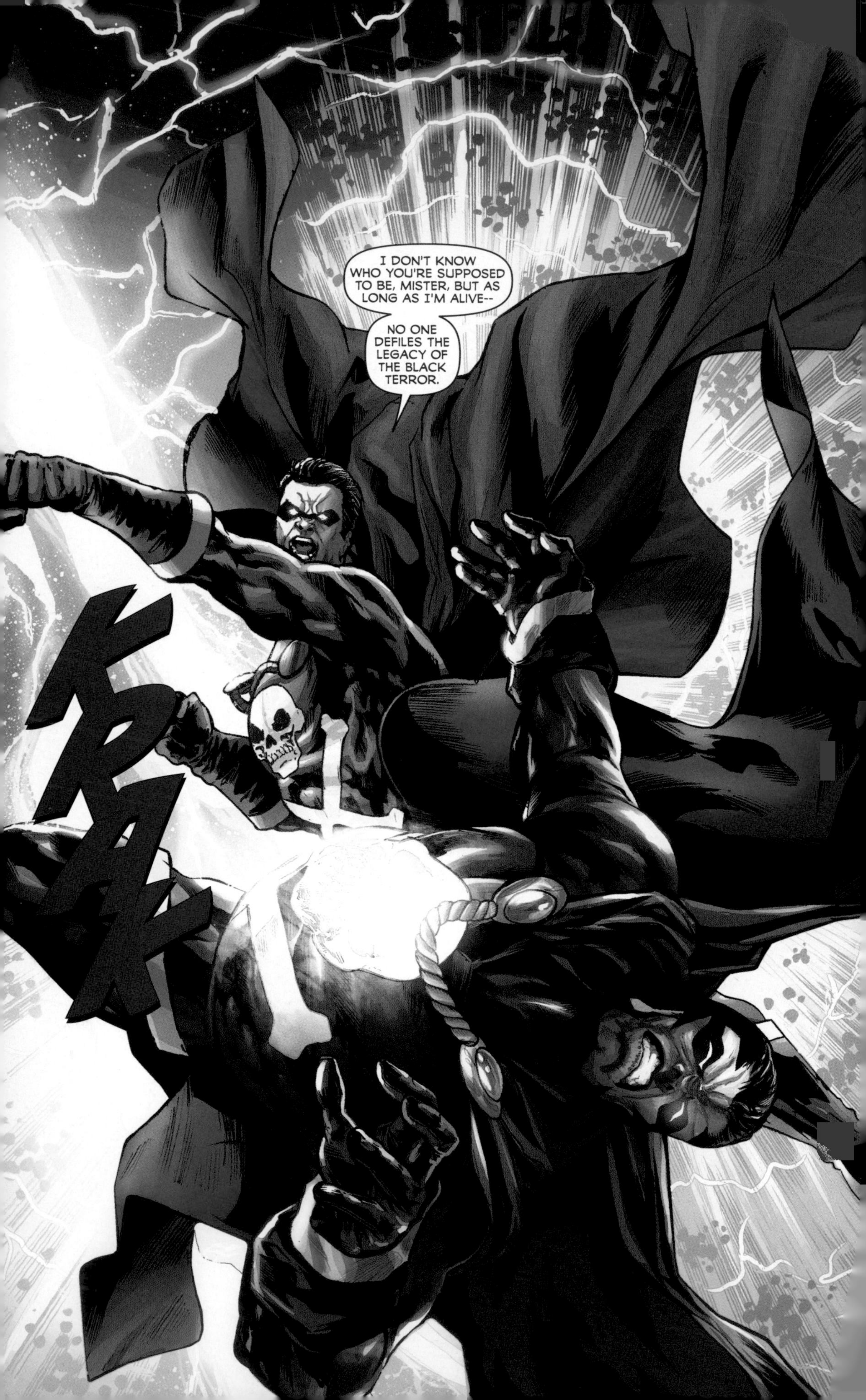
I DON'T KNOW WHO YOU'RE SUPPOSED TO BE, MISTER, BUT AS LONG AS I'M ALIVE--
NO ONE DEFILES THE LEGACY OF THE BLACK TERROR.
KRAK

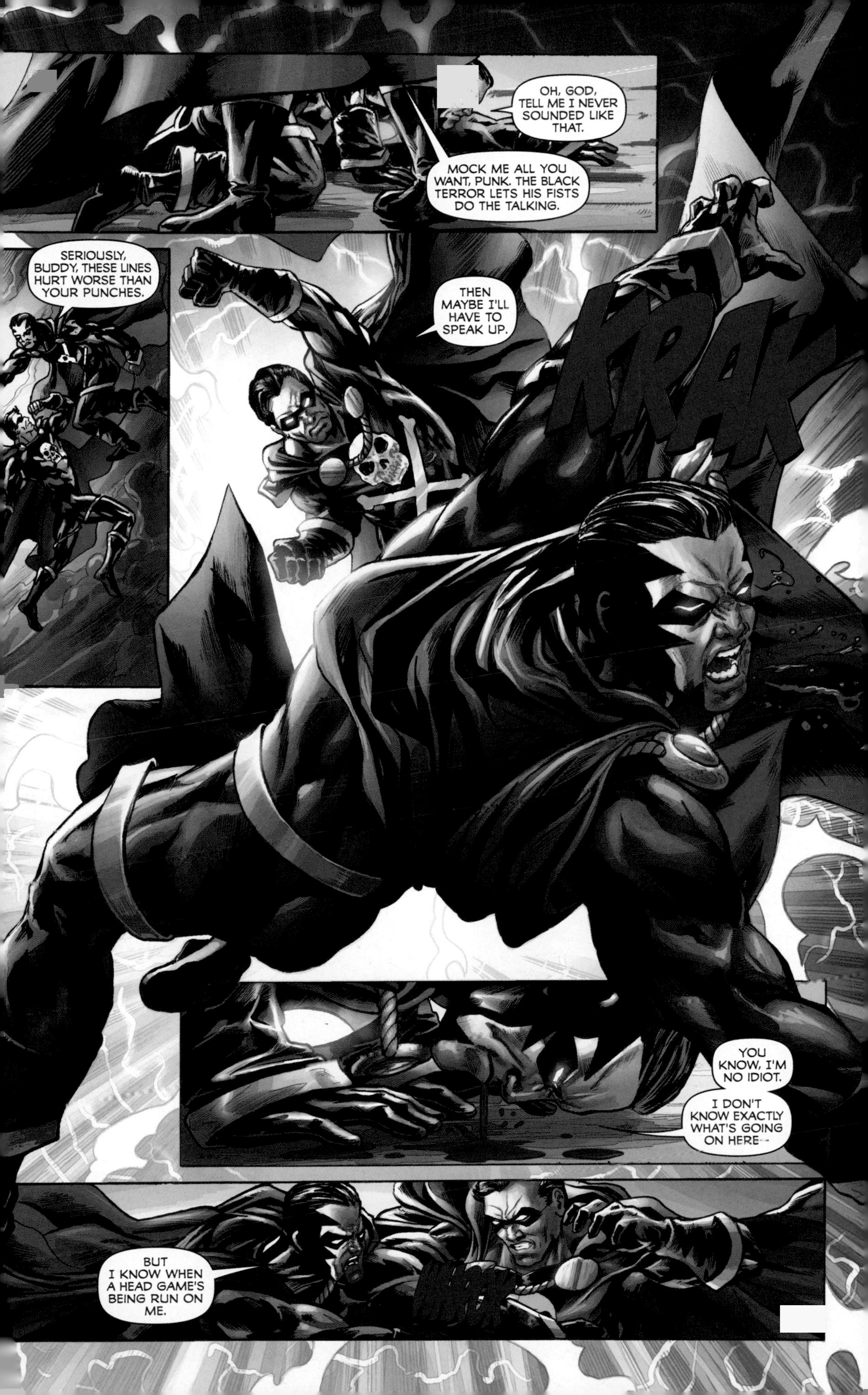
OH, GOD, TELL ME I NEVER SOUNDED LIKE THAT.
MOCK ME ALL YOU WANT, PUNK. THE BLACK TERROR LETS HIS FISTS DO THE TALKING.
SERIOUSLY, BUDDY, THESE LINES HURT WORSE THAN YOUR PUNCHES.
THEN MAYBE I'LL HAVE TO SPEAK UP.
KRAK
YOU KNOW, I'M NO IDIOT.
I DON'T KNOW EXACTLY WHAT'S GOING ON HERE--
BUT I KNOW WHEN A HEAD GAME'S BEING RUN ON ME.

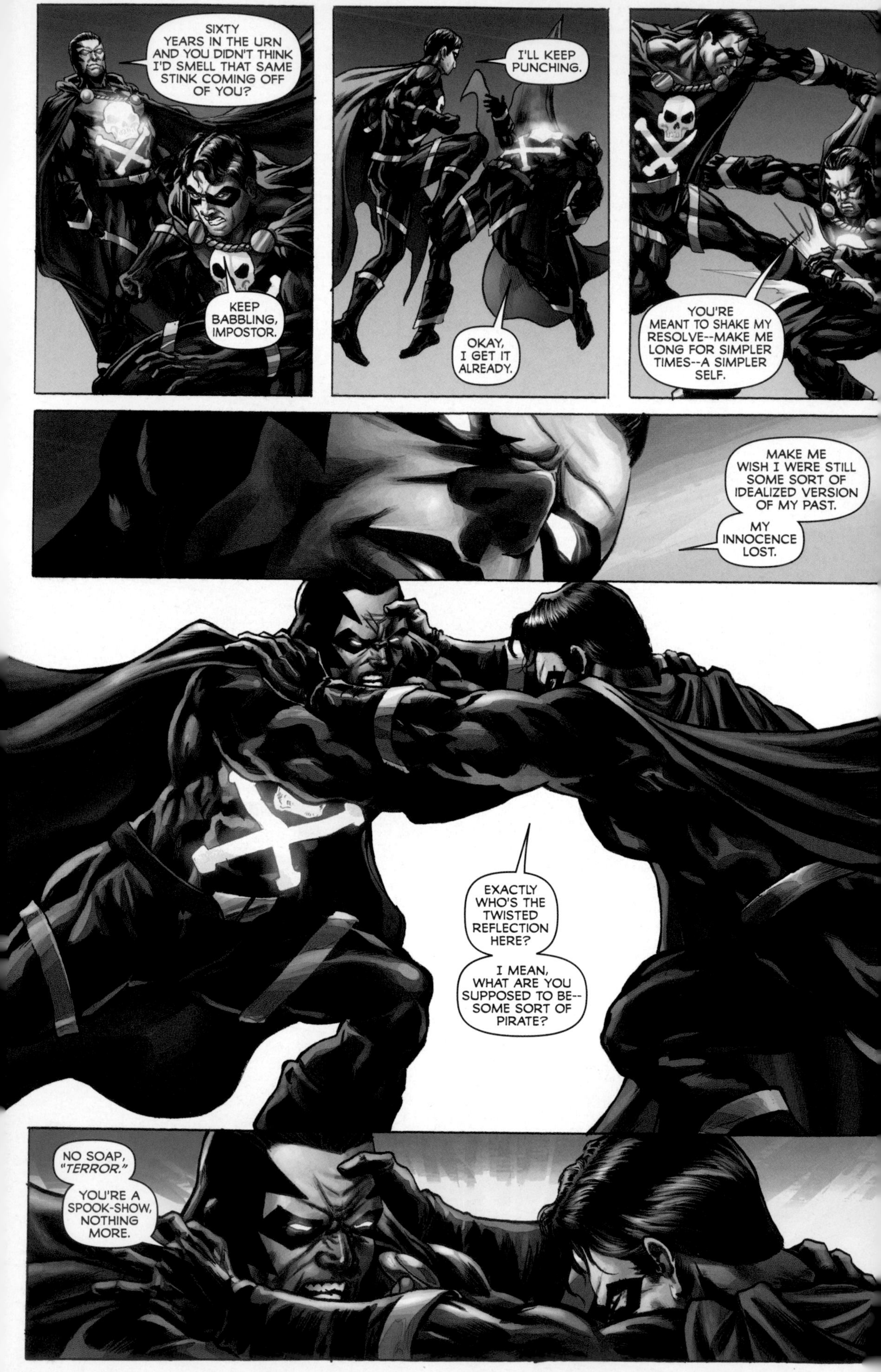
SIXTY YEARS IN THE URN AND YOU DIDN'T THINK I'D SMELL THAT SAME STINK COMING OFF OF YOU?
KEEP BABBLING, IMPOSTOR.
I'LL KEEP PUNCHING.
OKAY, I GET IT ALREADY.
YOU'RE MEANT TO SHAKE MY RESOLVE--MAKE ME LONG FOR SIMPLER TIMES--A SIMPLER SELF.
MAKE ME WISH I WERE STILL SOME SORT OF IDEALIZED VERSION OF MY PAST.
MY INNOCENCE LOST.
EXACTLY WHO'S THE TWISTED REFLECTION HERE?
I MEAN, WHAT ARE YOU SUPPOSED TO BE--SOME SORT OF PIRATE?
NO SOAP, "TERROR."
YOU'RE A SPOOK-SHOW, NOTHING MORE.

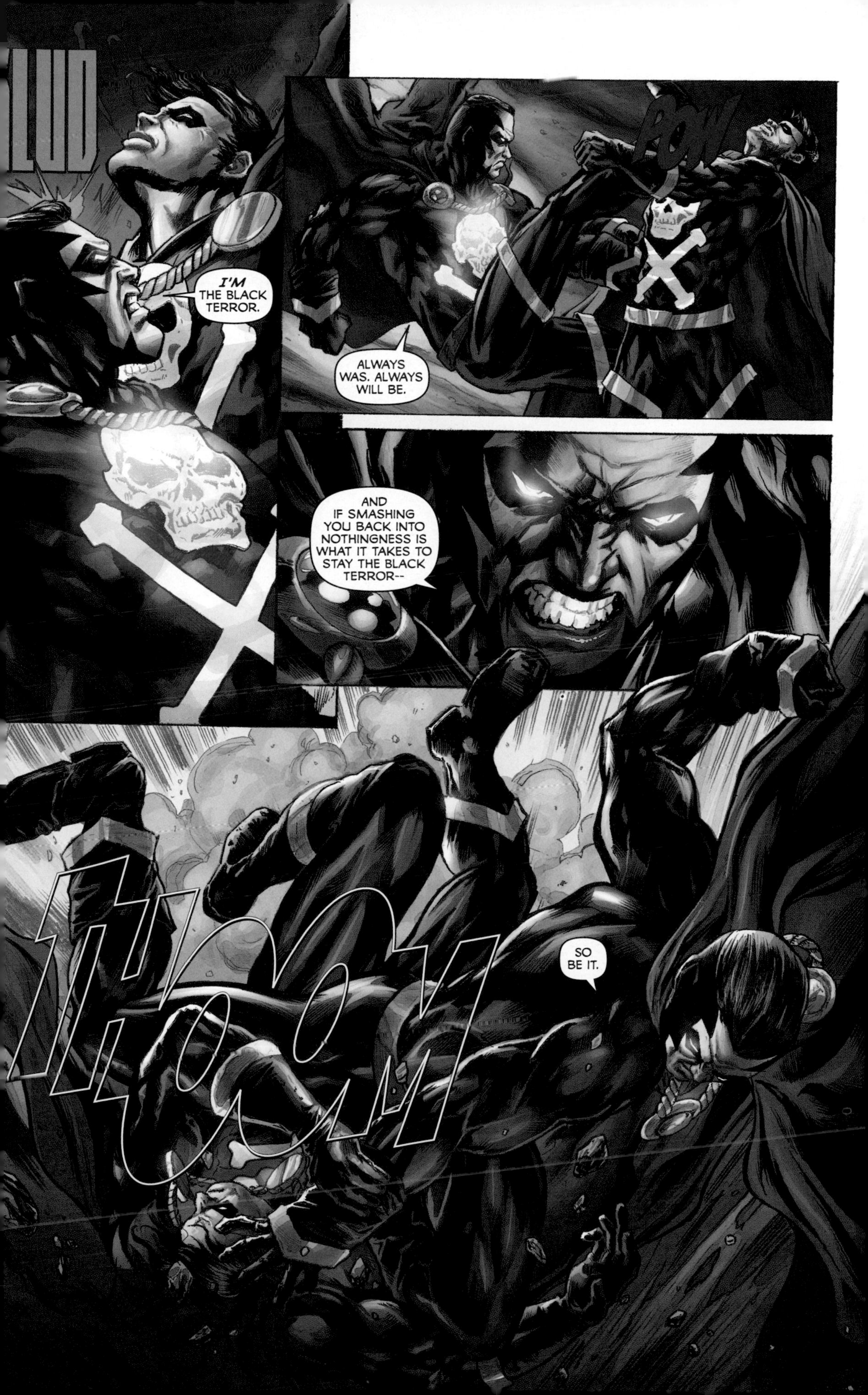

KLUD
I'M THE BLACK TERROR.
POW
ALWAYS WAS. ALWAYS WILL BE.
AND IF SMASHING YOU BACK INTO NOTHINGNESS IS WHAT IT TAKES TO STAY THE BLACK TERROR--
THOOM
SO BE IT.

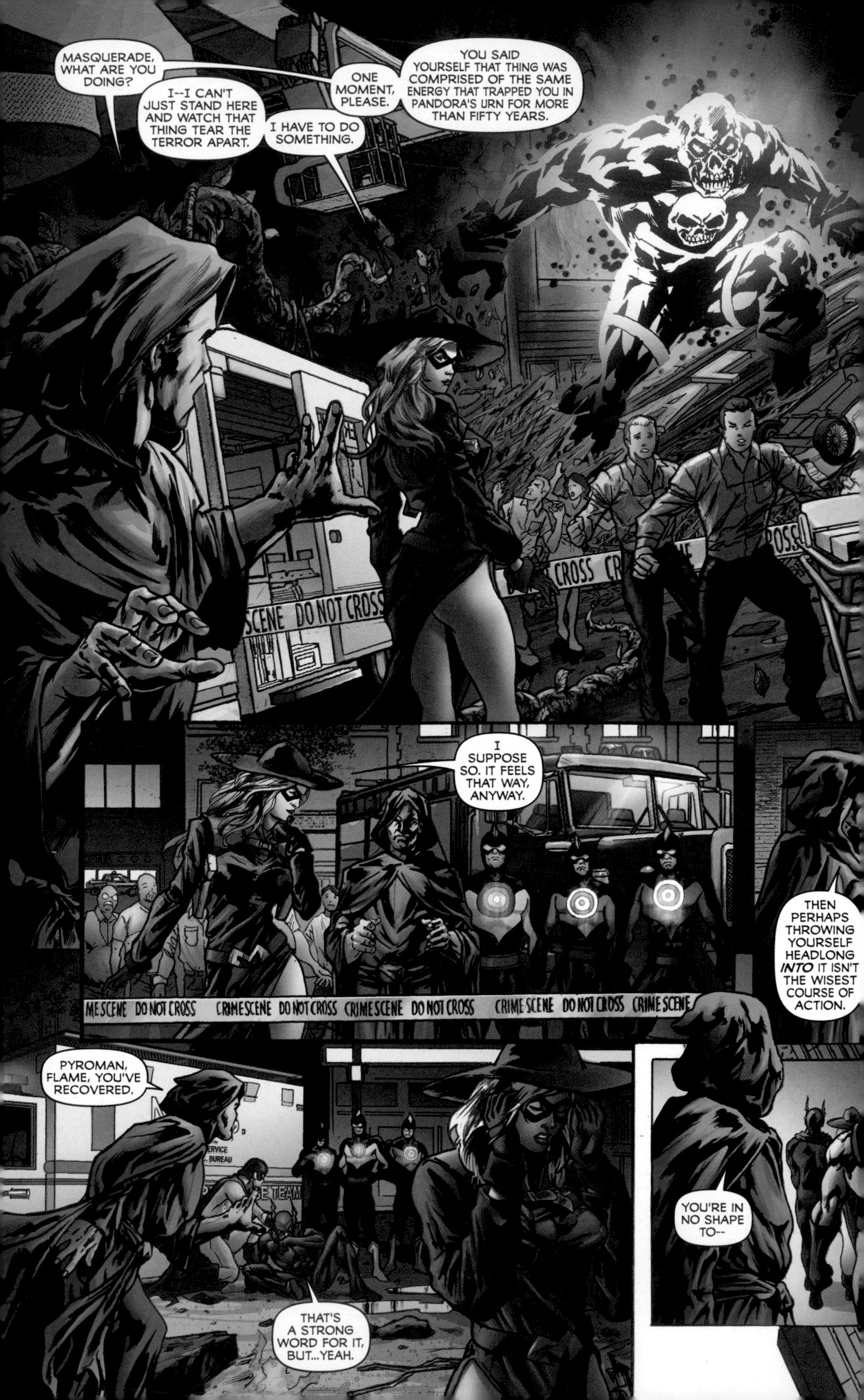
MASQUERADE, WHAT ARE YOU DOING?
I--I CAN'T JUST STAND HERE AND WATCH THAT THING TEAR THE TERROR APART.
I HAVE TO DO SOMETHING.
ONE MOMENT, PLEASE.
YOU SAID YOURSELF THAT THING WAS COMPRISED OF THE SAME ENERGY THAT TRAPPED YOU IN PANDORA'S URN FOR MORE THAN FIFTY YEARS.
SCENE DO NOT CROSS
CROSS
I SUPPOSE SO. IT FEELS THAT WAY, ANYWAY.
THEN PERHAPS THROWING YOURSELF HEADLONG *INTO* IT ISN'T THE WISEST COURSE OF ACTION.
MESCENE DO NOT CROSS CRIMESCENE DO NOT CROSS CRIMESCENE DO NOT CROSS CRIMESCENE DO NOT CROSS CRIMESCENE
PYROMAN, FLAME, YOU'VE RECOVERED.
THAT'S A STRONG WORD FOR IT, BUT...YEAH.
YOU'RE IN NO SHAPE TO--

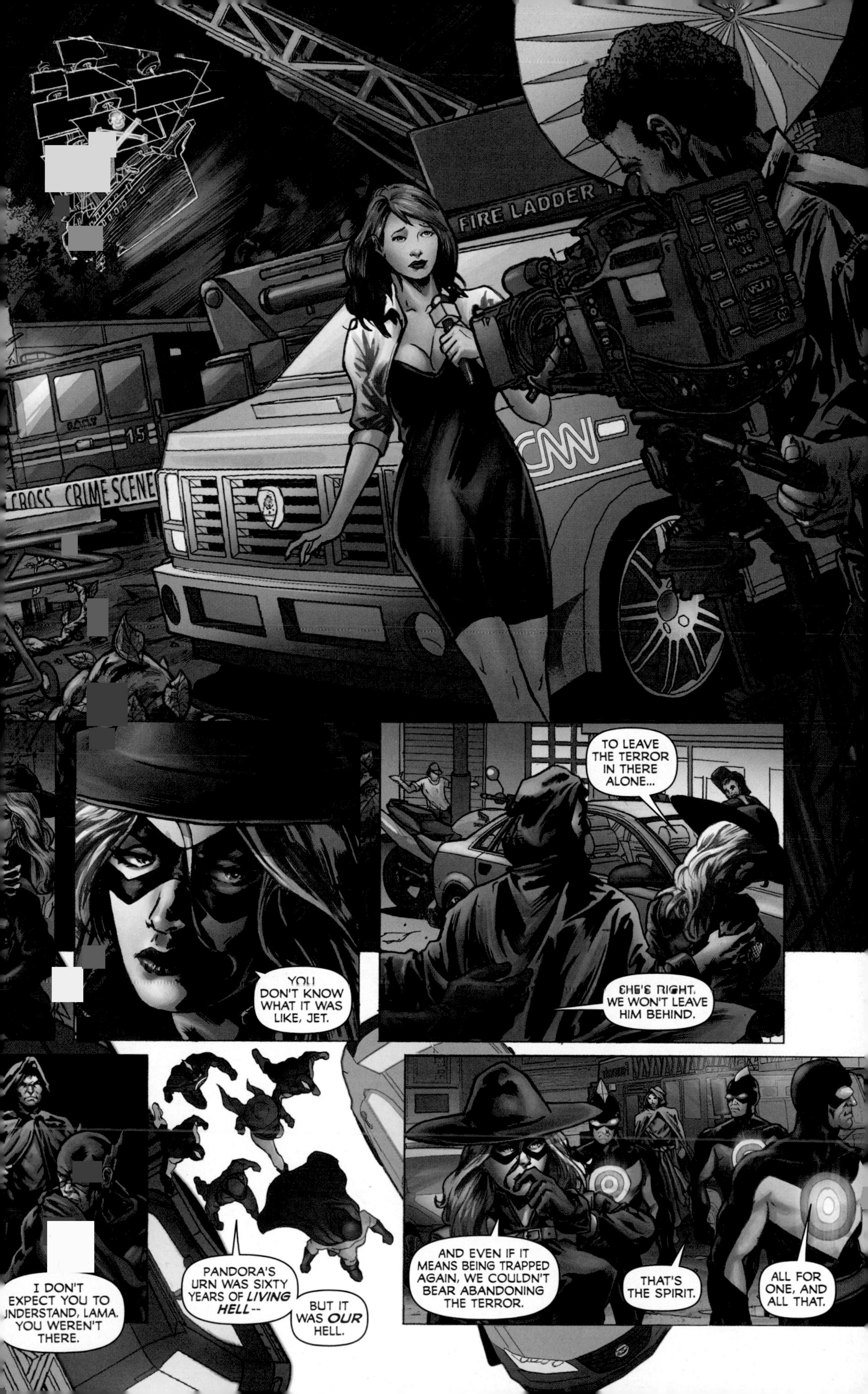
CNN
CROSS CRIME SCENE
YOU DON'T KNOW WHAT IT WAS LIKE, JET.
TO LEAVE THE TERROR IN THERE ALONE...
SHE'S RIGHT. WE WON'T LEAVE HIM BEHIND.
I DON'T EXPECT YOU TO UNDERSTAND, LAMA. YOU WEREN'T THERE.
PANDORA'S URN WAS SIXTY YEARS OF *LIVING HELL*--
BUT IT WAS *OUR* HELL.
AND EVEN IF IT MEANS BEING TRAPPED AGAIN, WE COULDN'T BEAR ABANDONING THE TERROR.
THAT'S THE SPIRIT.
ALL FOR ONE, AND ALL THAT.

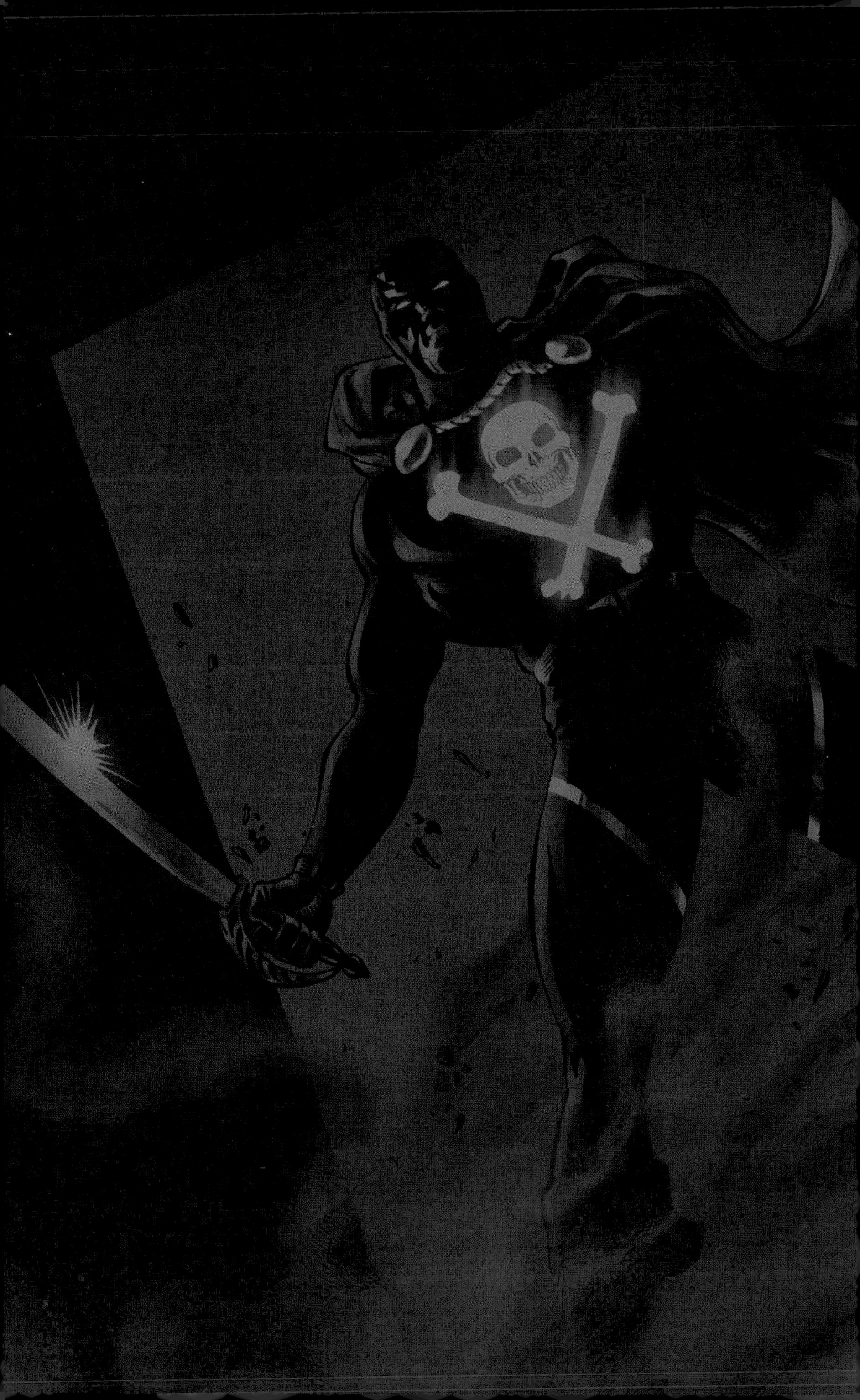

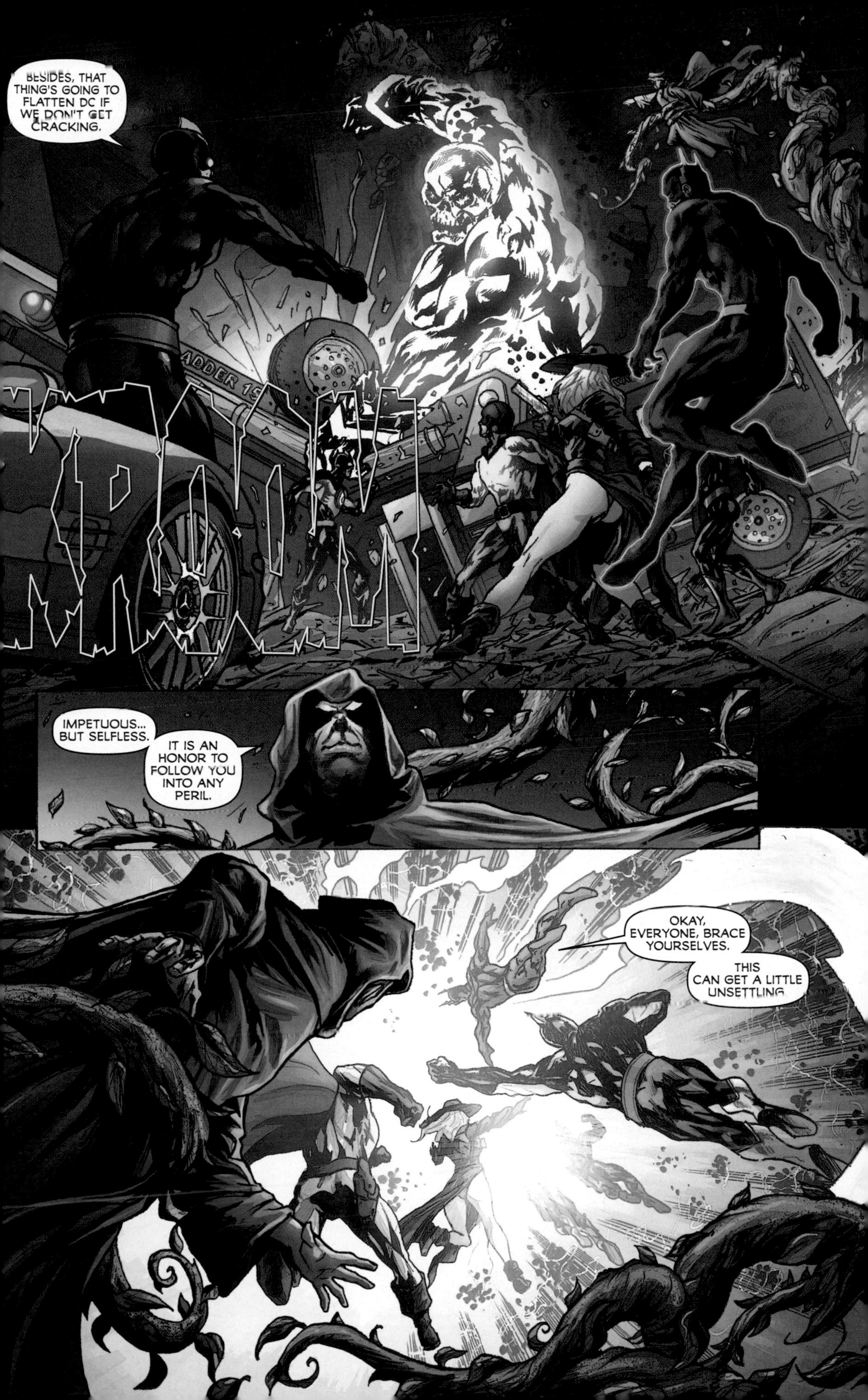
BESIDES, THAT THING'S GOING TO FLATTEN DC IF WE DON'T GET CRACKING.
IMPETUOUS... BUT SELFLESS.
IT IS AN HONOR TO FOLLOW YOU INTO ANY PERIL.
OKAY, EVERYONE, BRACE YOURSELVES.
THIS CAN GET A LITTLE UNSETTLING

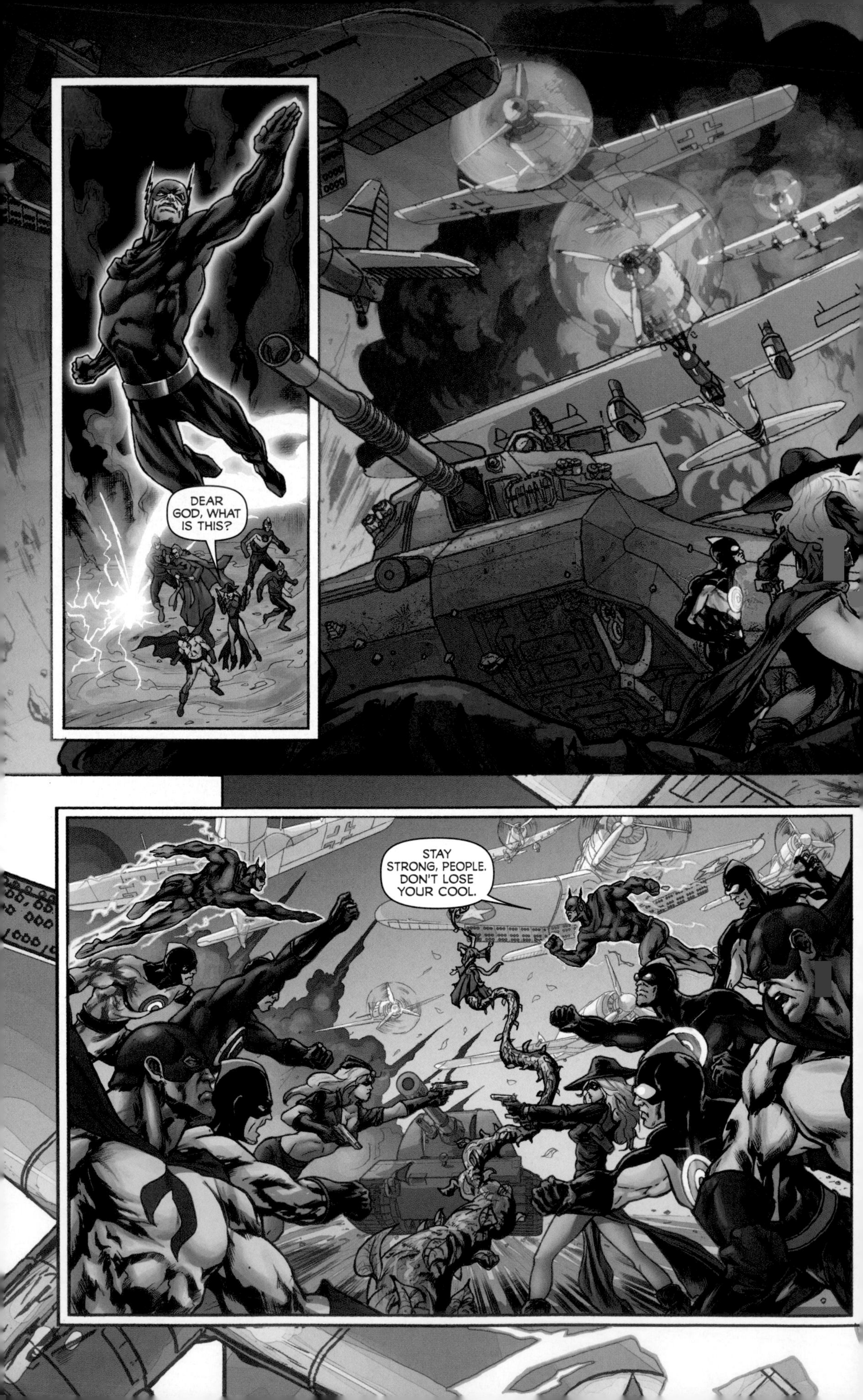
DEAR GOD, WHAT IS THIS?
STAY STRONG, PEOPLE. DON'T LOSE YOUR COOL.

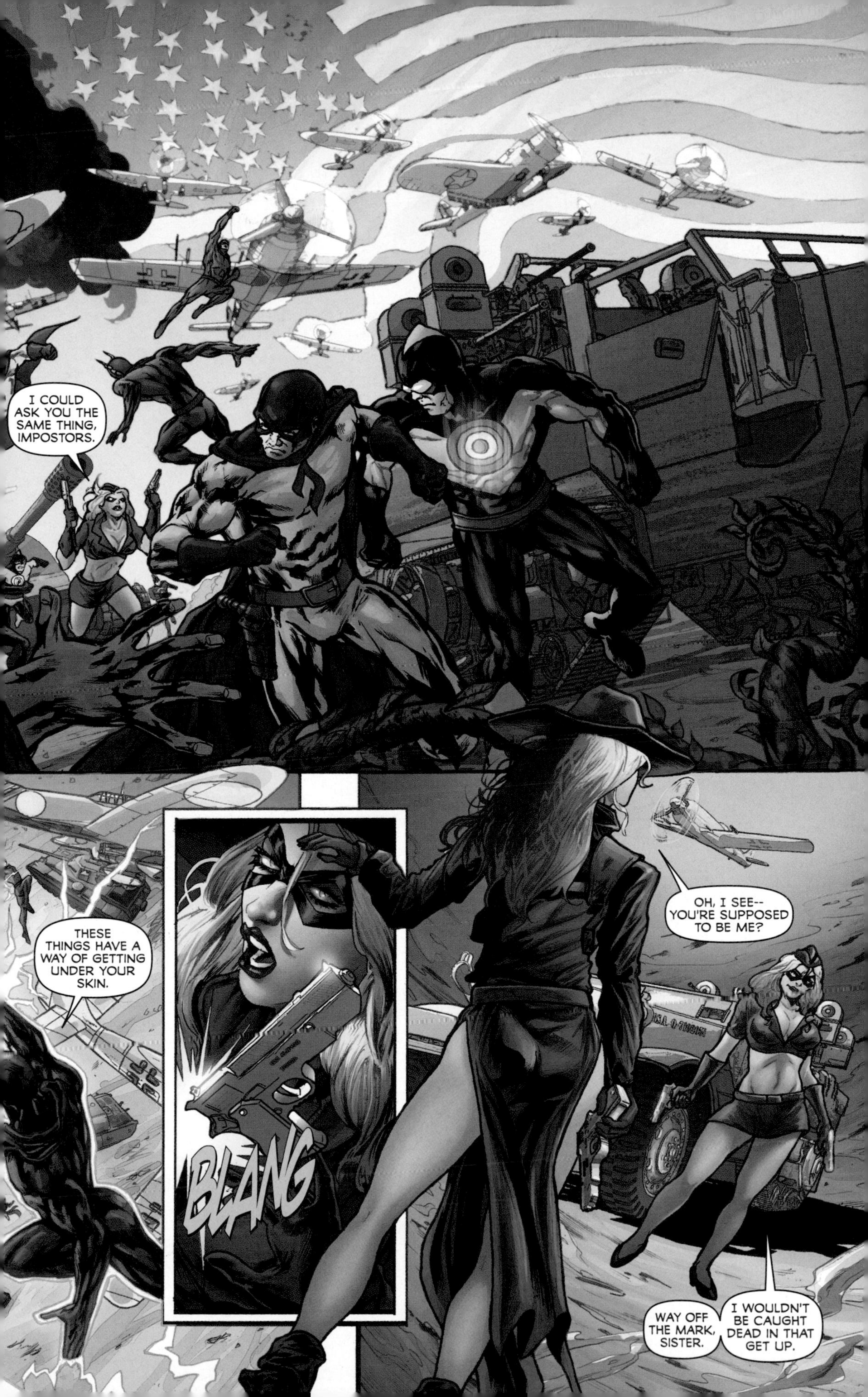
I COULD ASK YOU THE SAME THING, IMPOSTORS.
THESE THINGS HAVE A WAY OF GETTING UNDER YOUR SKIN.
BLANG
OH, I SEE-- YOU'RE SUPPOSED TO BE ME?
WAY OFF THE MARK, SISTER.
I WOULDN'T BE CAUGHT DEAD IN THAT GET UP.

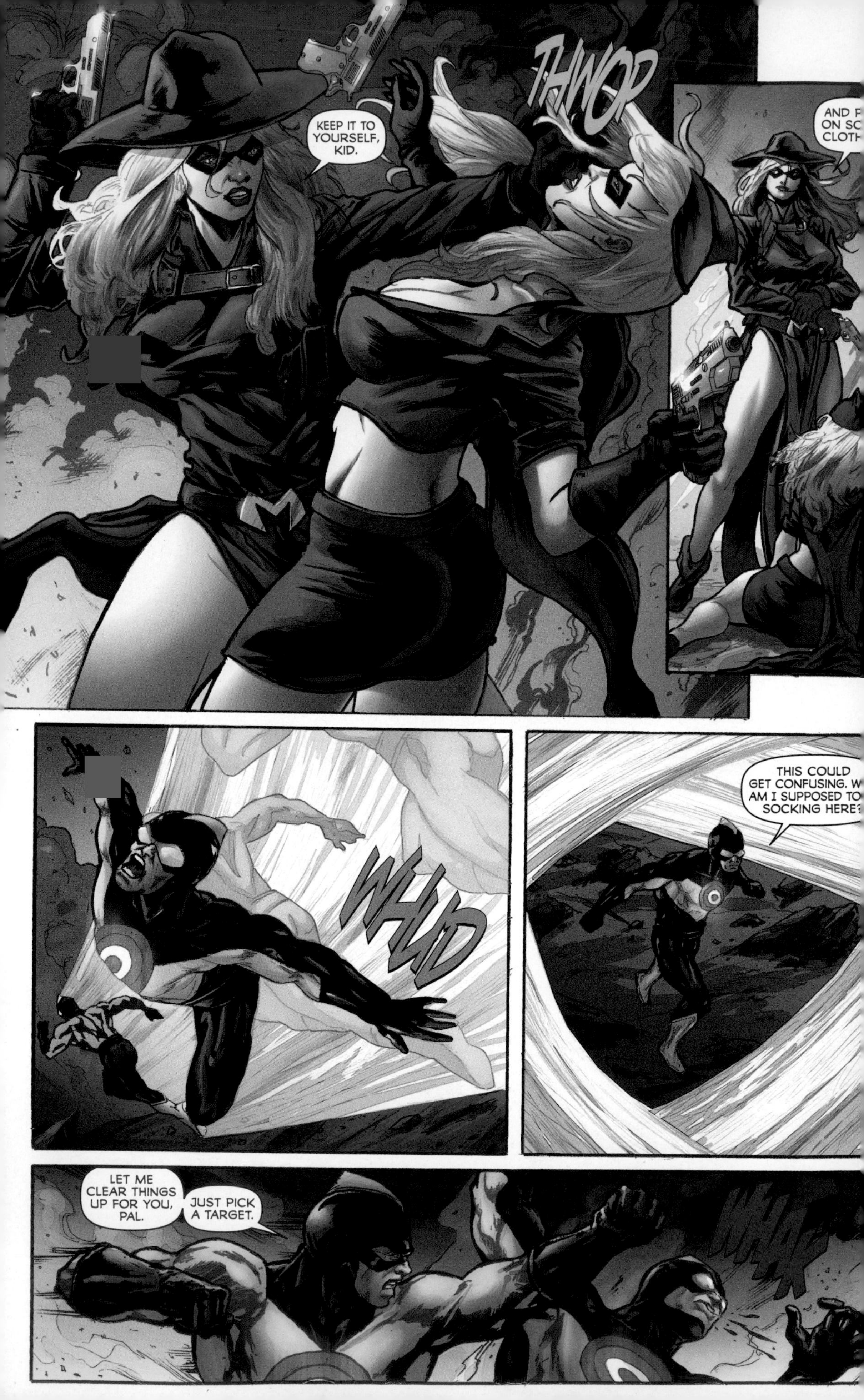

KEEP IT TO YOURSELF, KID.
THWOP
AND P ON SC CLOTH
WHUD
THIS COULD GET CONFUSING. W AM I SUPPOSED TO SOCKING HERE?
LET ME CLEAR THINGS UP FOR YOU, PAL.
JUST PICK A TARGET.

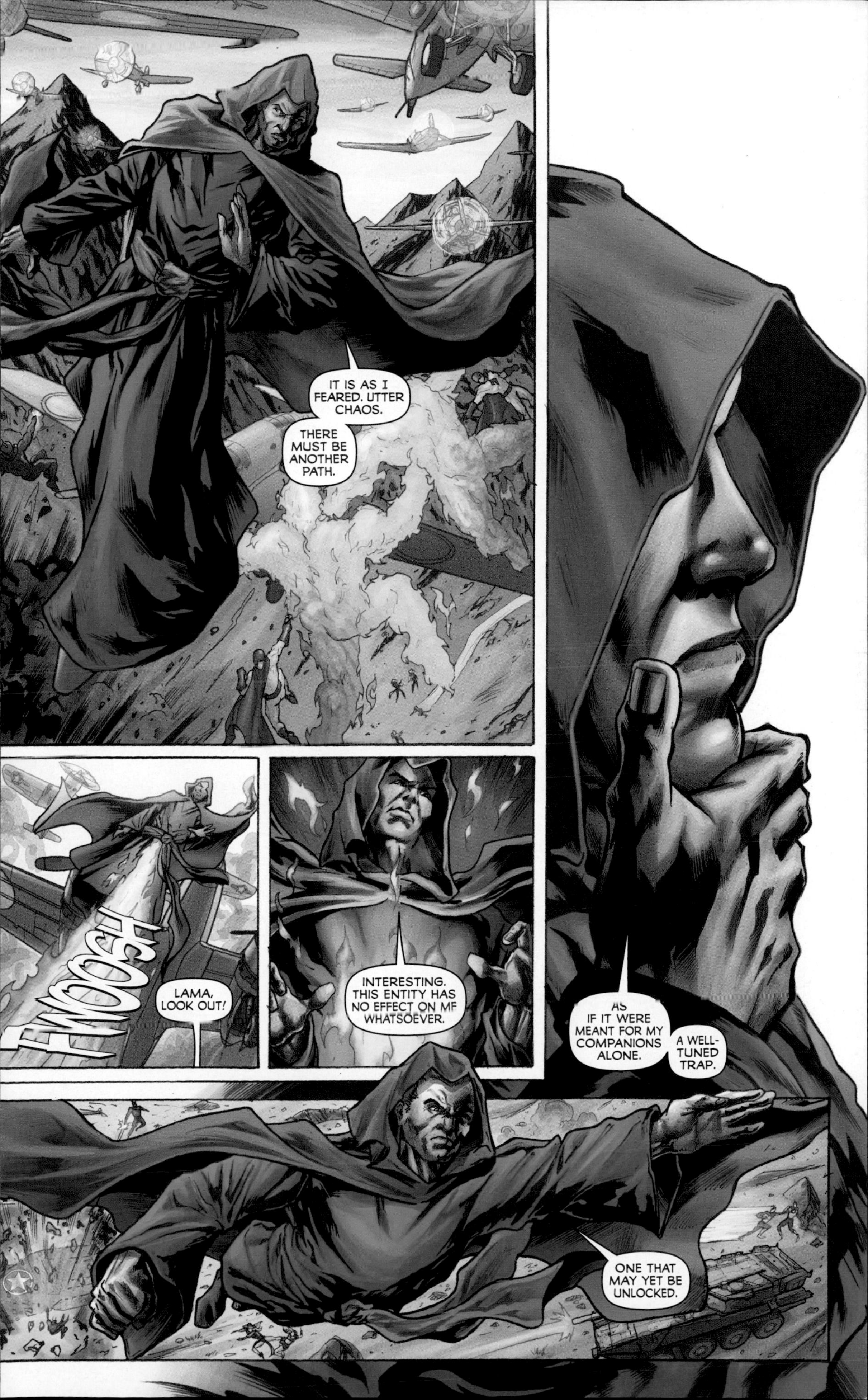
IT IS AS I FEARED. UTTER CHAOS.
THERE MUST BE ANOTHER PATH.
FWOOSH
LAMA, LOOK OUT!
INTERESTING. THIS ENTITY HAS NO EFFECT ON ME WHATSOEVER.
AS IF IT WERE MEANT FOR MY COMPANIONS ALONE.
A WELL-TUNED TRAP.
ONE THAT MAY YET BE UNLOCKED.

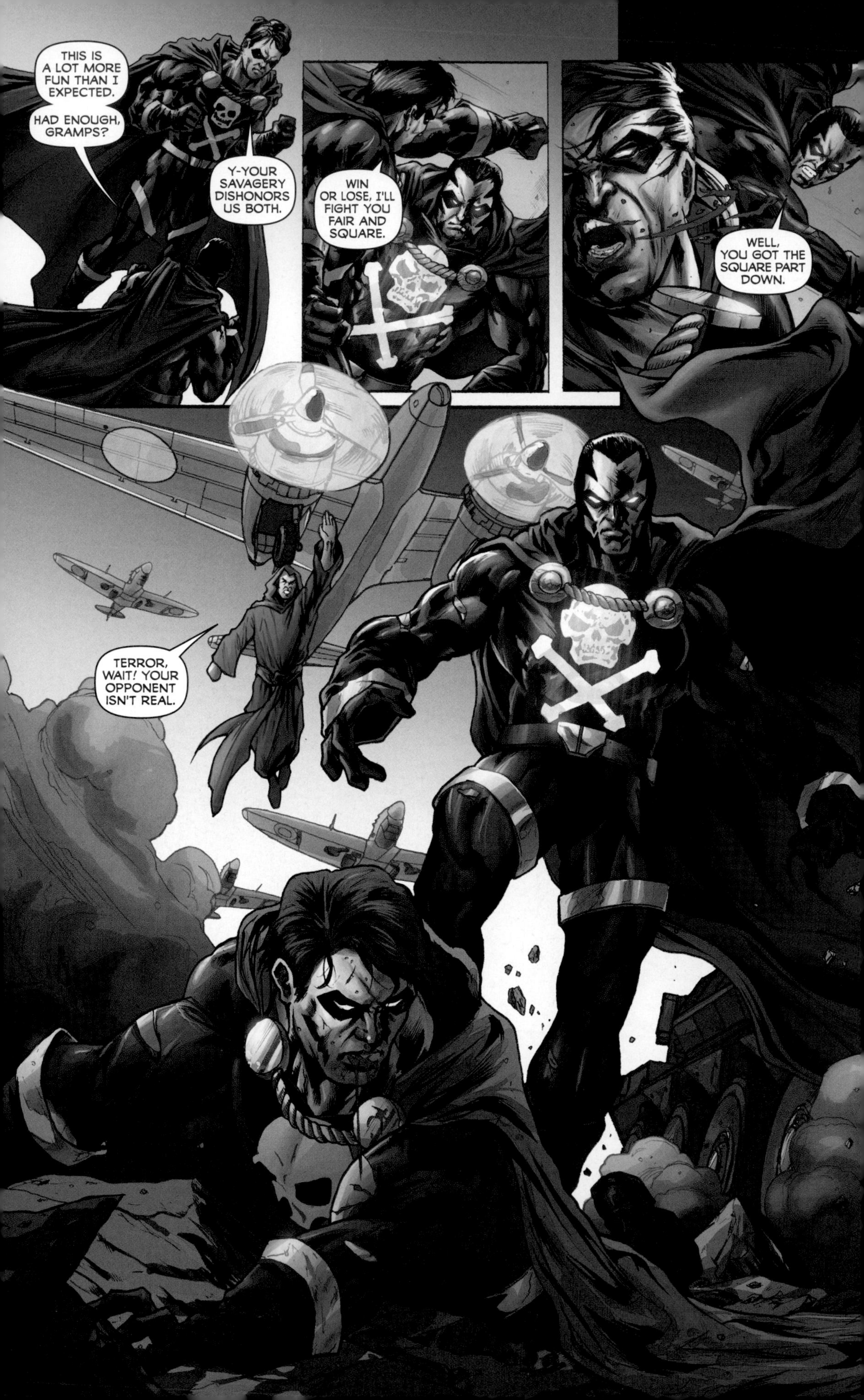
THIS IS A LOT MORE FUN THAN I EXPECTED.
HAD ENOUGH, GRAMPS?
Y-YOUR SAVAGERY DISHONORS US BOTH.
WIN OR LOSE, I'LL FIGHT YOU FAIR AND SQUARE.
WELL, YOU GOT THE SQUARE PART DOWN.
TERROR, WAIT! YOUR OPPONENT ISN'T REAL.

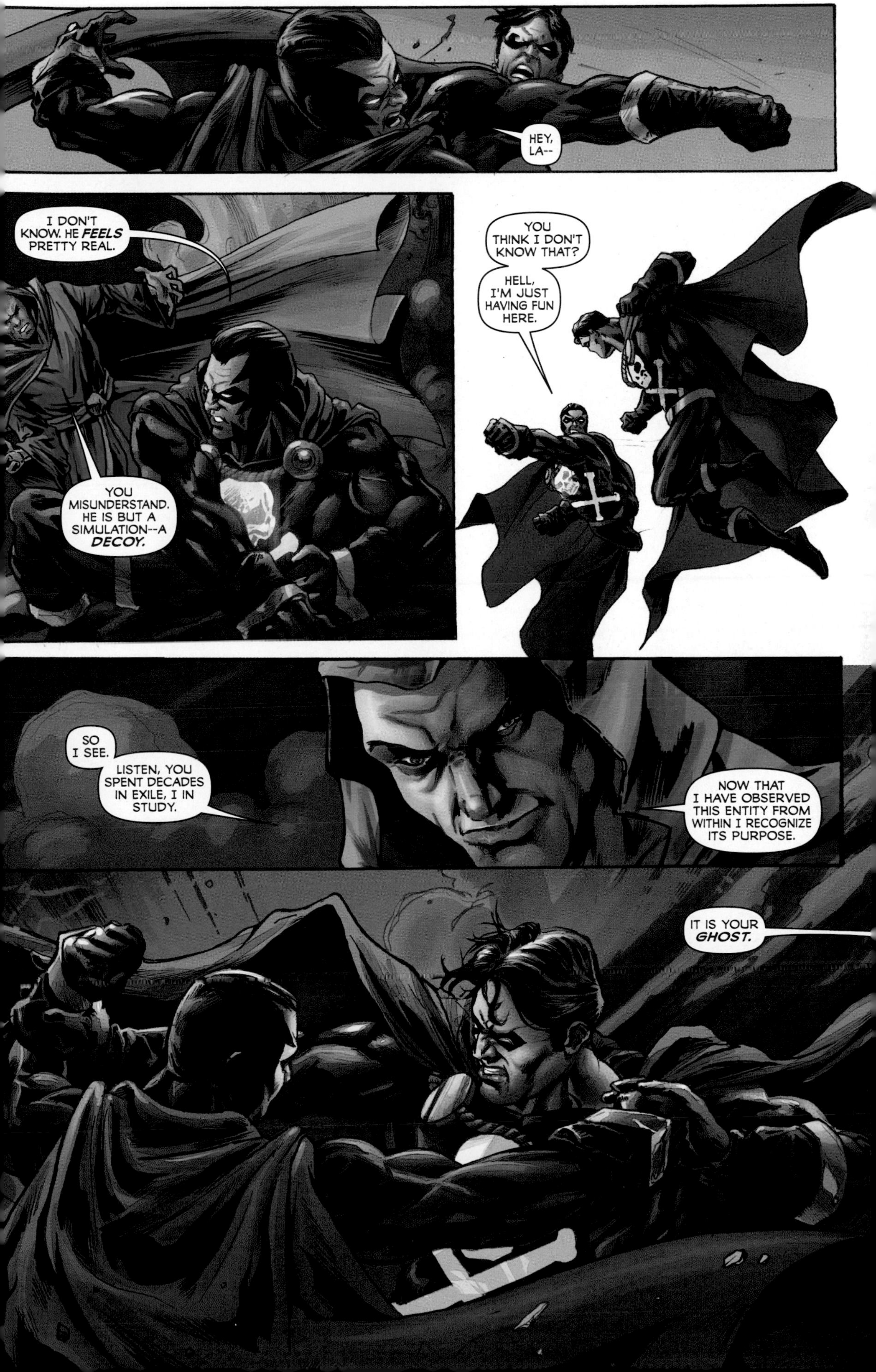
HEY, LA--
I DON'T KNOW. HE *FEELS* PRETTY REAL.
YOU MISUNDERSTAND. HE IS BUT A SIMULATION--A *DECOY.*
YOU THINK I DON'T KNOW THAT?
HELL, I'M JUST HAVING FUN HERE.
SO I SEE.
LISTEN, YOU SPENT DECADES IN EXILE, I IN STUDY.
NOW THAT I HAVE OBSERVED THIS ENTITY FROM WITHIN I RECOGNIZE ITS PURPOSE.
IT IS YOUR *GHOST.*

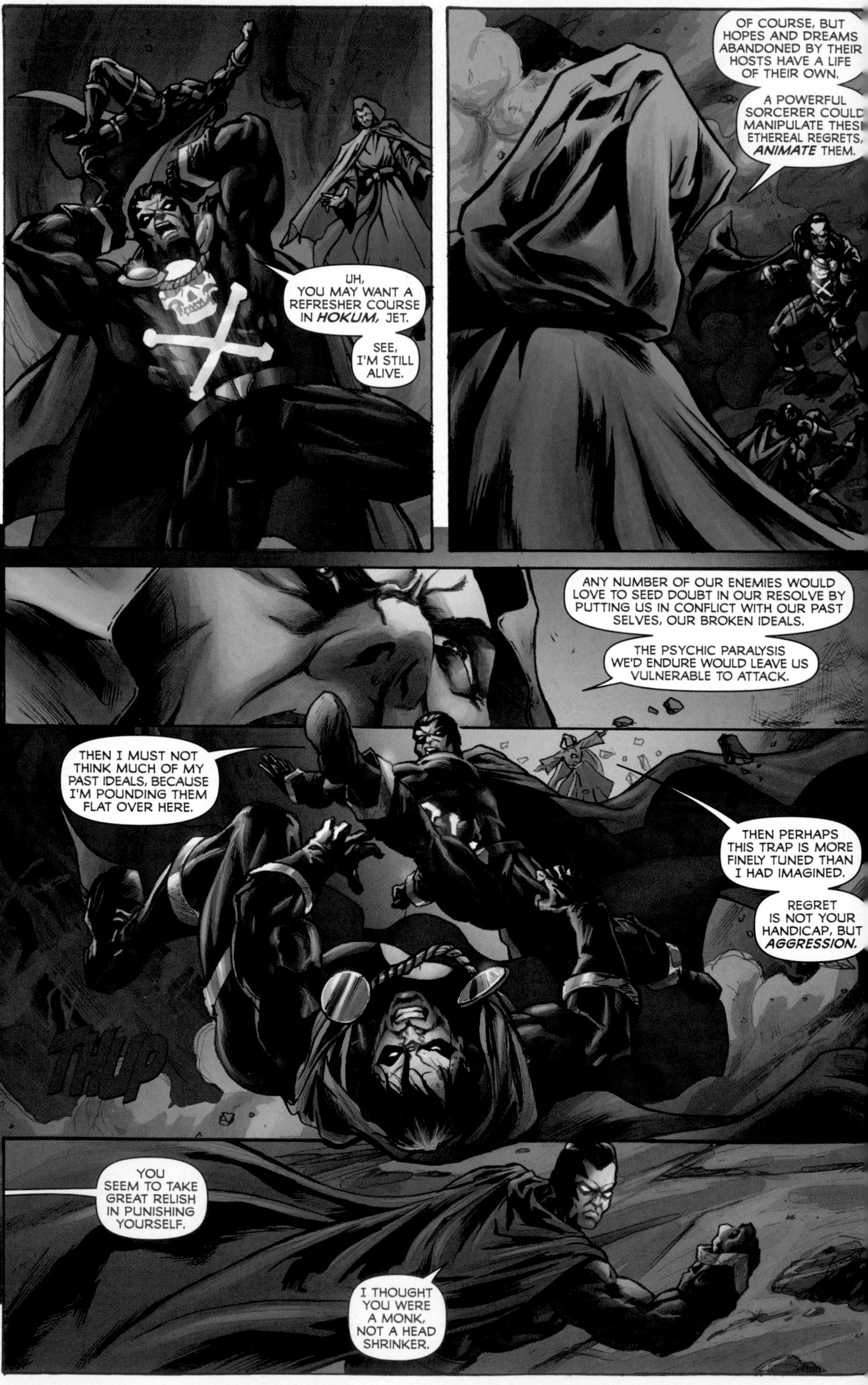
UH, YOU MAY WANT A REFRESHER COURSE IN HOKUM, JET.
SEE, I'M STILL ALIVE.
OF COURSE, BUT HOPES AND DREAMS ABANDONED BY THEIR HOSTS HAVE A LIFE OF THEIR OWN.
A POWERFUL SORCERER COULD MANIPULATE THESE ETHEREAL REGRETS, ANIMATE THEM.
ANY NUMBER OF OUR ENEMIES WOULD LOVE TO SEED DOUBT IN OUR RESOLVE BY PUTTING US IN CONFLICT WITH OUR PAST SELVES, OUR BROKEN IDEALS.
THE PSYCHIC PARALYSIS WE'D ENDURE WOULD LEAVE US VULNERABLE TO ATTACK.
THEN I MUST NOT THINK MUCH OF MY PAST IDEALS, BECAUSE I'M POUNDING THEM FLAT OVER HERE.
THEN PERHAPS THIS TRAP IS MORE FINELY TUNED THAN I HAD IMAGINED.
REGRET IS NOT YOUR HANDICAP, BUT AGGRESSION.
THUP
YOU SEEM TO TAKE GREAT RELISH IN PUNISHING YOURSELF.
I THOUGHT YOU WERE A MONK, NOT A HEAD SHRINKER.

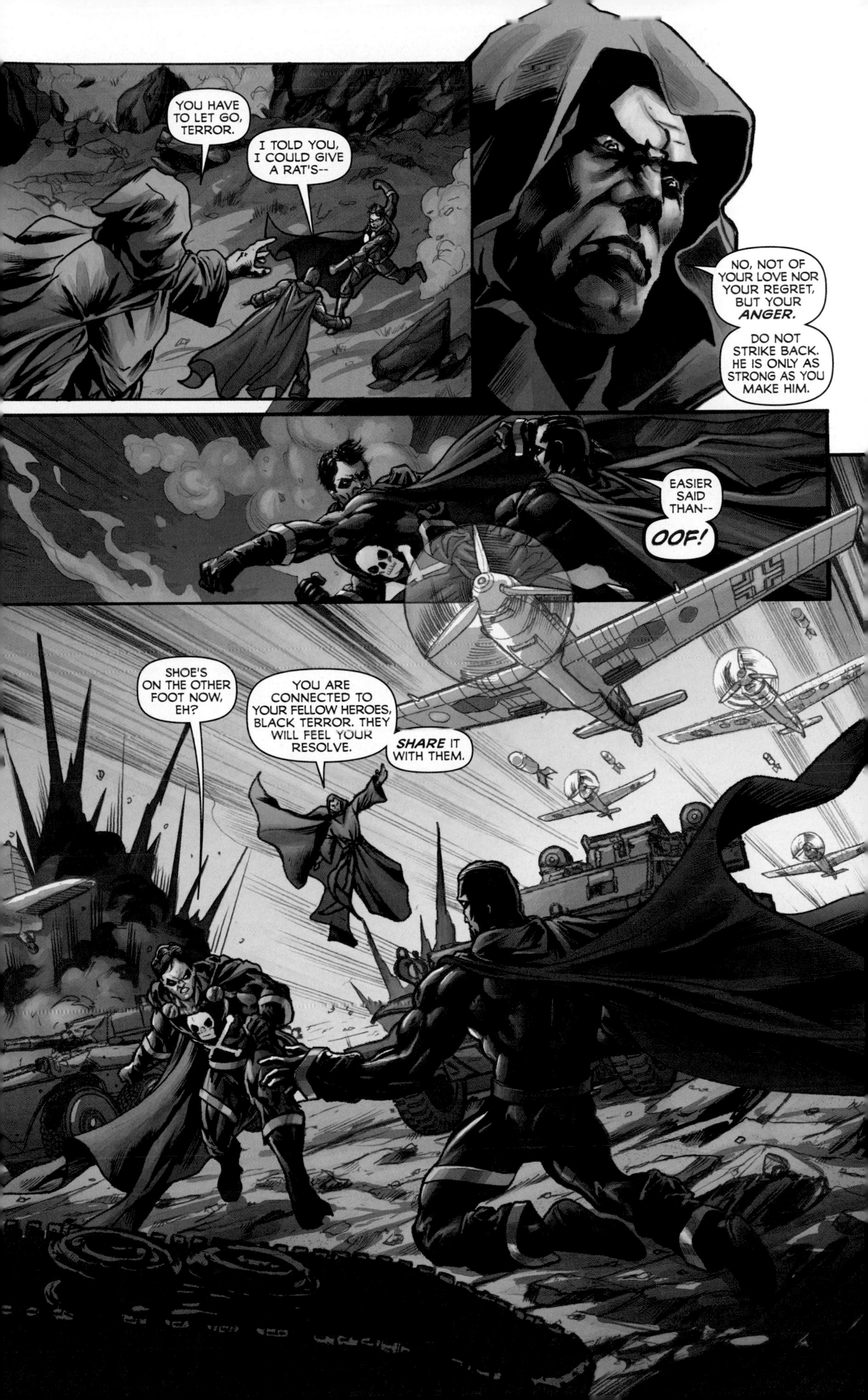
YOU HAVE TO LET GO, TERROR.
I TOLD YOU, I COULD GIVE A RAT'S--
NO, NOT OF YOUR LOVE NOR YOUR REGRET, BUT YOUR ANGER.
DO NOT STRIKE BACK. HE IS ONLY AS STRONG AS YOU MAKE HIM.
EASIER SAID THAN--
OOF!
SHOE'S ON THE OTHER FOOT NOW, EH?
YOU ARE CONNECTED TO YOUR FELLOW HEROES, BLACK TERROR. THEY WILL FEEL YOUR RESOLVE.
SHARE IT WITH THEM.

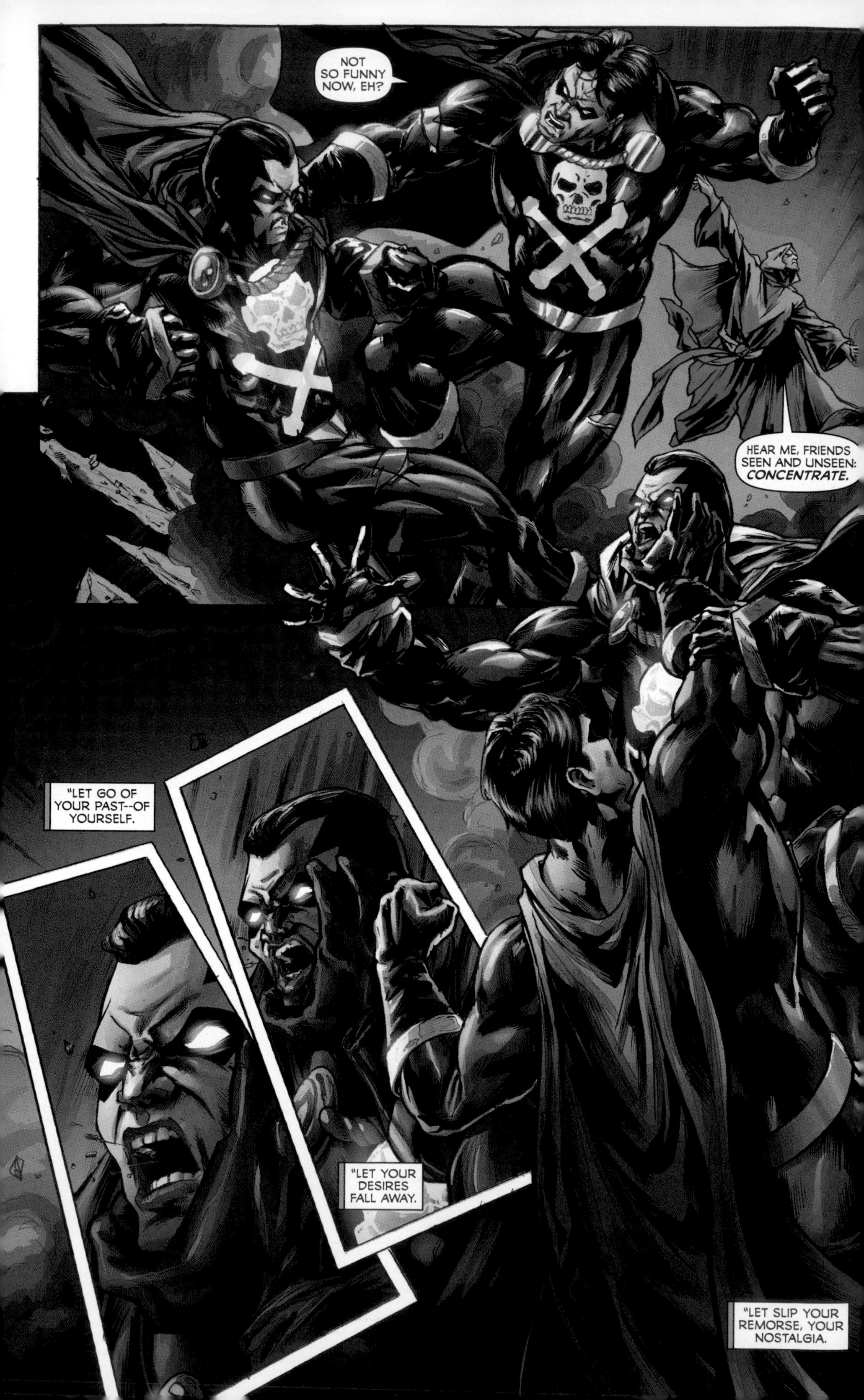
NOT SO FUNNY NOW, EH?
HEAR ME, FRIENDS SEEN AND UNSEEN: *CONCENTRATE.*
"LET GO OF YOUR PAST--OF YOURSELF.
"LET YOUR DESIRES FALL AWAY.
"LET SLIP YOUR REMORSE, YOUR NOSTALGIA.

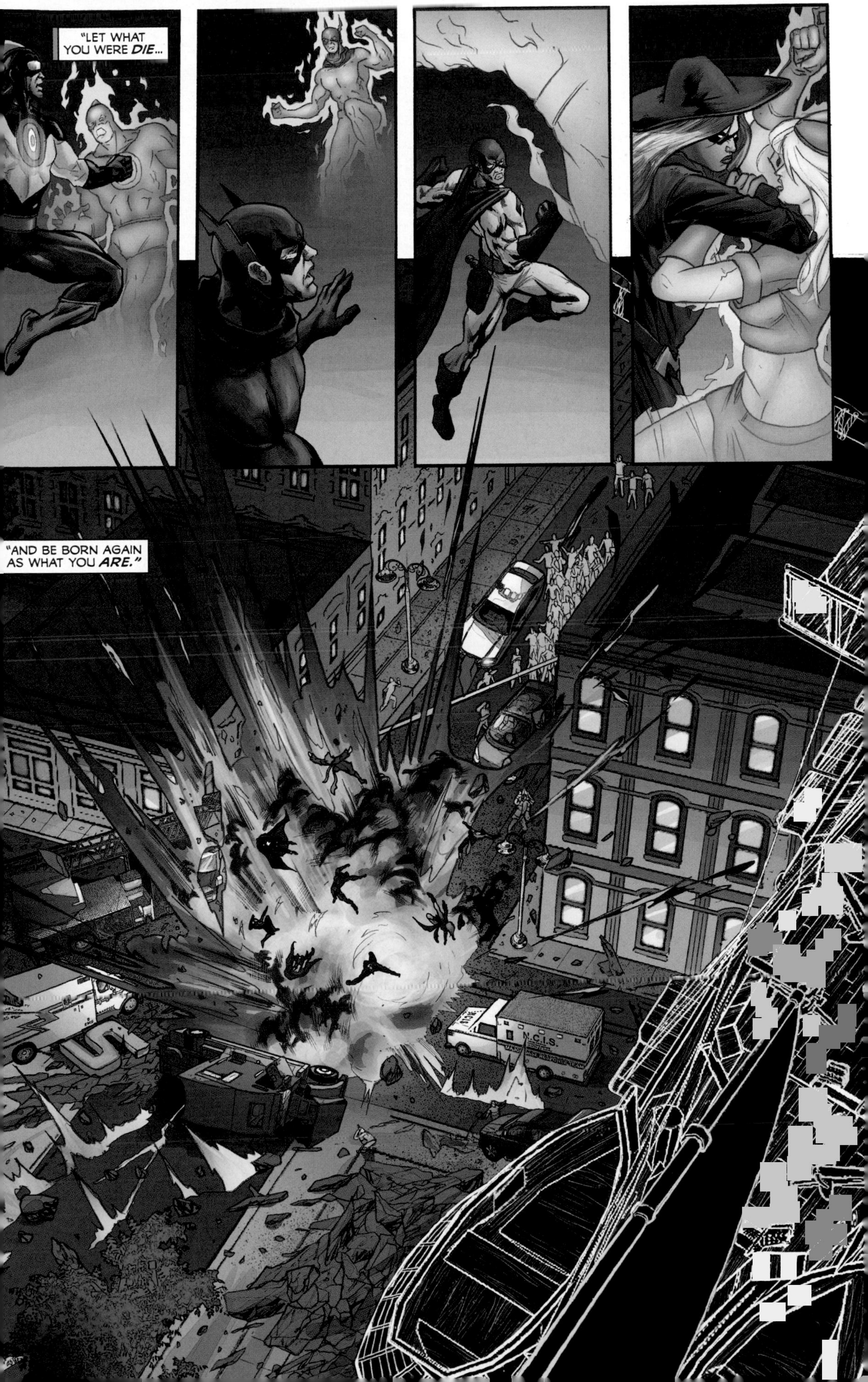
"LET WHAT YOU WERE *DIE*...
"AND BE BORN AGAIN AS WHAT YOU *ARE*."
N.C.I.S.

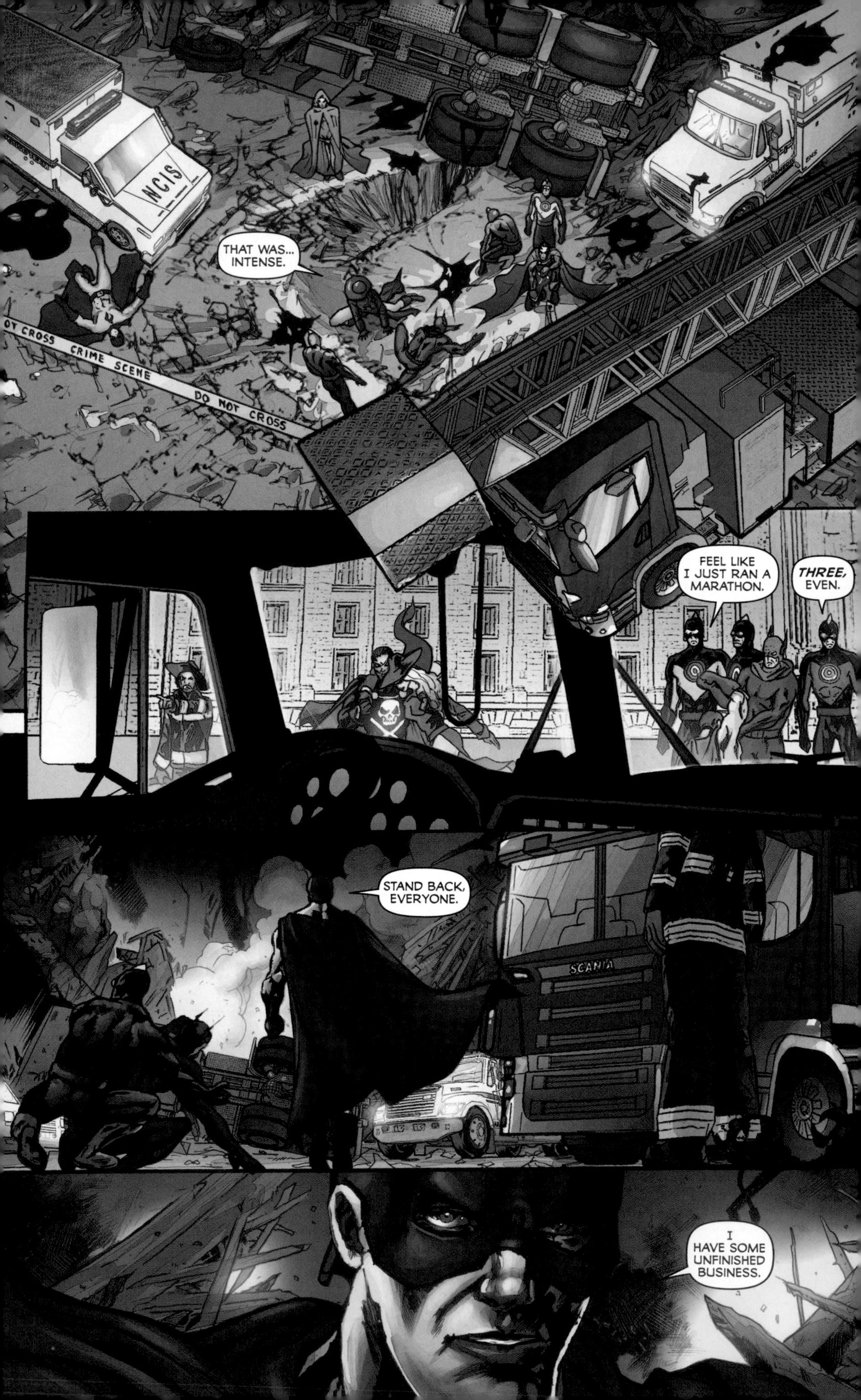
NCIS
THAT WAS... INTENSE.
OT CROSS CRIME SCENE DO NOT CROSS
FEEL LIKE I JUST RAN A MARATHON.
THREE, EVEN.
STAND BACK, EVERYONE.
SCANIA
I HAVE SOME UNFINISHED BUSINESS.

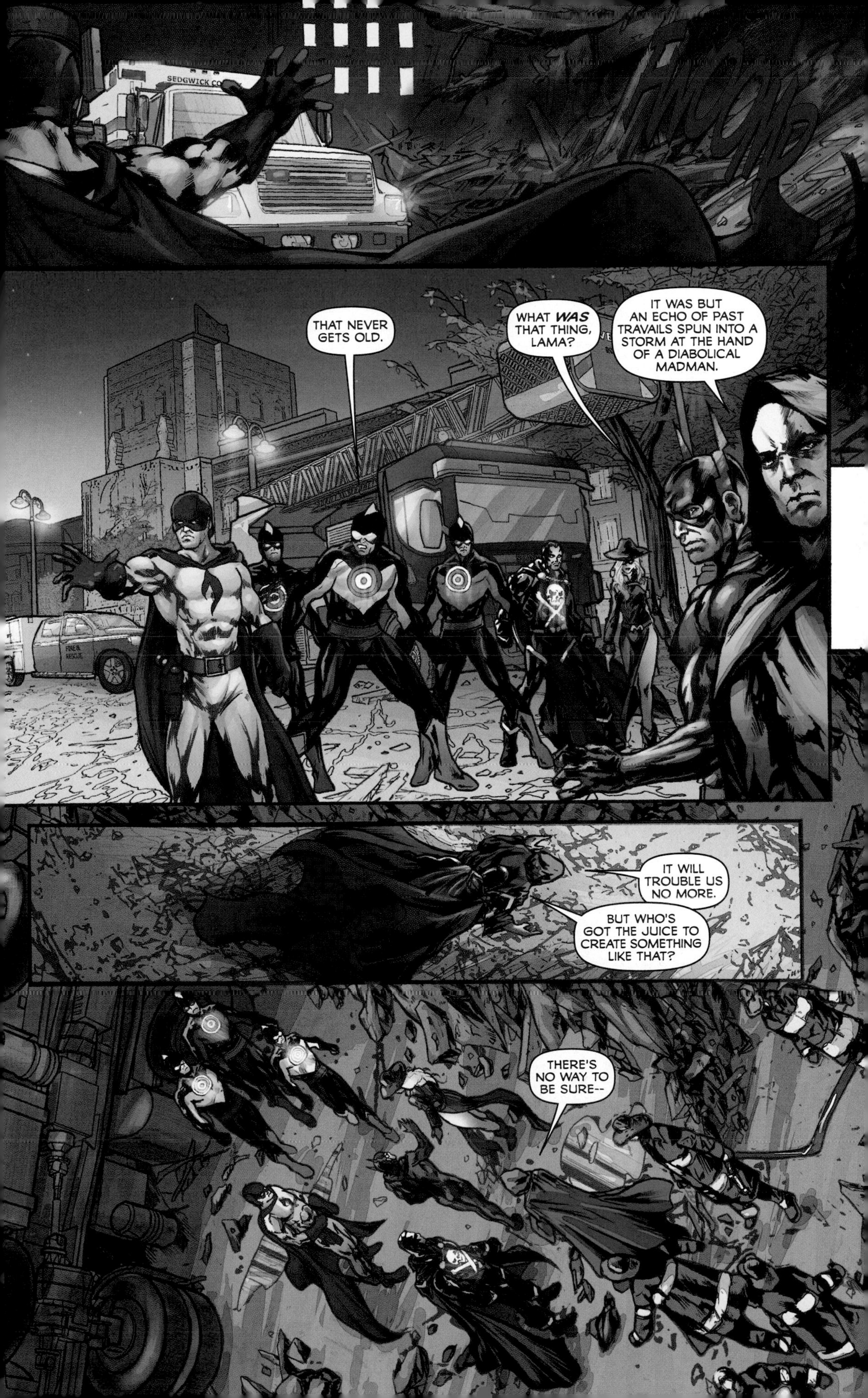
THAT NEVER GETS OLD.
WHAT *WAS* THAT THING, LAMA?
IT WAS BUT AN ECHO OF PAST TRAVAILS SPUN INTO A STORM AT THE HAND OF A DIABOLICAL MADMAN.
IT WILL TROUBLE US NO MORE.
BUT WHO'S GOT THE JUICE TO CREATE SOMETHING LIKE THAT?
THERE'S NO WAY TO BE SURE--

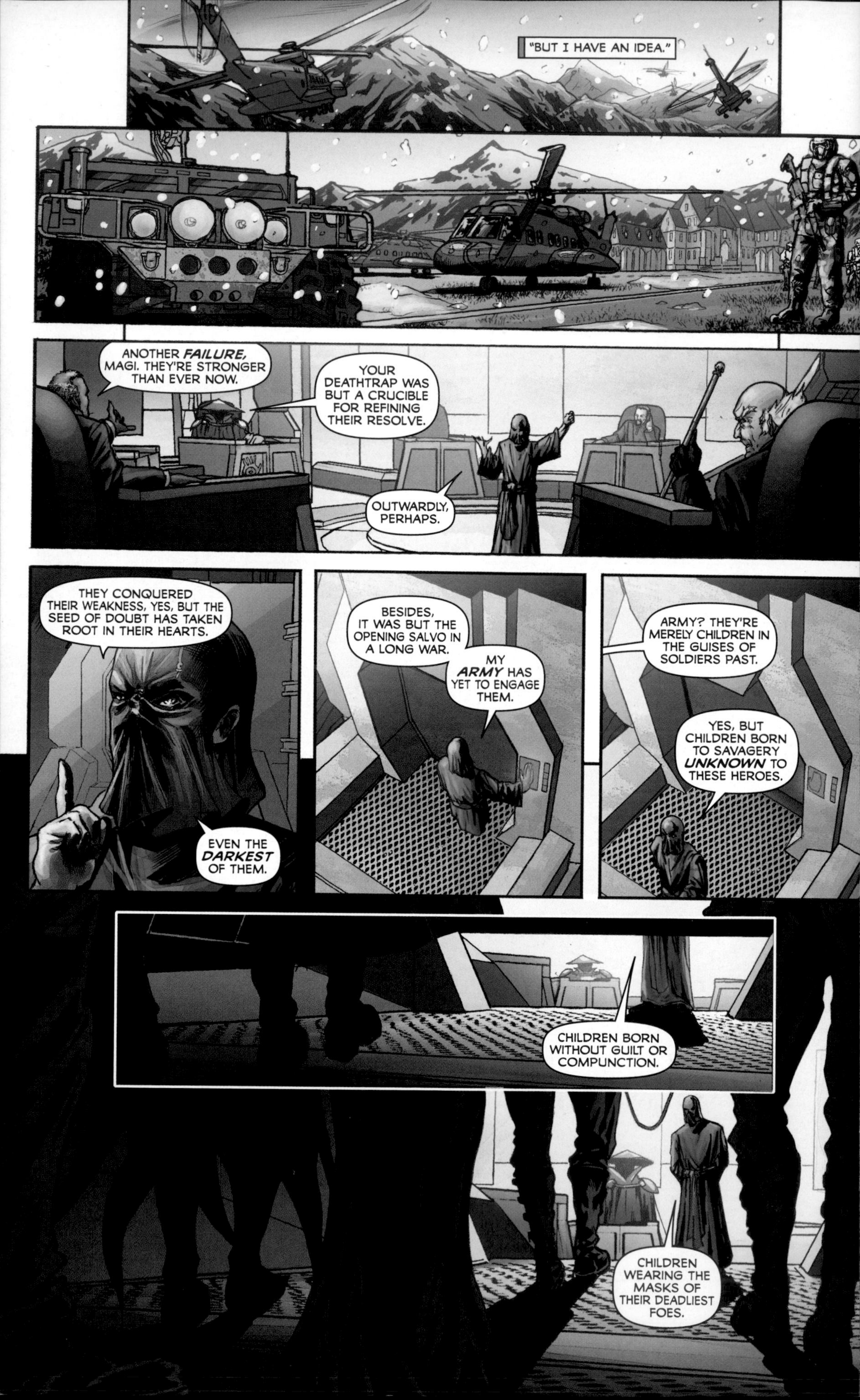
"BUT I HAVE AN IDEA."
ANOTHER FAILURE, MAGI. THEY'RE STRONGER THAN EVER NOW.
YOUR DEATHTRAP WAS BUT A CRUCIBLE FOR REFINING THEIR RESOLVE.
OUTWARDLY, PERHAPS.
THEY CONQUERED THEIR WEAKNESS, YES, BUT THE SEED OF DOUBT HAS TAKEN ROOT IN THEIR HEARTS.
EVEN THE DARKEST OF THEM.
BESIDES, IT WAS BUT THE OPENING SALVO IN A LONG WAR.
MY ARMY HAS YET TO ENGAGE THEM.
ARMY? THEY'RE MERELY CHILDREN IN THE GUISES OF SOLDIERS PAST.
YES, BUT CHILDREN BORN TO SAVAGERY UNKNOWN TO THESE HEROES.
CHILDREN BORN WITHOUT GUILT OR COMPUNCTION.
CHILDREN WEARING THE MASKS OF THEIR DEADLIEST FOES.

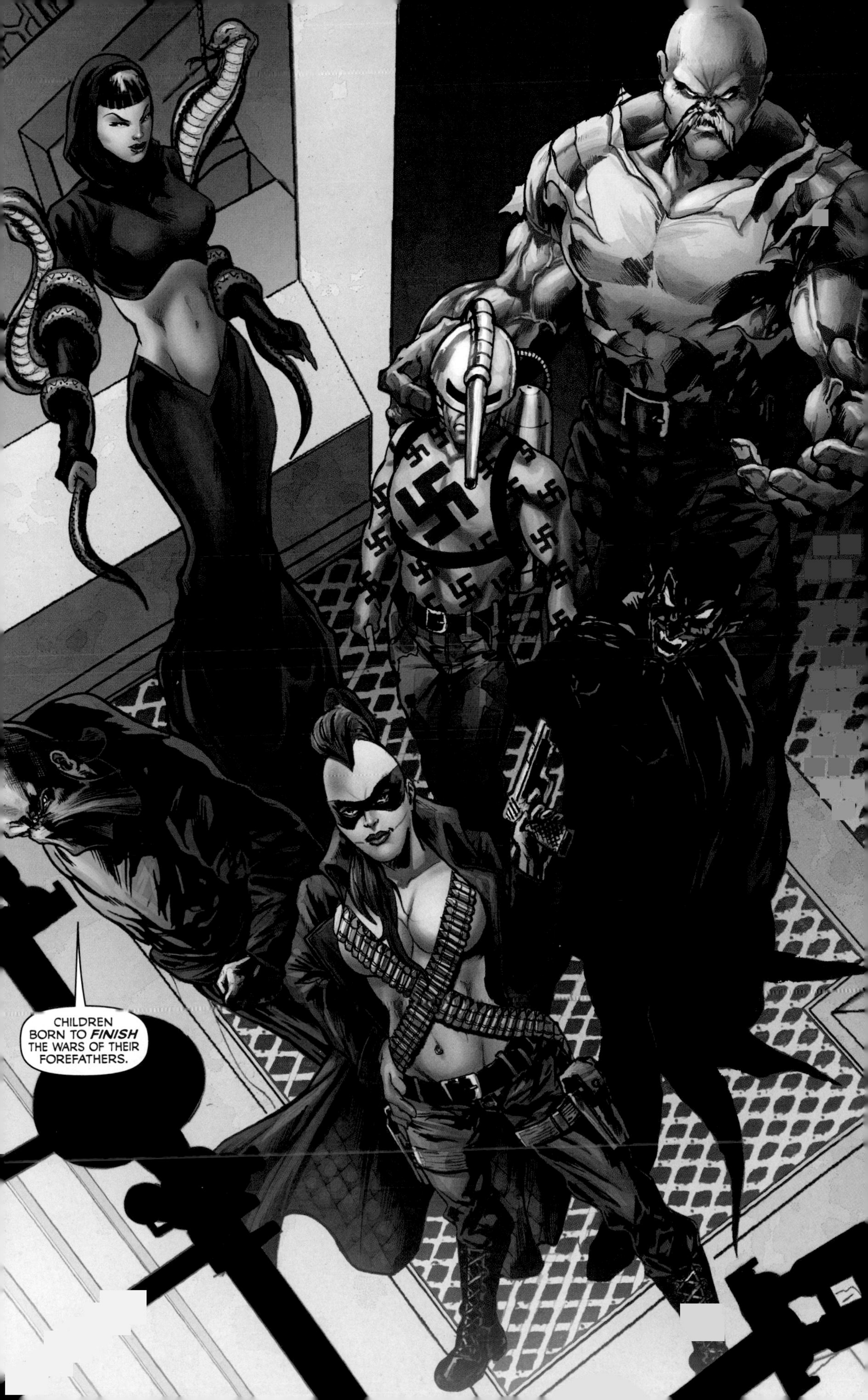
CHILDREN BORN TO *FINISH* THE WARS OF THEIR FOREFATHERS.

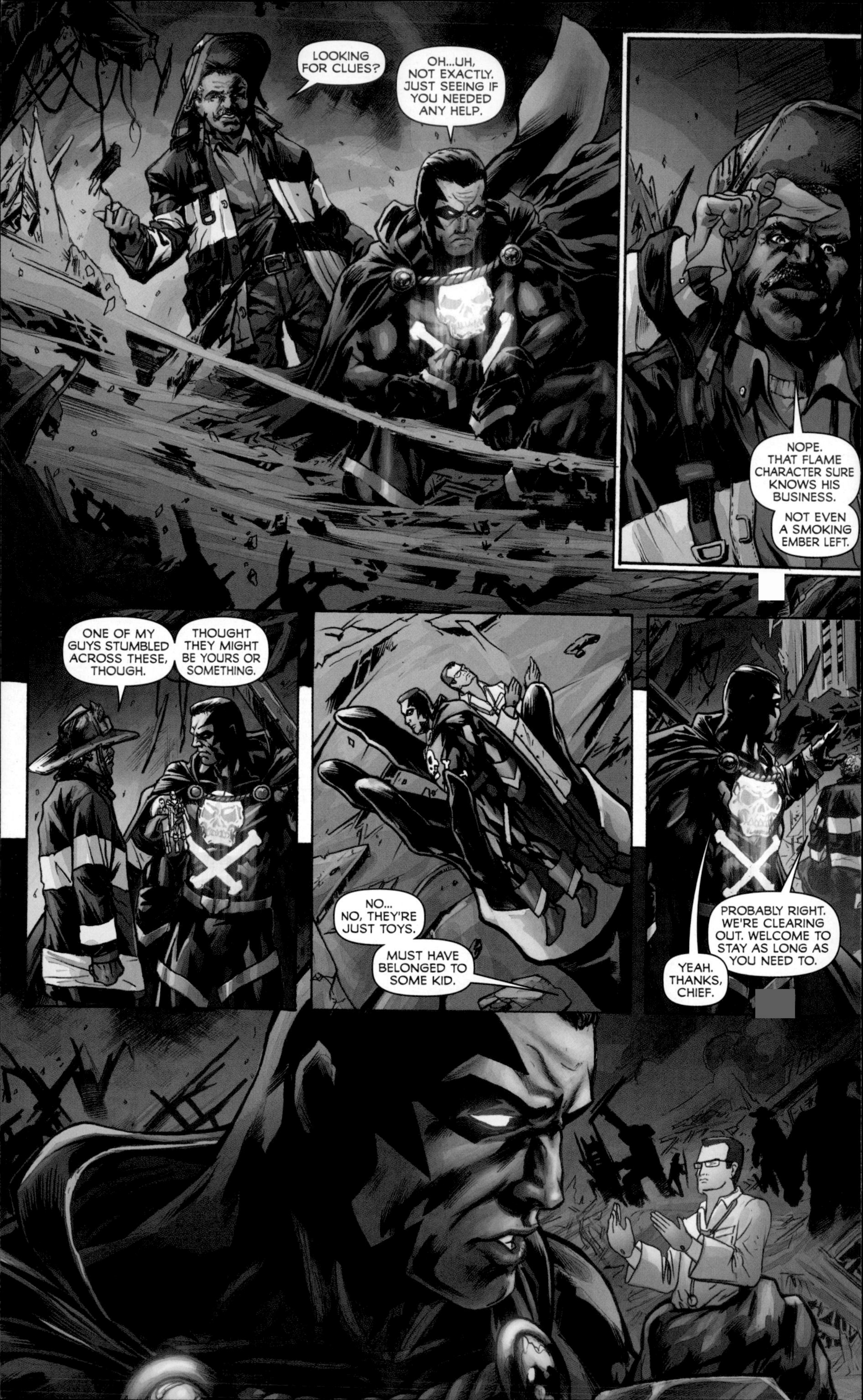
LOOKING FOR CLUES?
OH...UH, NOT EXACTLY. JUST SEEING IF YOU NEEDED ANY HELP.
NOPE. THAT FLAME CHARACTER SURE KNOWS HIS BUSINESS.
NOT EVEN A SMOKING EMBER LEFT.
ONE OF MY GUYS STUMBLED ACROSS THESE, THOUGH.
THOUGHT THEY MIGHT BE YOURS OR SOMETHING.
NO... NO, THEY'RE JUST TOYS.
MUST HAVE BELONGED TO SOME KID.
PROBABLY RIGHT. WE'RE CLEARING OUT. WELCOME TO STAY AS LONG AS YOU NEED TO.
YEAH. THANKS, CHIEF.

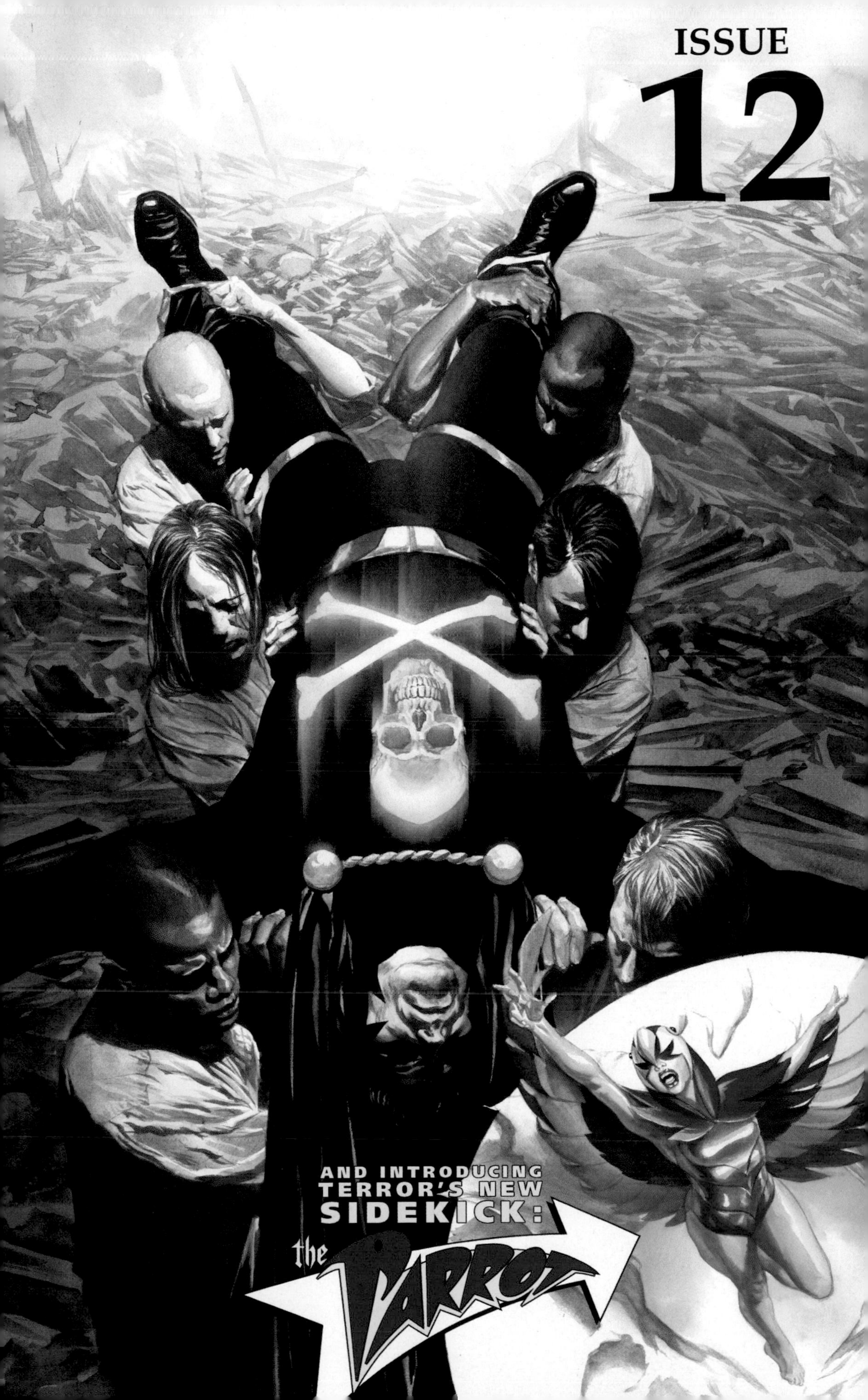
ISSUE
12
AND INTRODUCING
TERROR'S NEW
SIDEKICK:
the PARROT

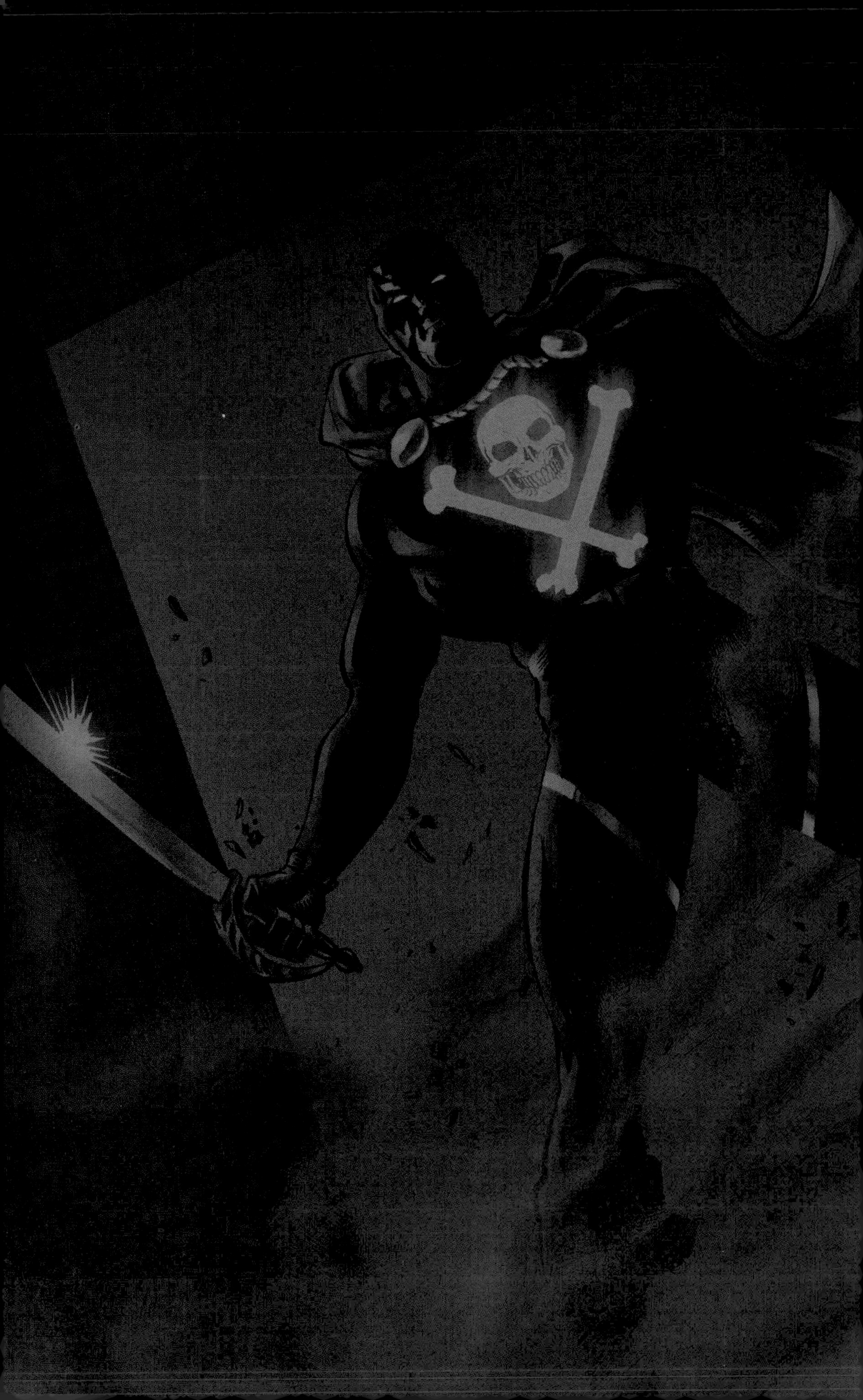

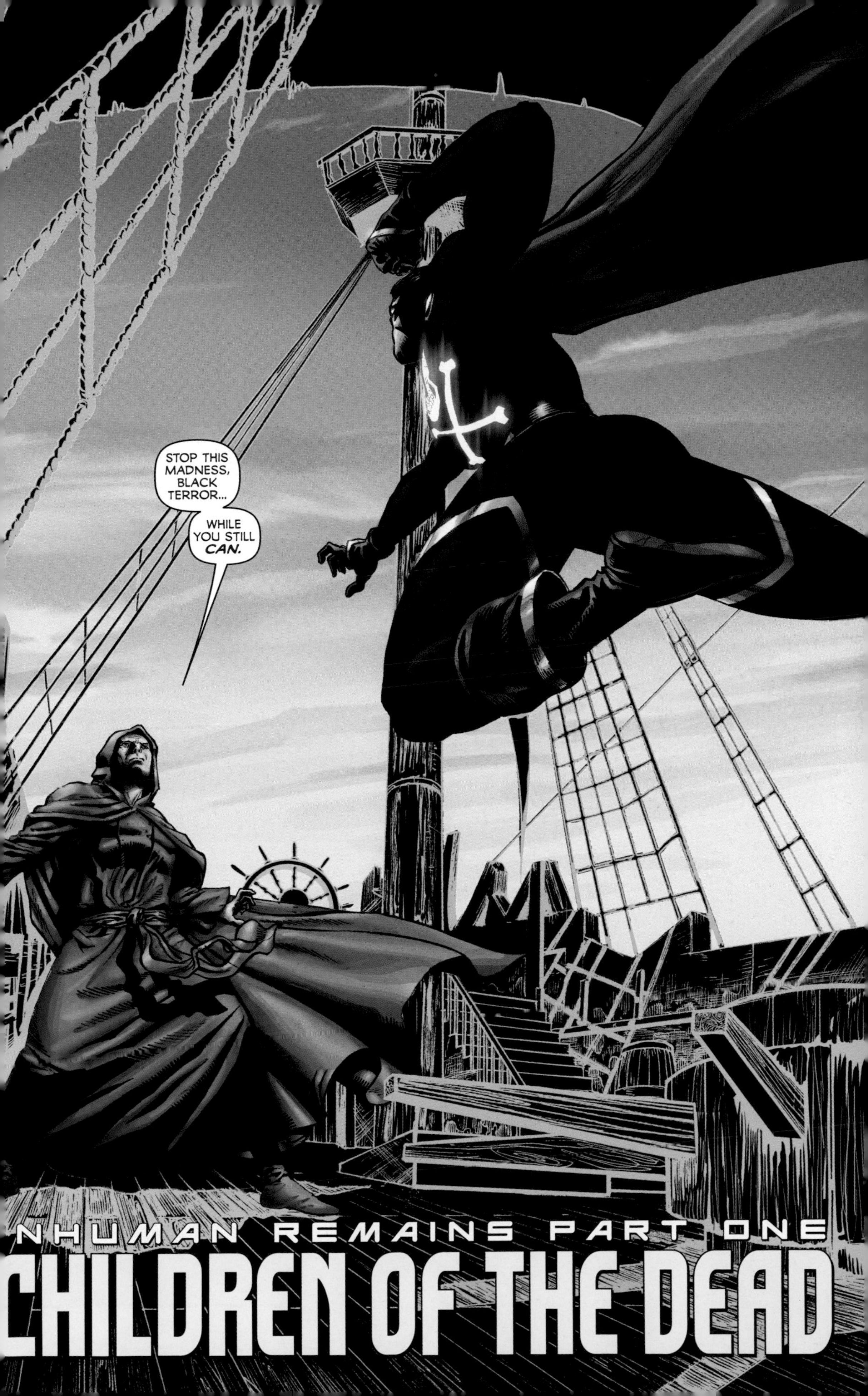
STOP THIS MADNESS, BLACK TERROR...
WHILE YOU STILL CAN.
NHUMAN REMAINS PART ONE
CHILDREN OF THE DEAD

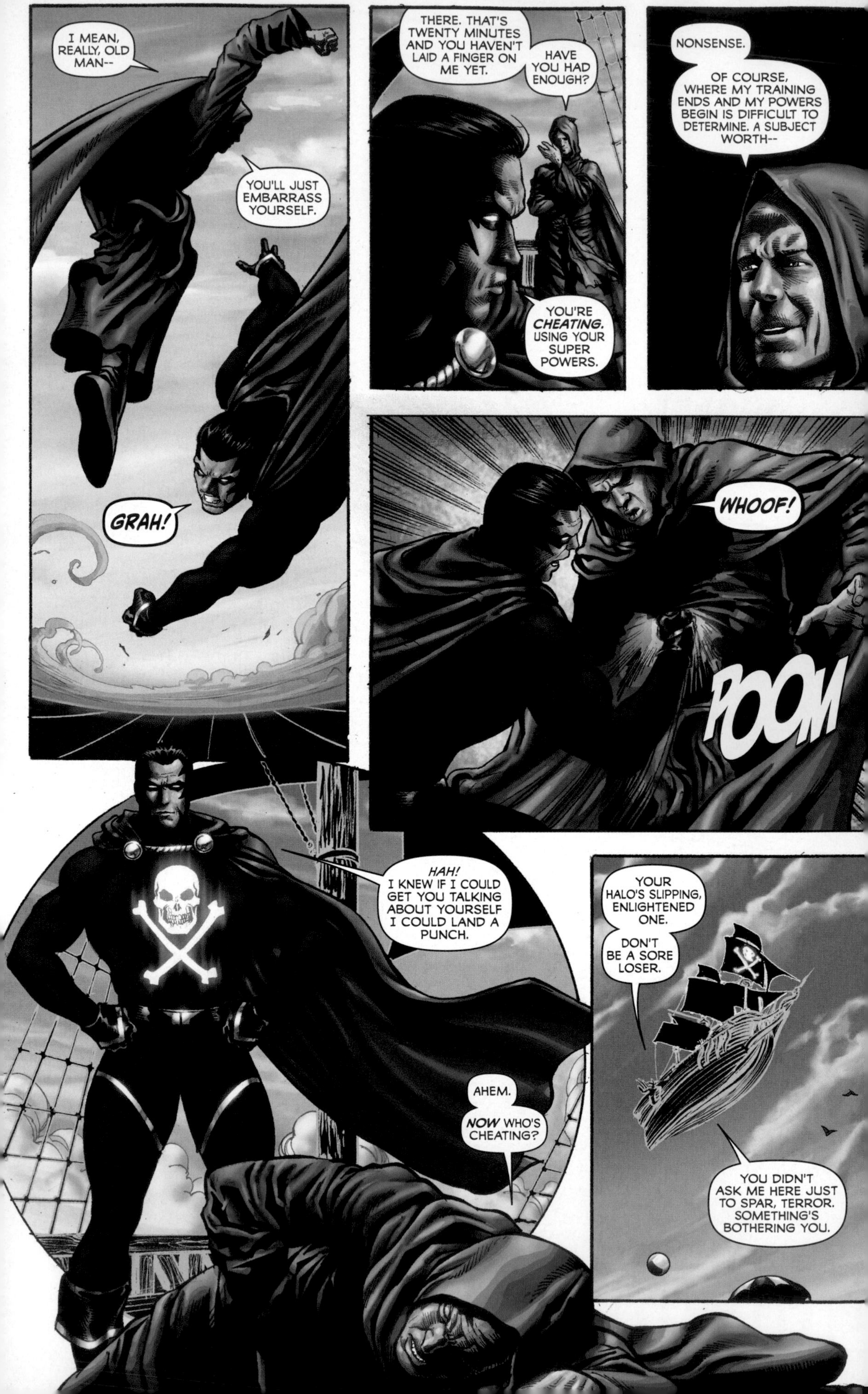
I MEAN, REALLY, OLD MAN--
YOU'LL JUST EMBARRASS YOURSELF.
GRAH!
THERE. THAT'S TWENTY MINUTES AND YOU HAVEN'T LAID A FINGER ON ME YET.
HAVE YOU HAD ENOUGH?
YOU'RE CHEATING. USING YOUR SUPER POWERS.
NONSENSE.
OF COURSE, WHERE MY TRAINING ENDS AND MY POWERS BEGIN IS DIFFICULT TO DETERMINE. A SUBJECT WORTH--
WHOOF!
POOM
HAH! I KNEW IF I COULD GET YOU TALKING ABOUT YOURSELF I COULD LAND A PUNCH.
AHEM.
NOW WHO'S CHEATING?
YOUR HALO'S SLIPPING, ENLIGHTENED ONE.
DON'T BE A SORE LOSER.
YOU DIDN'T ASK ME HERE JUST TO SPAR, TERROR. SOMETHING'S BOTHERING YOU.

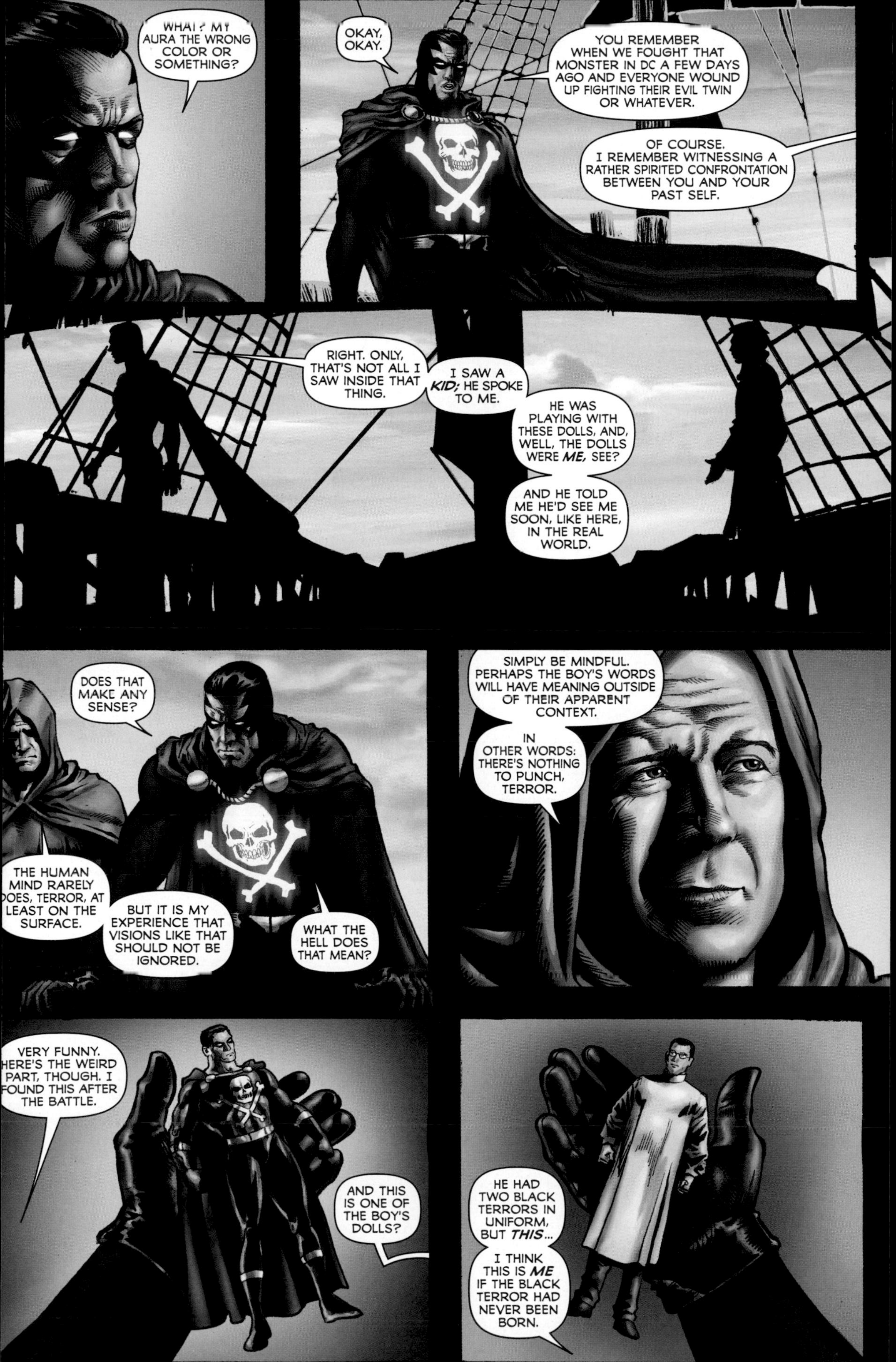
WHAT? MY AURA THE WRONG COLOR OR SOMETHING?
OKAY, OKAY.
YOU REMEMBER WHEN WE FOUGHT THAT MONSTER IN DC A FEW DAYS AGO AND EVERYONE WOUND UP FIGHTING THEIR EVIL TWIN OR WHATEVER.
OF COURSE. I REMEMBER WITNESSING A RATHER SPIRITED CONFRONTATION BETWEEN YOU AND YOUR PAST SELF.
RIGHT. ONLY, THAT'S NOT ALL I SAW INSIDE THAT THING.
I SAW A KID; HE SPOKE TO ME.
HE WAS PLAYING WITH THESE DOLLS, AND, WELL, THE DOLLS WERE ME, SEE?
AND HE TOLD ME HE'D SEE ME SOON, LIKE HERE, IN THE REAL WORLD.
DOES THAT MAKE ANY SENSE?
THE HUMAN MIND RARELY DOES, TERROR, AT LEAST ON THE SURFACE.
BUT IT IS MY EXPERIENCE THAT VISIONS LIKE THAT SHOULD NOT BE IGNORED.
WHAT THE HELL DOES THAT MEAN?
SIMPLY BE MINDFUL. PERHAPS THE BOY'S WORDS WILL HAVE MEANING OUTSIDE OF THEIR APPARENT CONTEXT.
IN OTHER WORDS: THERE'S NOTHING TO PUNCH, TERROR.
VERY FUNNY. HERE'S THE WEIRD PART, THOUGH. I FOUND THIS AFTER THE BATTLE.
AND THIS IS ONE OF THE BOY'S DOLLS?
HE HAD TWO BLACK TERRORS IN UNIFORM, BUT THIS...
I THINK THIS IS ME IF THE BLACK TERROR HAD NEVER BEEN BORN.

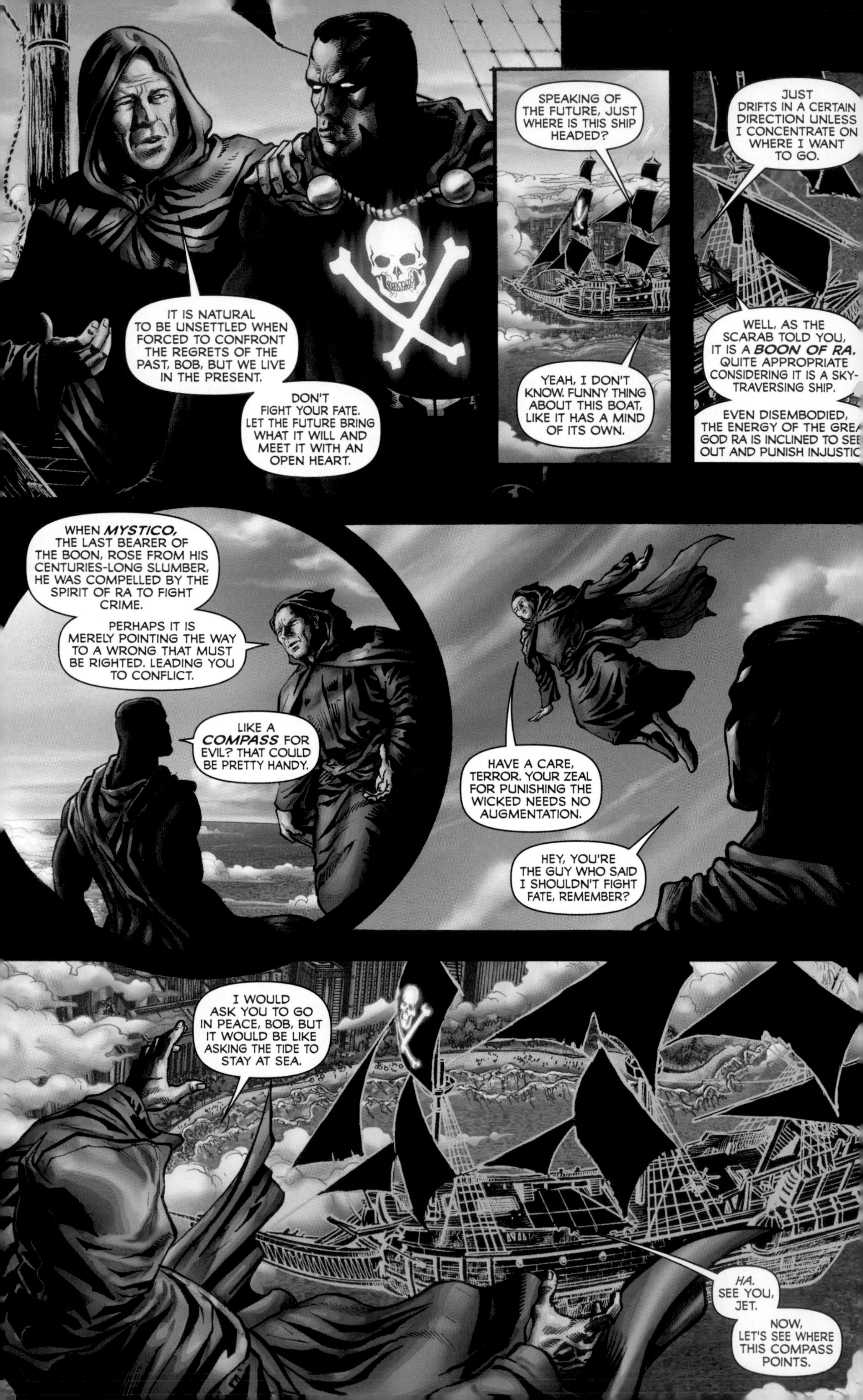
IT IS NATURAL TO BE UNSETTLED WHEN FORCED TO CONFRONT THE REGRETS OF THE PAST, BOB, BUT WE LIVE IN THE PRESENT.
DON'T FIGHT YOUR FATE. LET THE FUTURE BRING WHAT IT WILL AND MEET IT WITH AN OPEN HEART.
SPEAKING OF THE FUTURE, JUST WHERE IS THIS SHIP HEADED?
YEAH, I DON'T KNOW. FUNNY THING ABOUT THIS BOAT, LIKE IT HAS A MIND OF ITS OWN.
JUST DRIFTS IN A CERTAIN DIRECTION UNLESS I CONCENTRATE ON WHERE I WANT TO GO.
WELL, AS THE SCARAB TOLD YOU, IT IS A BOON OF RA. QUITE APPROPRIATE CONSIDERING IT IS A SKY-TRAVERSING SHIP.
EVEN DISEMBODIED, THE ENERGY OF THE GREA GOD RA IS INCLINED TO SEE OUT AND PUNISH INJUSTIC
WHEN MYSTICO, THE LAST BEARER OF THE BOON, ROSE FROM HIS CENTURIES-LONG SLUMBER, HE WAS COMPELLED BY THE SPIRIT OF RA TO FIGHT CRIME.
PERHAPS IT IS MERELY POINTING THE WAY TO A WRONG THAT MUST BE RIGHTED. LEADING YOU TO CONFLICT.
LIKE A COMPASS FOR EVIL? THAT COULD BE PRETTY HANDY.
HAVE A CARE, TERROR. YOUR ZEAL FOR PUNISHING THE WICKED NEEDS NO AUGMENTATION.
HEY, YOU'RE THE GUY WHO SAID I SHOULDN'T FIGHT FATE, REMEMBER?
I WOULD ASK YOU TO GO IN PEACE, BOB, BUT IT WOULD BE LIKE ASKING THE TIDE TO STAY AT SEA.
HA. SEE YOU, JET.
NOW, LET'S SEE WHERE THIS COMPASS POINTS.

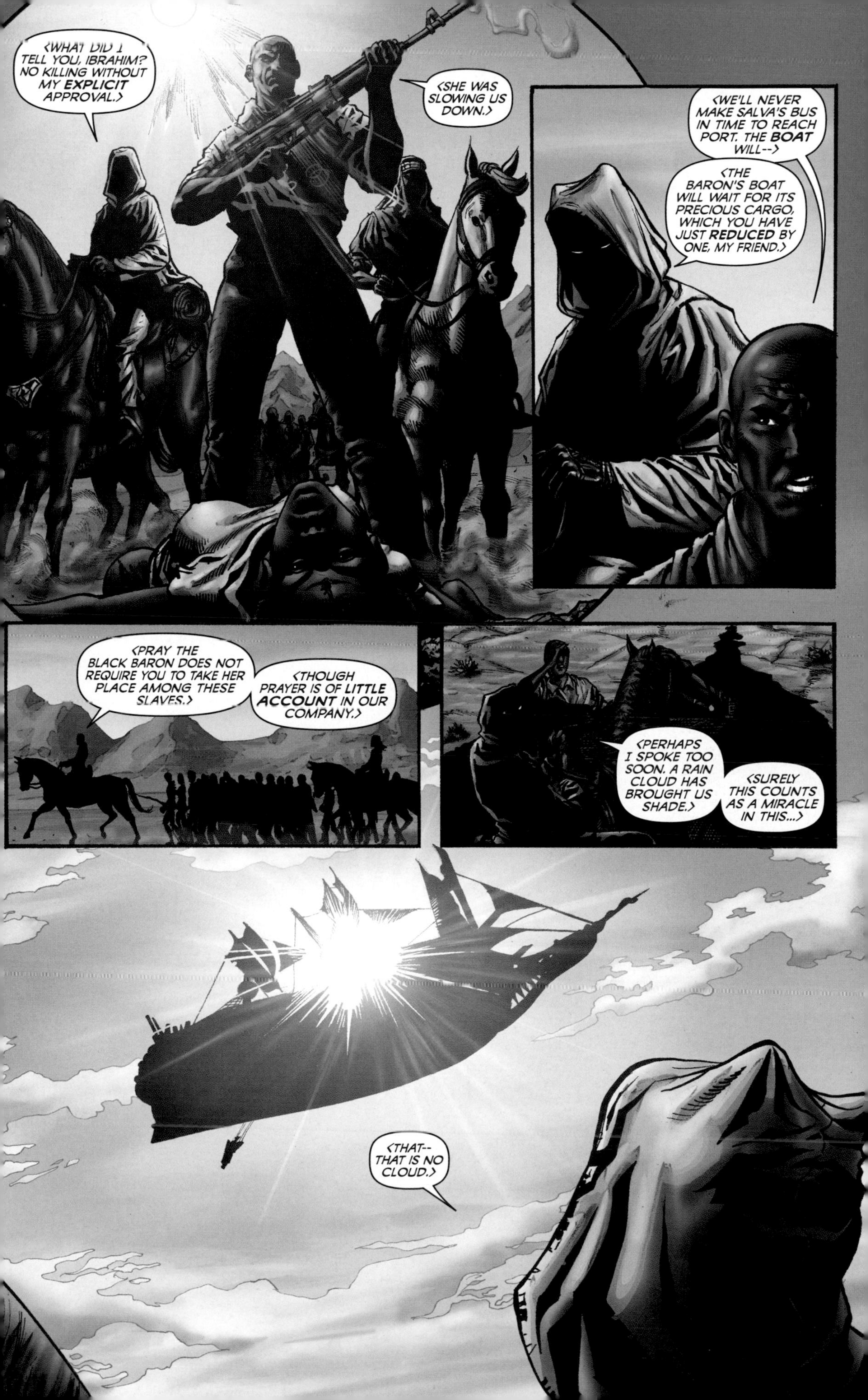
<WHAT DID I TELL YOU, IBRAHIM? NO KILLING WITHOUT MY **EXPLICIT** APPROVAL.>
<SHE WAS SLOWING US DOWN.>
<WE'LL NEVER MAKE SALVA'S BUS IN TIME TO REACH PORT. THE **BOAT** WILL-->
<THE BARON'S BOAT WILL WAIT FOR ITS PRECIOUS CARGO, WHICH YOU HAVE JUST **REDUCED** BY ONE, MY FRIEND.>
<PRAY THE BLACK BARON DOES NOT REQUIRE YOU TO TAKE HER PLACE AMONG THESE SLAVES.>
<THOUGH PRAYER IS OF **LITTLE ACCOUNT** IN OUR COMPANY.>
<PERHAPS I SPOKE TOO SOON. A RAIN CLOUD HAS BROUGHT US SHADE.>
<SURELY THIS COUNTS AS A MIRACLE IN THIS...>
<THAT-- THAT IS NO CLOUD.>

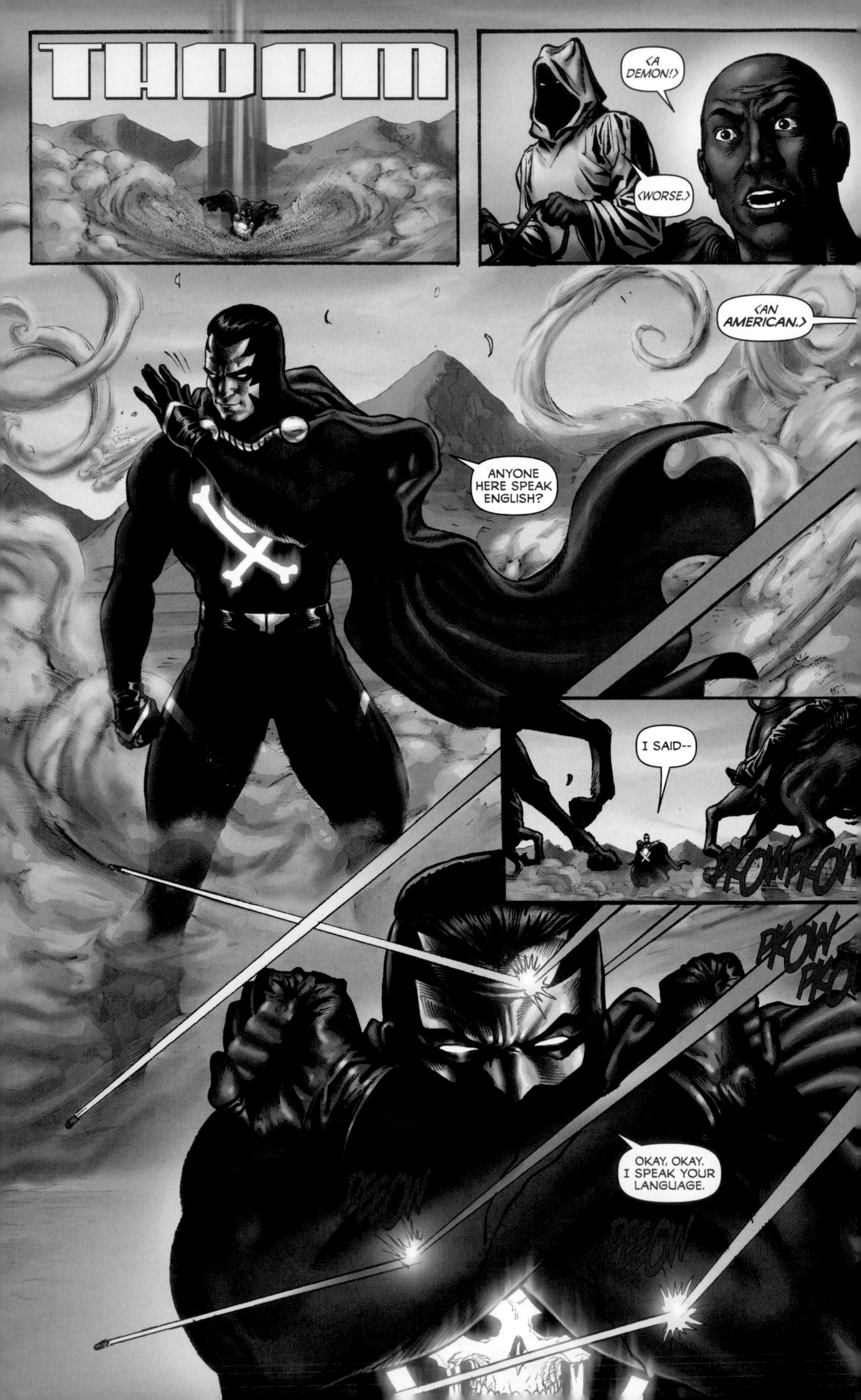
THOOM
<A DEMON!>
<WORSE.>
<AN AMERICAN.>
ANYONE HERE SPEAK ENGLISH?
I SAID--
PKOW PKOW
PKOW PKOW
OKAY, OKAY. I SPEAK YOUR LANGUAGE.

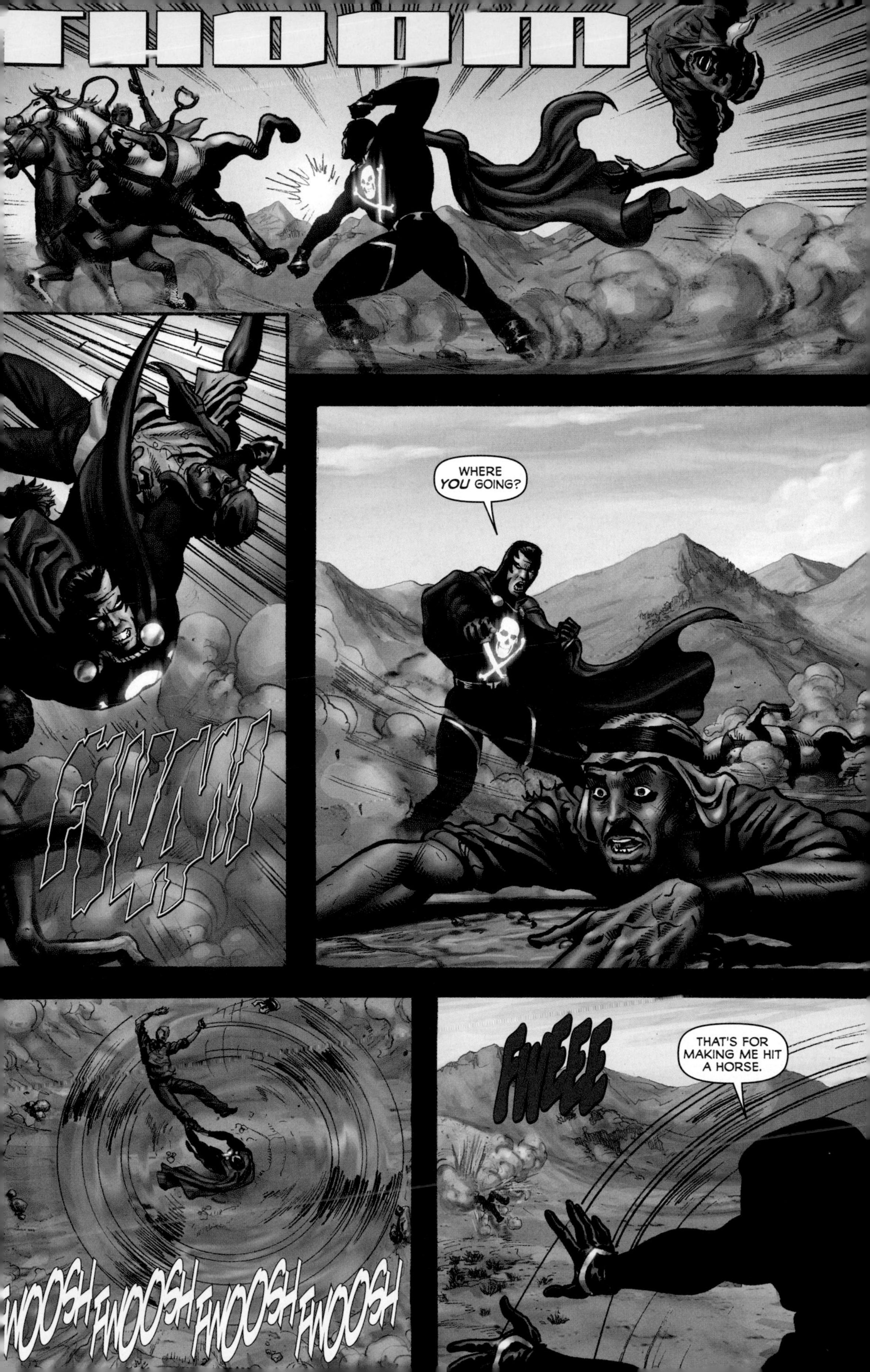
THOOM
GWM
WHERE YOU GOING?
FWOOSH FWOOSH FWOOSH FWOOSH
FWEEE
THAT'S FOR MAKING ME HIT A HORSE.

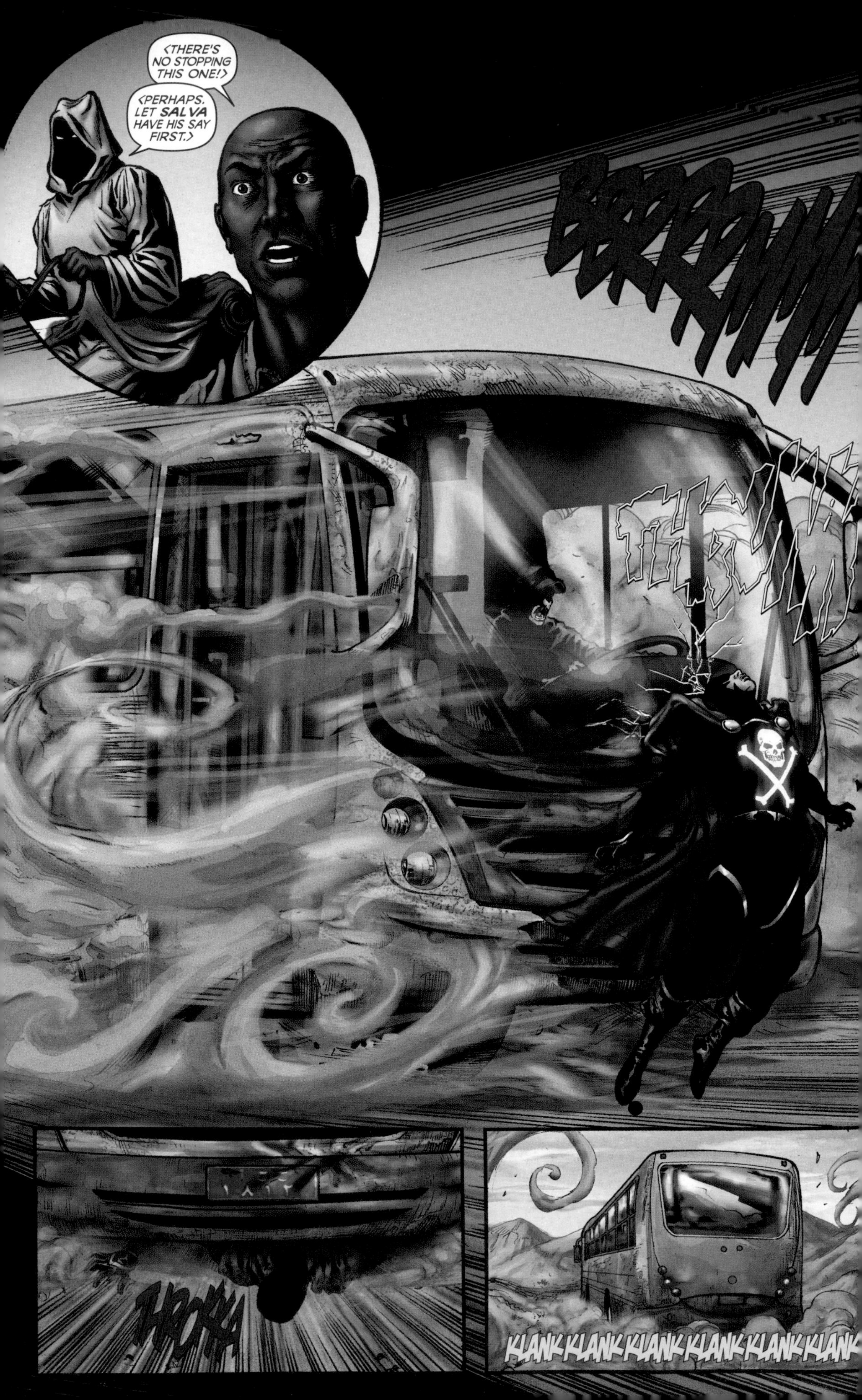

<THERE'S NO STOPPING THIS ONE!>
<PERHAPS. LET SALVA HAVE HIS SAY FIRST.>
KLANK KLANK KLANK KLANK KLANK KLANK

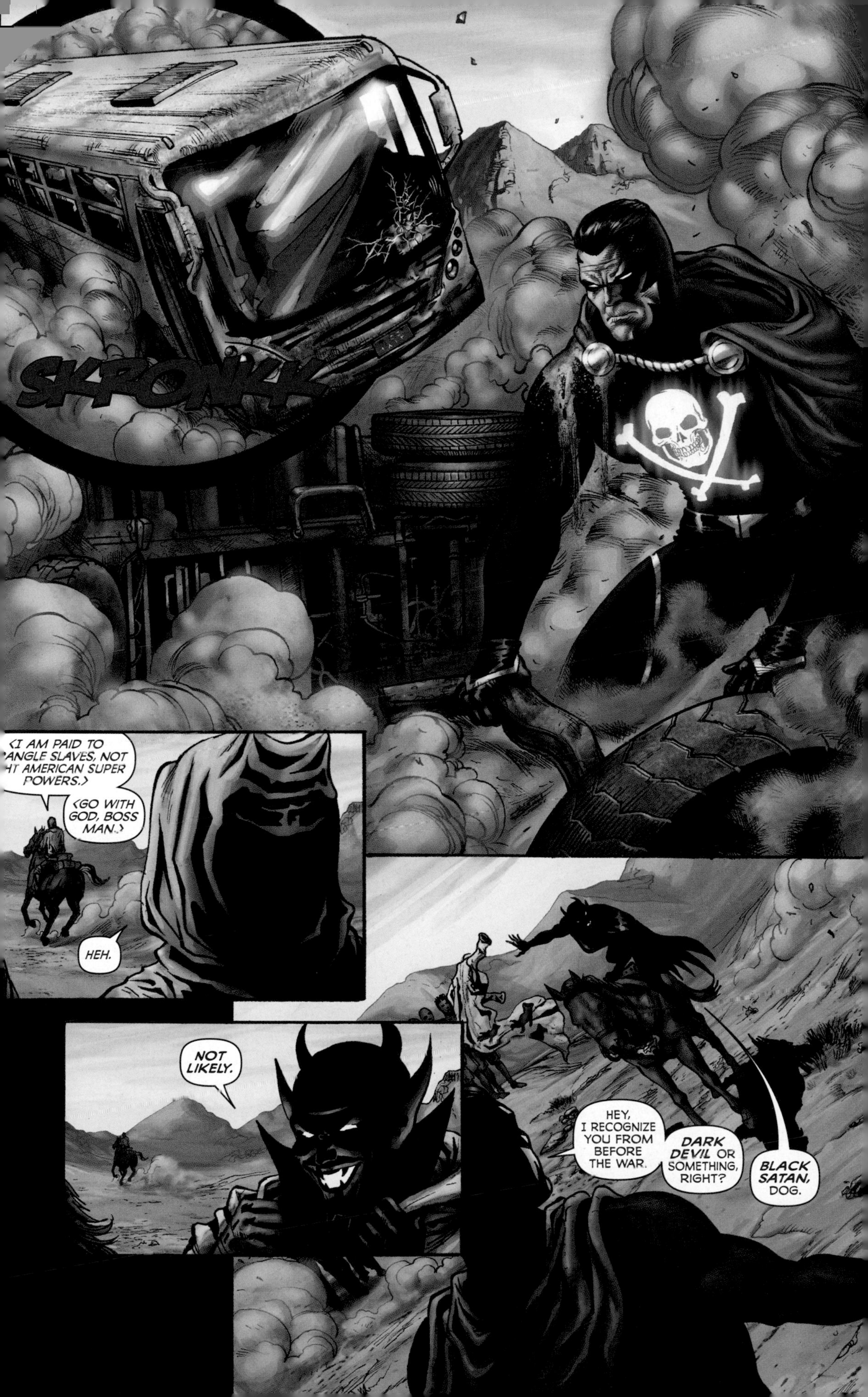
SKRONKK
<I AM PAID TO WRANGLE SLAVES, NOT FIGHT AMERICAN SUPER POWERS.>
<GO WITH GOD, BOSS MAN.>
HEH.
NOT LIKELY.
HEY, I RECOGNIZE YOU FROM BEFORE THE WAR.
DARK DEVIL OR SOMETHING, RIGHT?
BLACK SATAN, DOG.

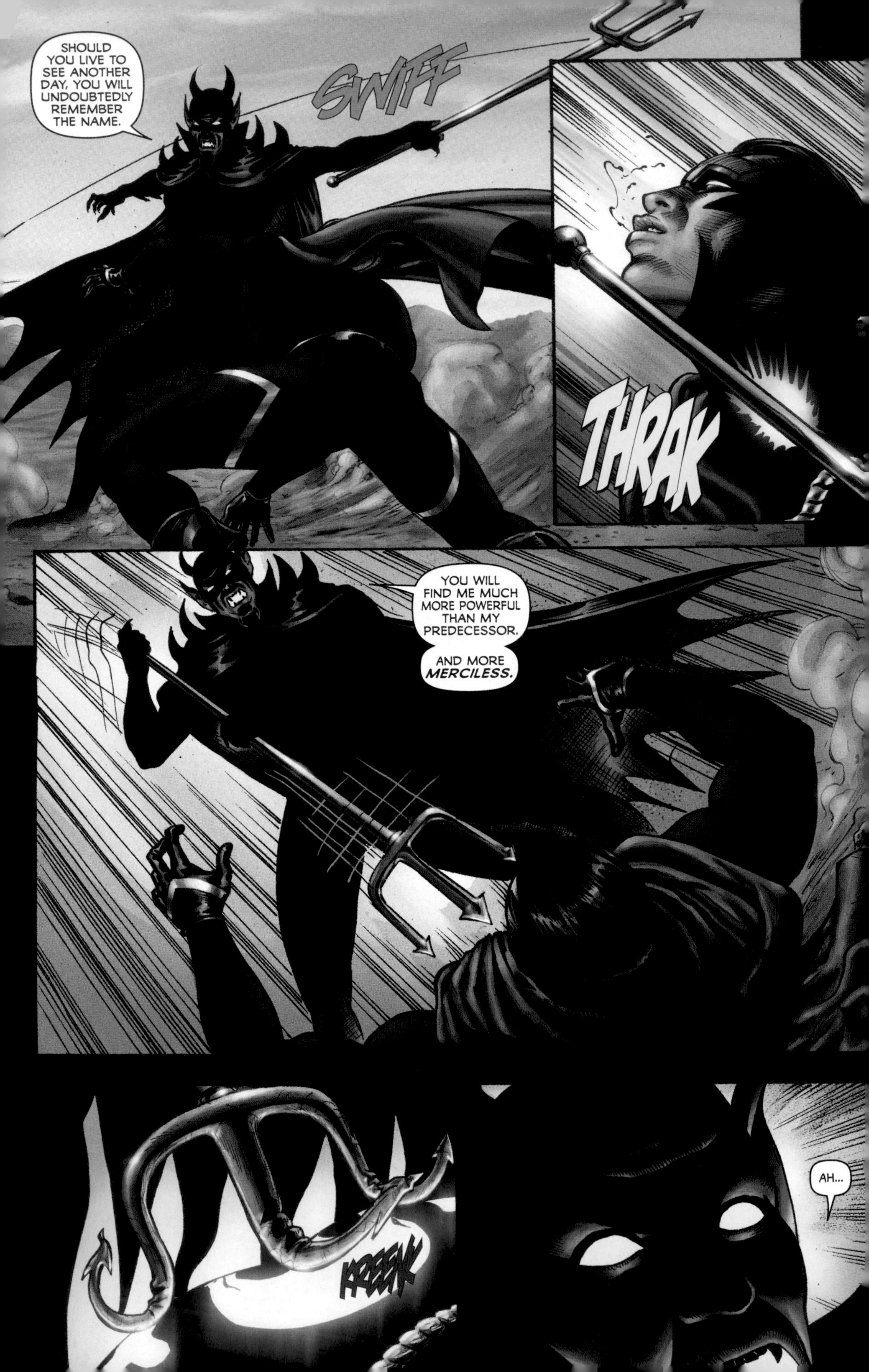
SHOULD YOU LIVE TO SEE ANOTHER DAY, YOU WILL UNDOUBTEDLY REMEMBER THE NAME.
SWIFF
THRAK
YOU WILL FIND ME MUCH MORE POWERFUL THAN MY PREDECESSOR.
AND MORE *MERCILESS.*
KREEK
AH...

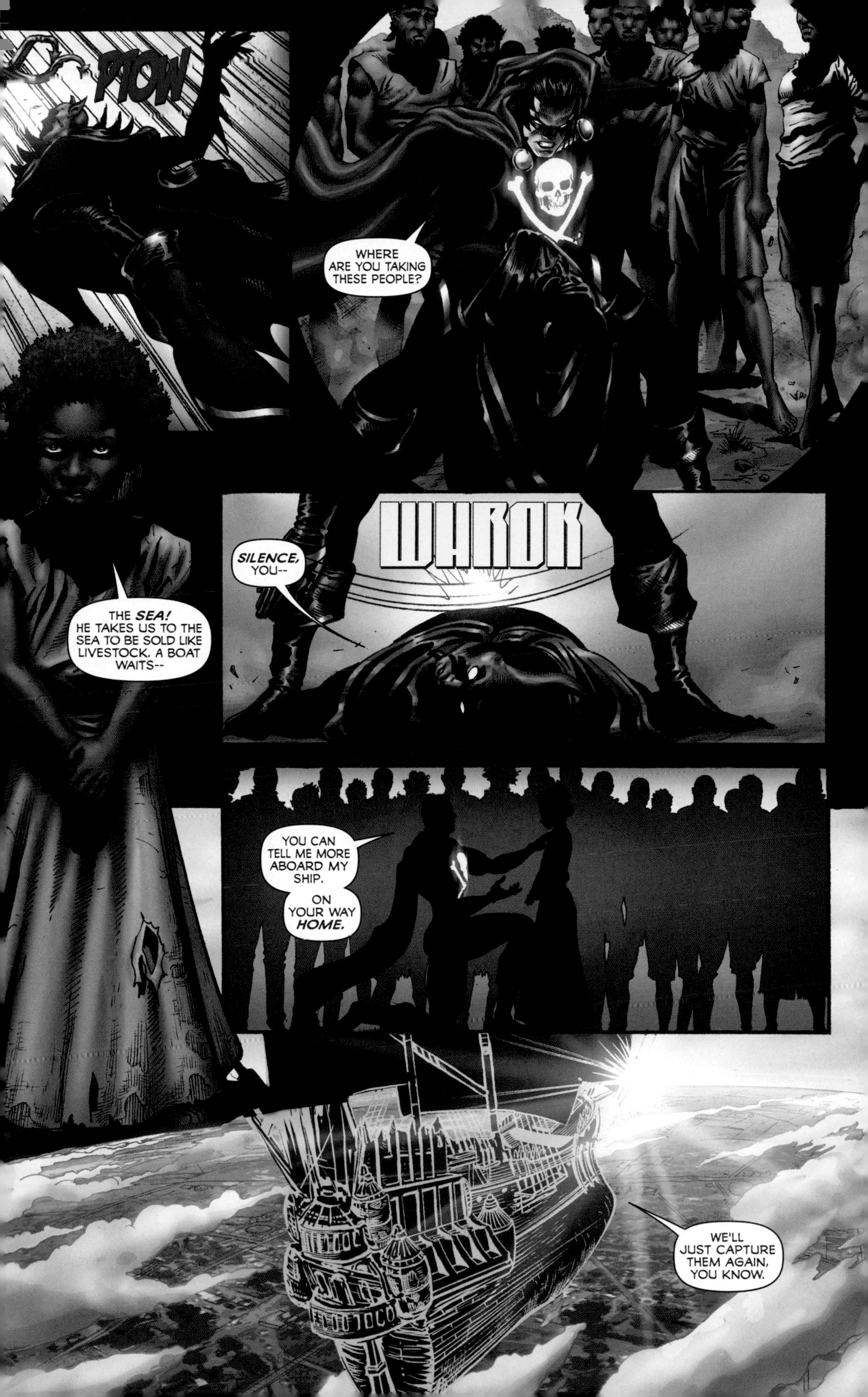
PTOW
WHERE ARE YOU TAKING THESE PEOPLE?
THE SEA! HE TAKES US TO THE SEA TO BE SOLD LIKE LIVESTOCK. A BOAT WAITS--
SILENCE, YOU--
WHROK
YOU CAN TELL ME MORE ABOARD MY SHIP.
ON YOUR WAY HOME.
WE'LL JUST CAPTURE THEM AGAIN, YOU KNOW.

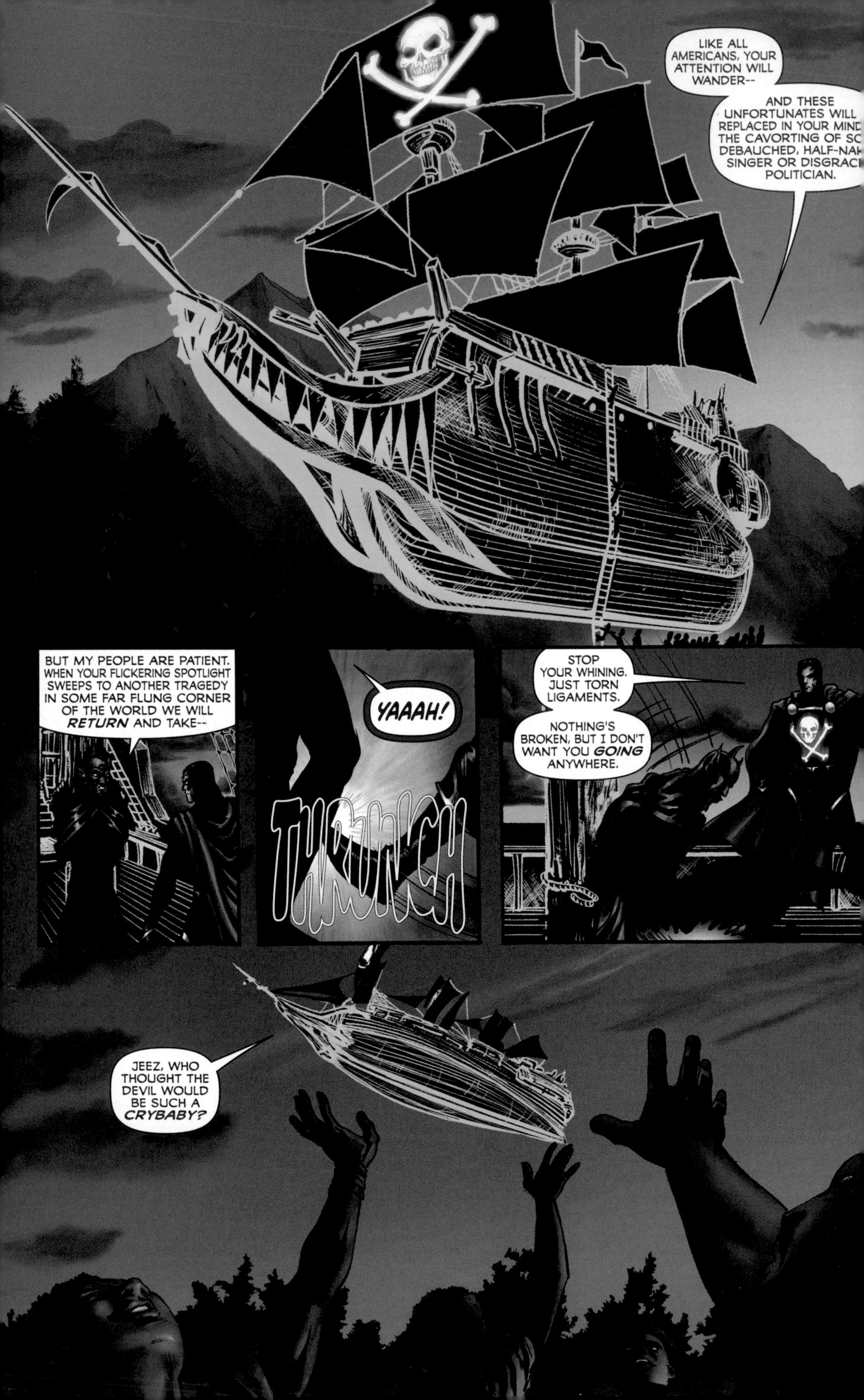
LIKE ALL AMERICANS, YOUR ATTENTION WILL WANDER--
AND THESE UNFORTUNATES WILL REPLACED IN YOUR MIND THE CAVORTING OF SC DEBAUCHED, HALF-NAK SINGER OR DISGRAC POLITICIAN.
BUT MY PEOPLE ARE PATIENT. WHEN YOUR FLICKERING SPOTLIGHT SWEEPS TO ANOTHER TRAGEDY IN SOME FAR FLUNG CORNER OF THE WORLD WE WILL *RETURN* AND TAKE--
YAAAH!
THWUNCH
STOP YOUR WHINING. JUST TORN LIGAMENTS.
NOTHING'S BROKEN, BUT I DON'T WANT YOU *GOING* ANYWHERE.
JEEZ, WHO THOUGHT THE DEVIL WOULD BE SUCH A *CRYBABY?*

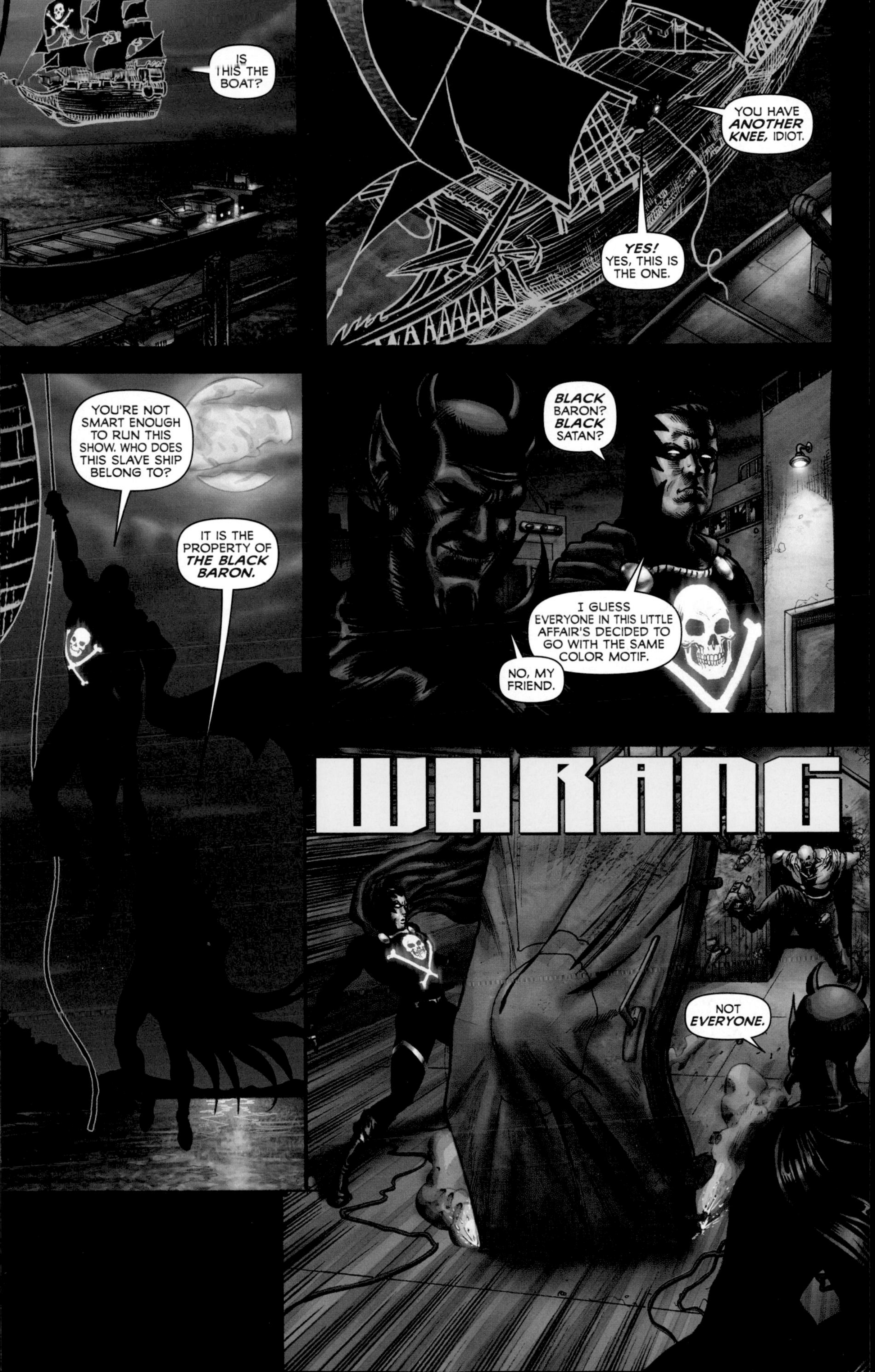
IS THIS THE BOAT?
YOU HAVE ***ANOTHER KNEE,*** IDIOT.
YES! YES, THIS IS THE ONE.
YOU'RE NOT SMART ENOUGH TO RUN THIS SHOW. WHO DOES THIS SLAVE SHIP BELONG TO?
IT IS THE PROPERTY OF ***THE BLACK BARON.***
BLACK BARON? ***BLACK*** SATAN?
I GUESS EVERYONE IN THIS LITTLE AFFAIR'S DECIDED TO GO WITH THE SAME COLOR MOTIF.
NO, MY FRIEND.
WHRANG
NOT ***EVERYONE.***

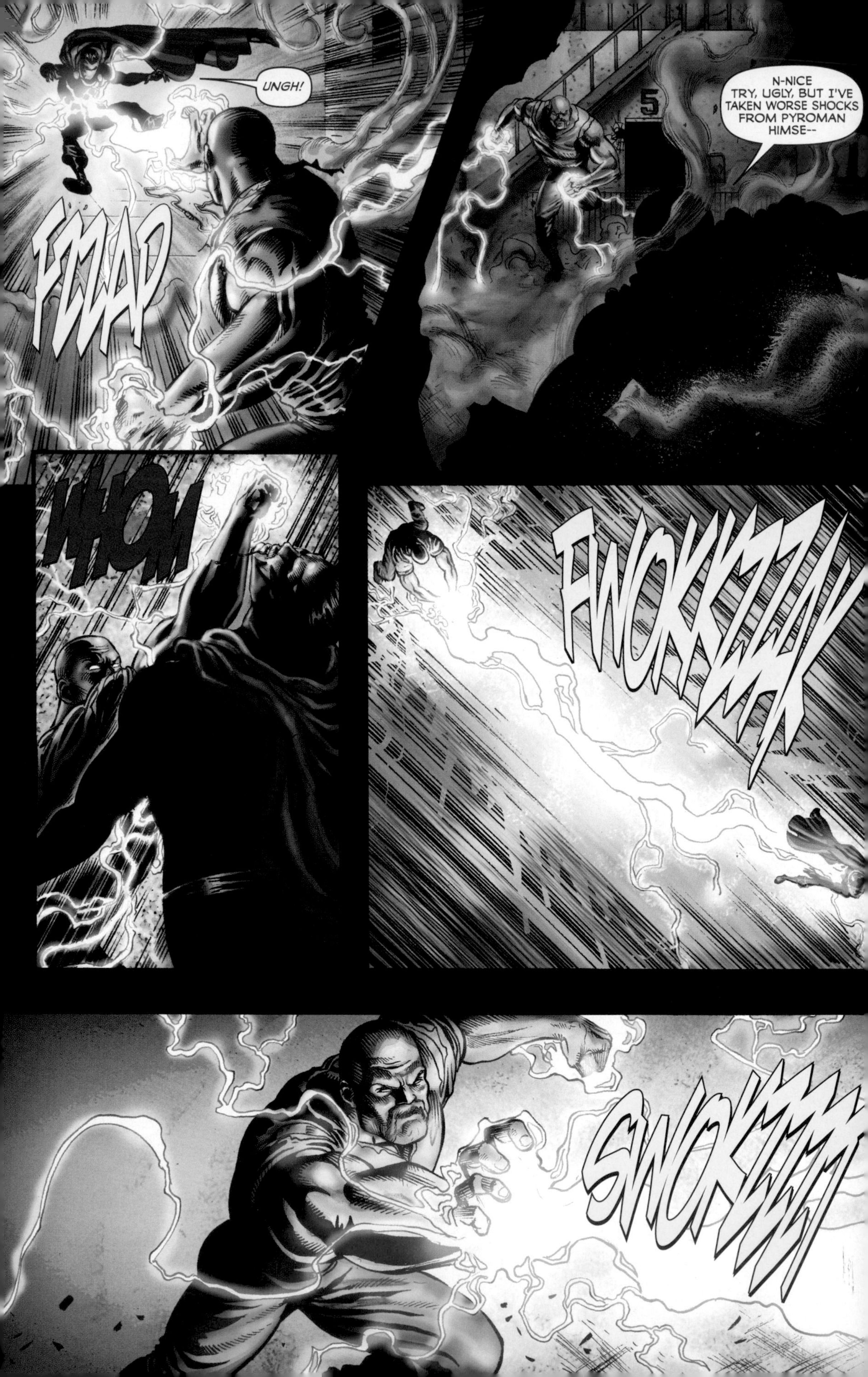
UNGH!
FZZAP
N-NICE TRY, UGLY, BUT I'VE TAKEN WORSE SHOCKS FROM PYROMAN HIMSE--
WHOM
FWOKKZZAK
SWOKZZT

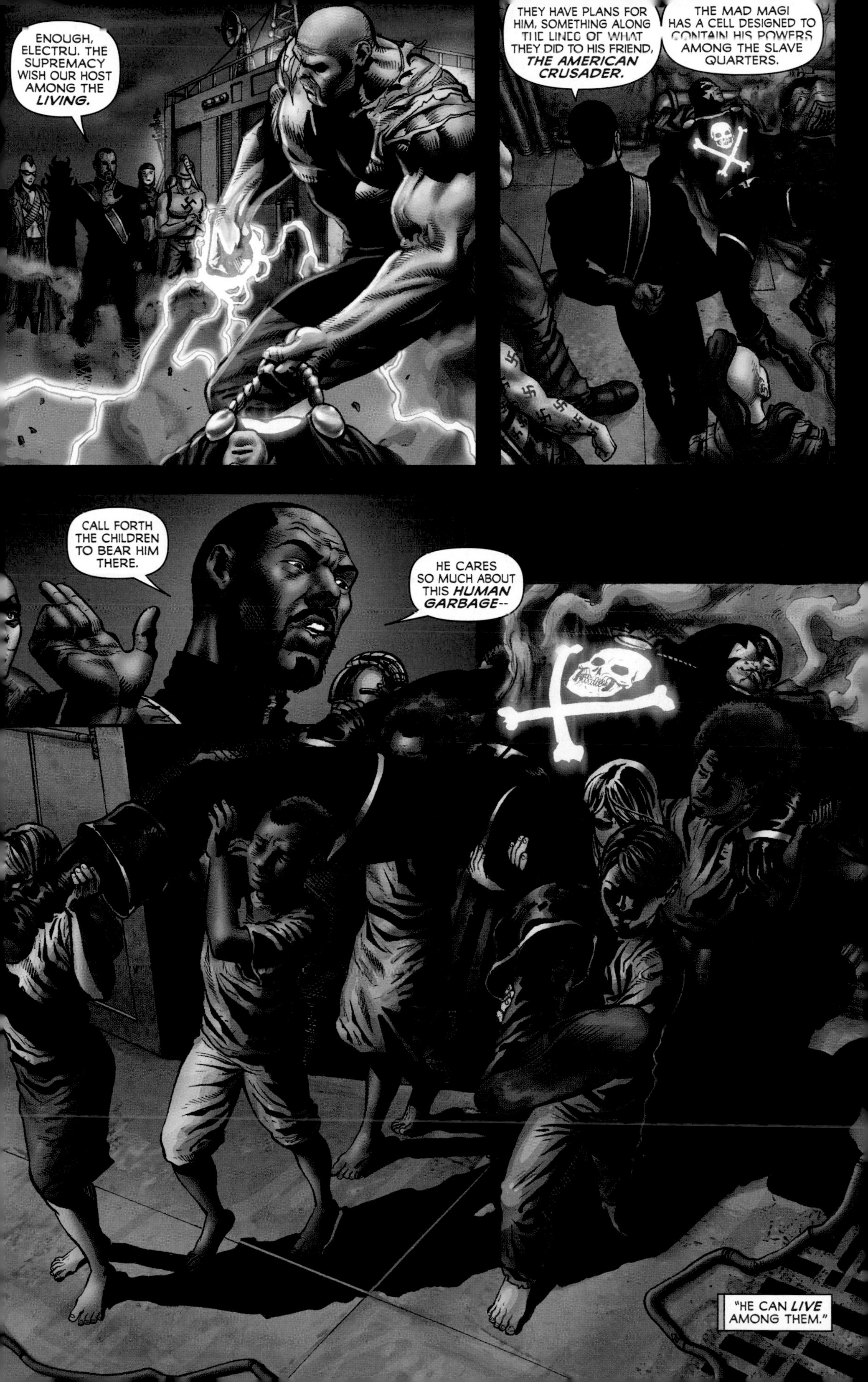

ENOUGH, ELECTRU. THE SUPREMACY WISH OUR HOST AMONG THE *LIVING.*
THEY HAVE PLANS FOR HIM, SOMETHING ALONG THE LINES OF WHAT THEY DID TO HIS FRIEND, ***THE AMERICAN CRUSADER.***
THE MAD MAGI HAS A CELL DESIGNED TO CONTAIN HIS POWERS AMONG THE SLAVE QUARTERS.
CALL FORTH THE CHILDREN TO BEAR HIM THERE.
HE CARES SO MUCH ABOUT THIS ***HUMAN GARBAGE***--
"HE CAN *LIVE* AMONG THEM."

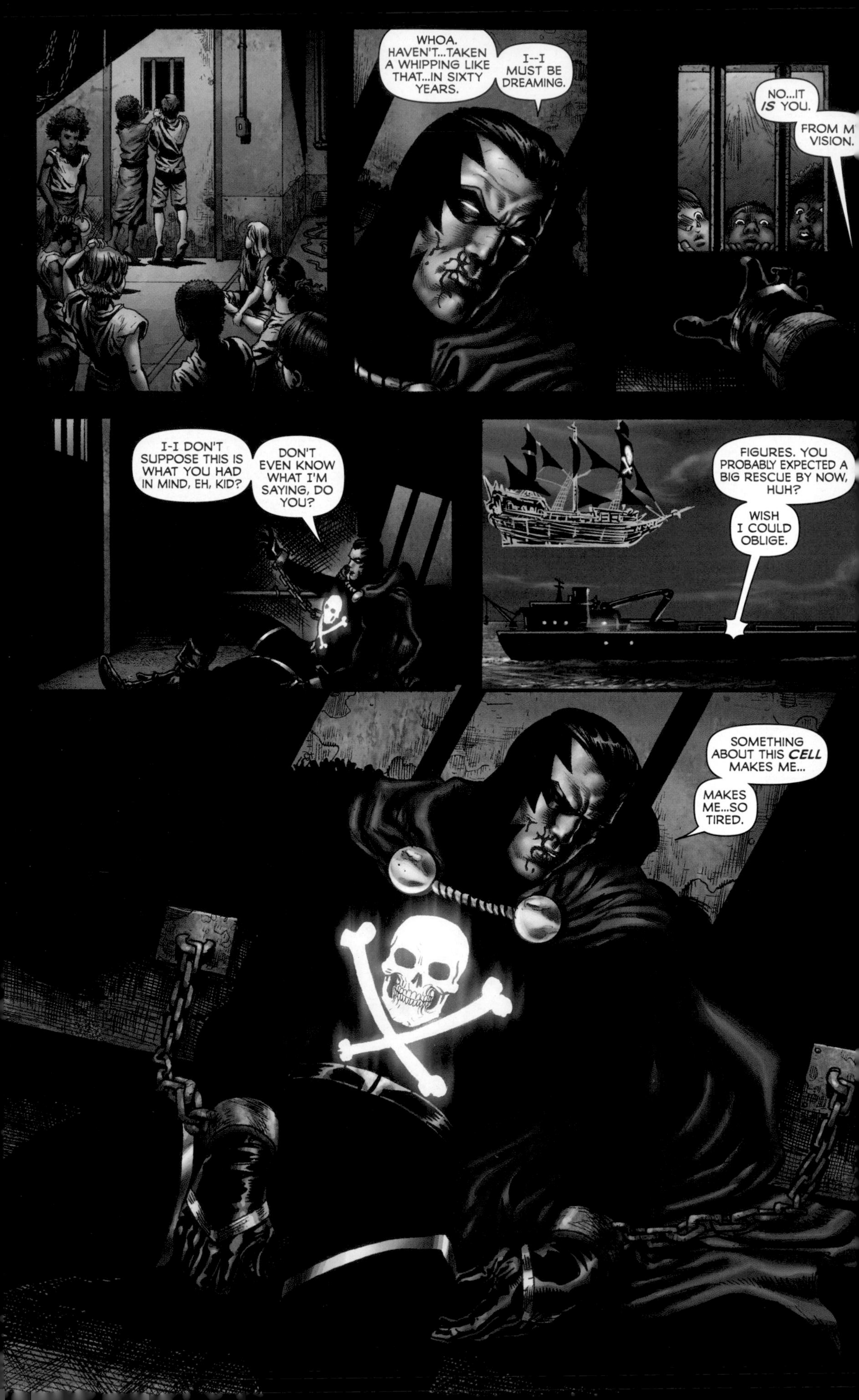
WHOA. HAVEN'T...TAKEN A WHIPPING LIKE THAT...IN SIXTY YEARS.
I--I MUST BE DREAMING.
NO...IT IS YOU.
FROM M VISION.
I-I DON'T SUPPOSE THIS IS WHAT YOU HAD IN MIND, EH, KID?
DON'T EVEN KNOW WHAT I'M SAYING, DO YOU?
FIGURES. YOU PROBABLY EXPECTED A BIG RESCUE BY NOW, HUH?
WISH I COULD OBLIGE.
SOMETHING ABOUT THIS CELL MAKES ME...
MAKES ME...SO TIRED.

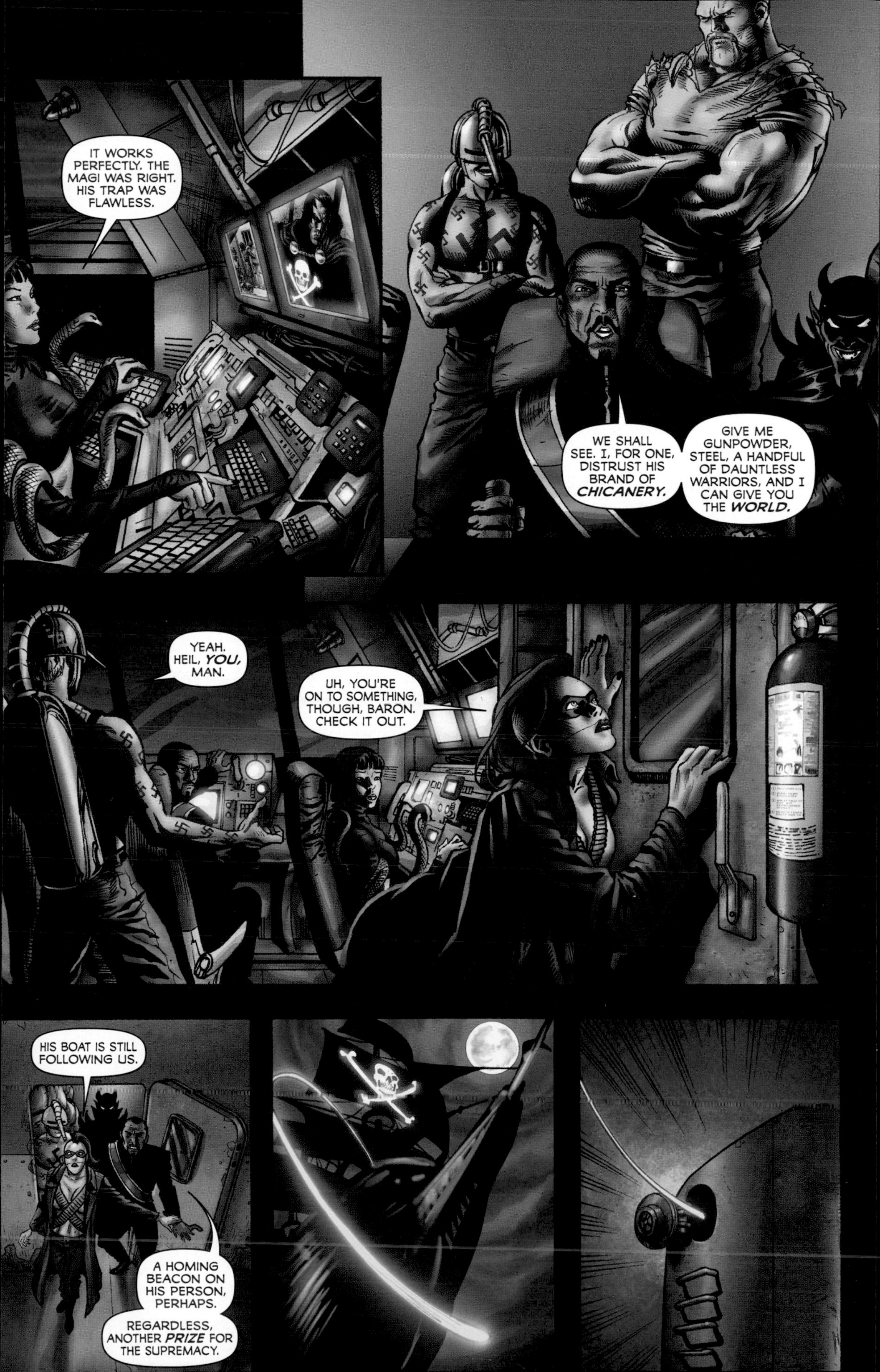
IT WORKS PERFECTLY. THE MAGI WAS RIGHT. HIS TRAP WAS FLAWLESS.
WE SHALL SEE. I, FOR ONE, DISTRUST HIS BRAND OF CHICANERY.
GIVE ME GUNPOWDER, STEEL, A HANDFUL OF DAUNTLESS WARRIORS, AND I CAN GIVE YOU THE WORLD.
YEAH. HEIL, YOU, MAN.
UH, YOU'RE ON TO SOMETHING, THOUGH, BARON. CHECK IT OUT.
HIS BOAT IS STILL FOLLOWING US.
A HOMING BEACON ON HIS PERSON, PERHAPS.
REGARDLESS, ANOTHER PRIZE FOR THE SUPREMACY.

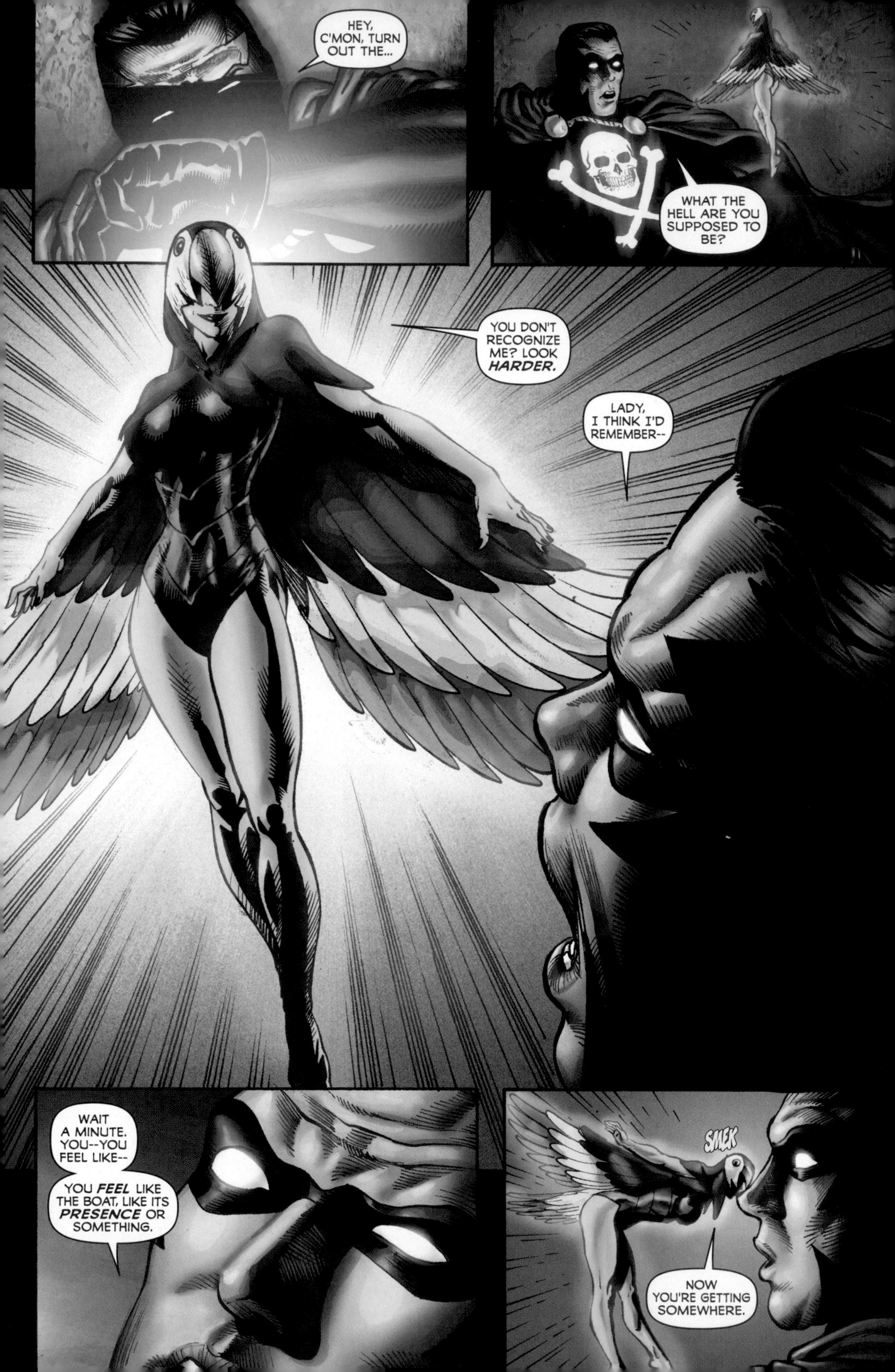

HEY, C'MON, TURN OUT THE...
WHAT THE HELL ARE YOU SUPPOSED TO BE?
YOU DON'T RECOGNIZE ME? LOOK *HARDER.*
LADY, I THINK I'D REMEMBER--
WAIT A MINUTE. YOU--YOU FEEL LIKE--
YOU *FEEL* LIKE THE BOAT, LIKE ITS *PRESENCE* OR SOMETHING.
SMEK
NOW YOU'RE GETTING SOMEWHERE.

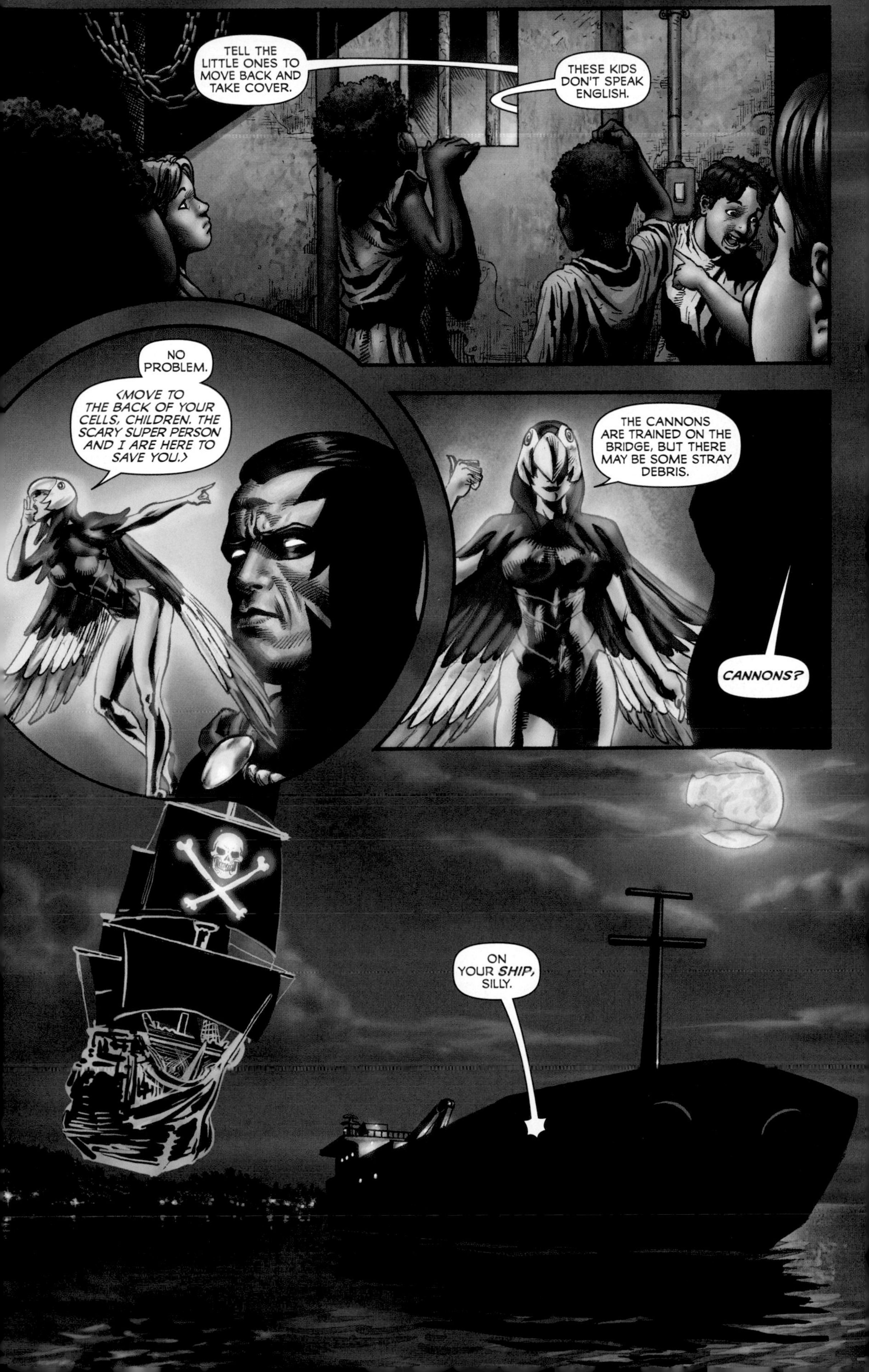
TELL THE LITTLE ONES TO MOVE BACK AND TAKE COVER.
THESE KIDS DON'T SPEAK ENGLISH.
NO PROBLEM.
‹MOVE TO THE BACK OF YOUR CELLS, CHILDREN. THE SCARY SUPER PERSON AND I ARE HERE TO SAVE YOU.›
THE CANNONS ARE TRAINED ON THE BRIDGE, BUT THERE MAY BE SOME STRAY DEBRIS.
CANNONS?
ON YOUR SHIP, SILLY.

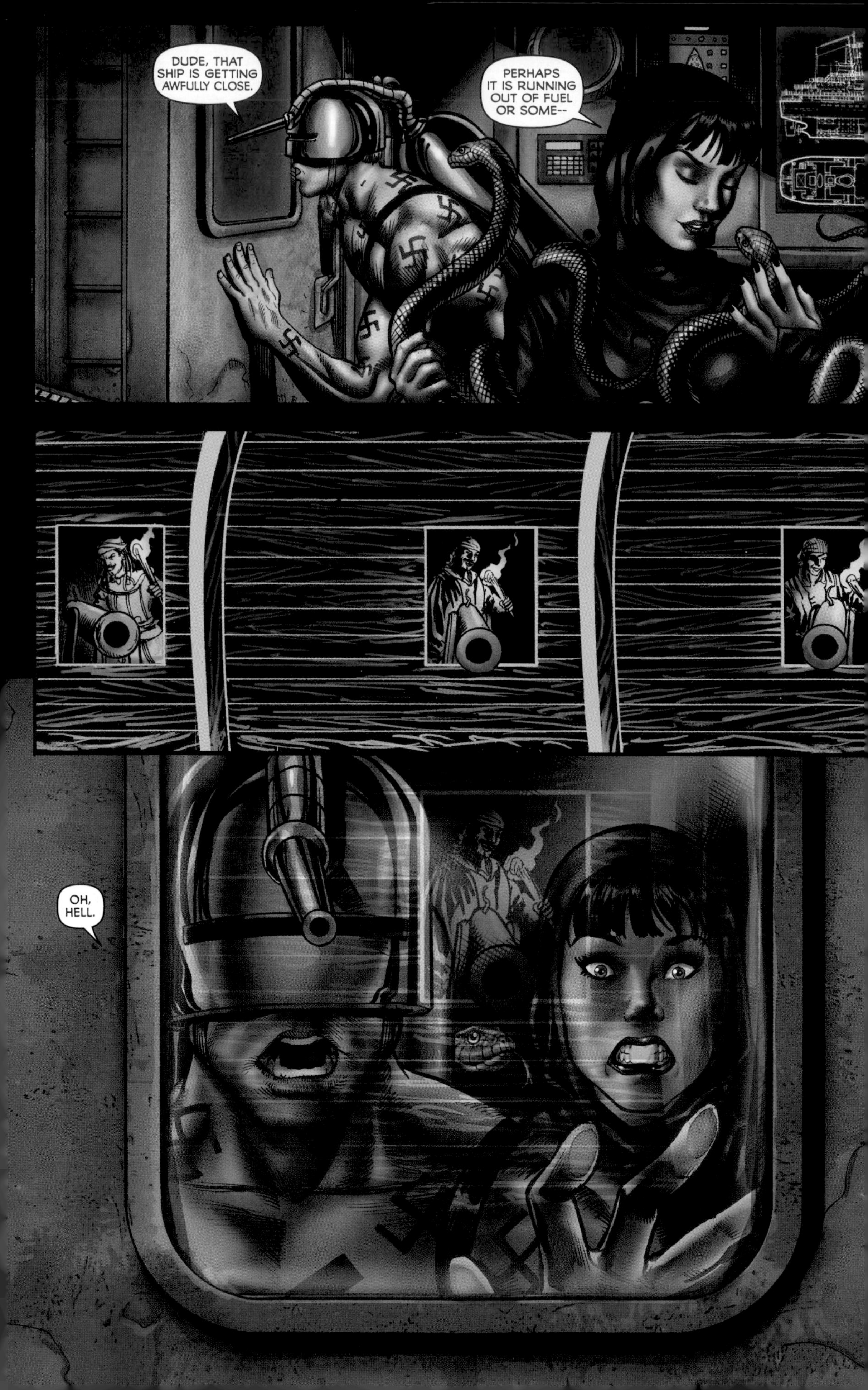
DUDE, THAT SHIP IS GETTING AWFULLY CLOSE.
PERHAPS IT IS RUNNING OUT OF FUEL OR SOME--
OH, HELL.

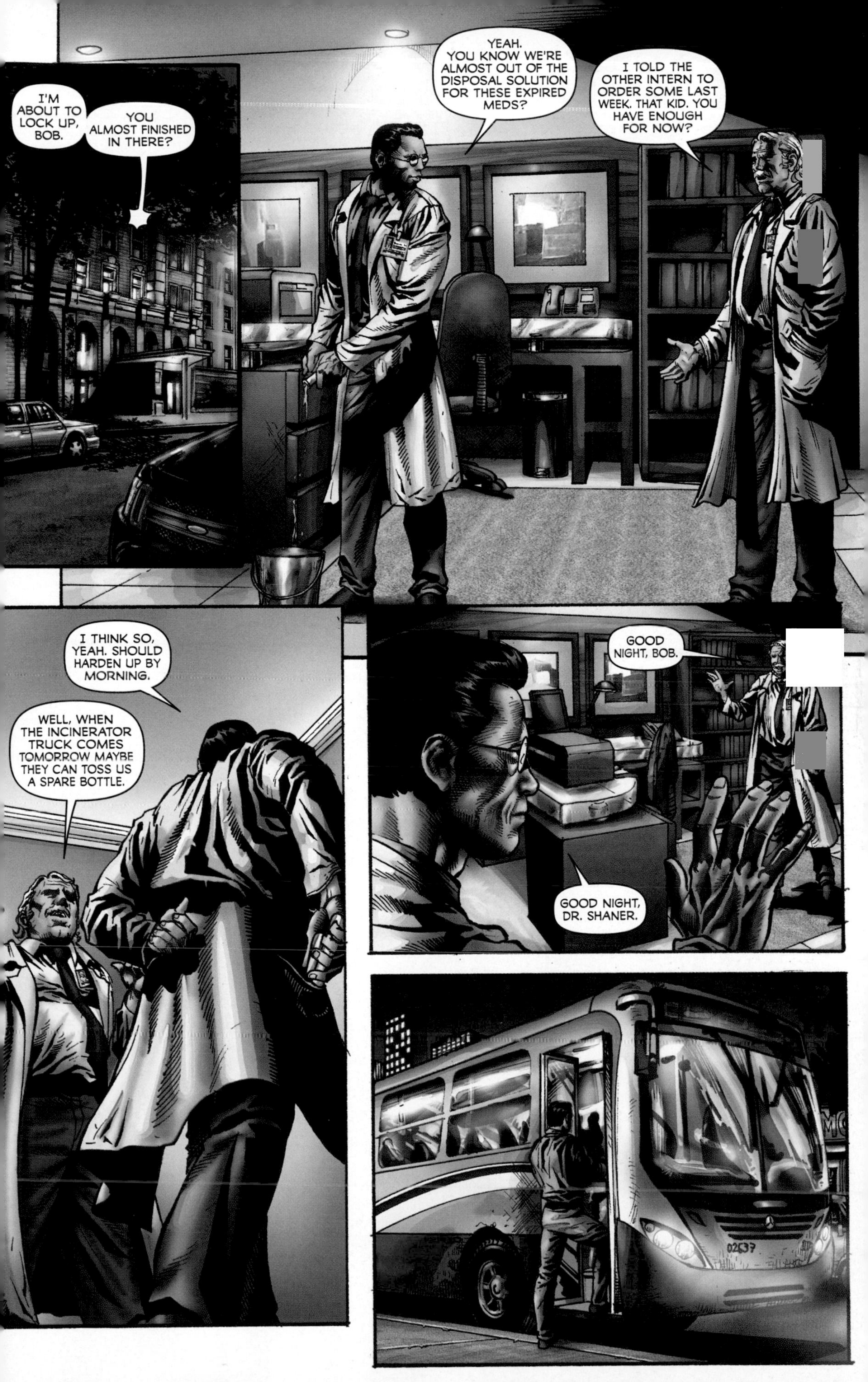
I'M ABOUT TO LOCK UP, BOB.
YOU ALMOST FINISHED IN THERE?
YEAH. YOU KNOW WE'RE ALMOST OUT OF THE DISPOSAL SOLUTION FOR THESE EXPIRED MEDS?
I TOLD THE OTHER INTERN TO ORDER SOME LAST WEEK. THAT KID. YOU HAVE ENOUGH FOR NOW?
I THINK SO, YEAH. SHOULD HARDEN UP BY MORNING.
WELL, WHEN THE INCINERATOR TRUCK COMES TOMORROW MAYBE THEY CAN TOSS US A SPARE BOTTLE.
GOOD NIGHT, BOB.
GOOD NIGHT, DR. SHANER.

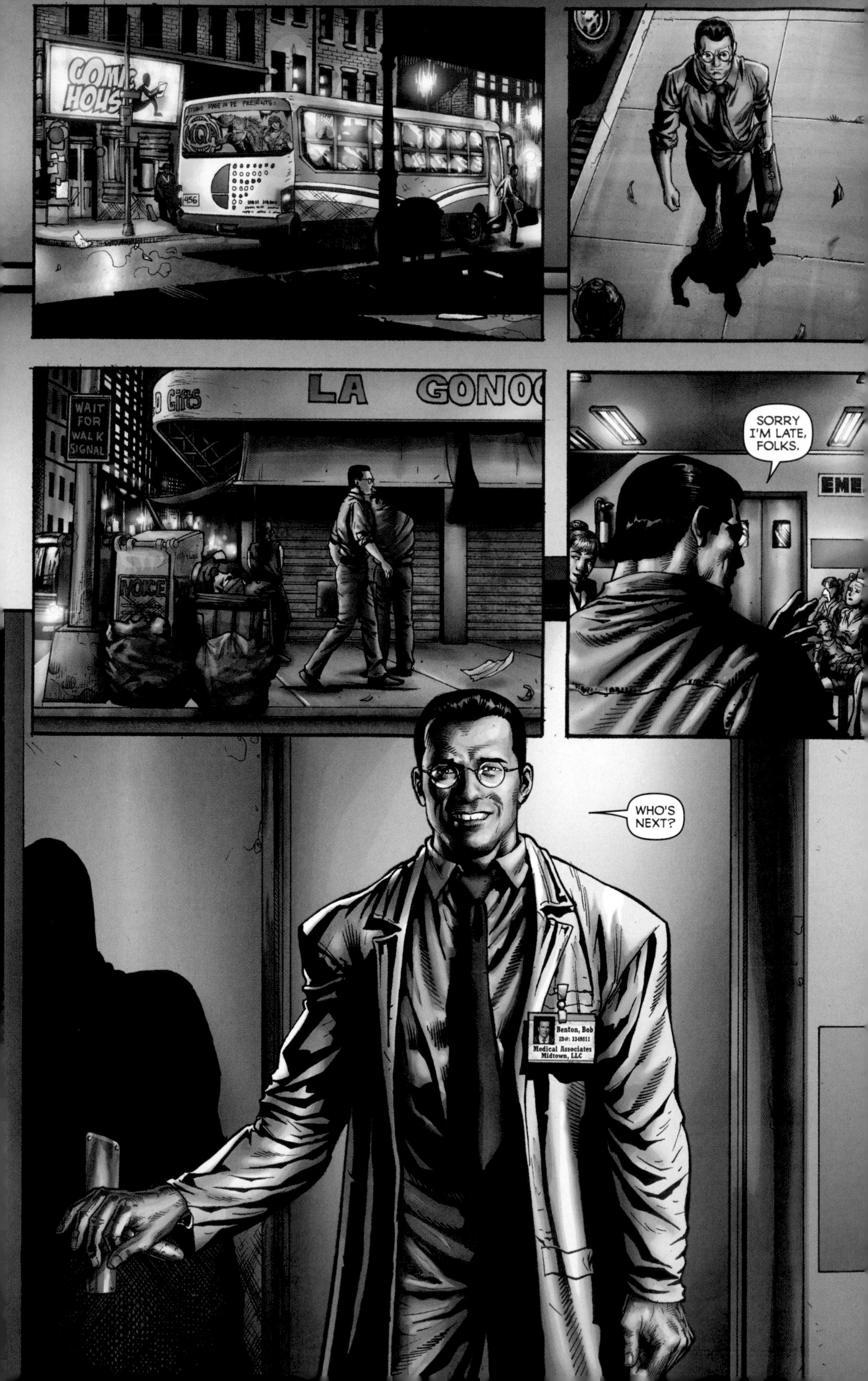
COMIC HOUSE
STUDIO MADE IN PE PRESENTS
456
LA GONO
WAIT FOR WALK SIGNAL
VOICE
SORRY I'M LATE, FOLKS.
EME
WHO'S NEXT?
Benton, Bob
ID#: 3349811
Medical Associates Midtown, LLC

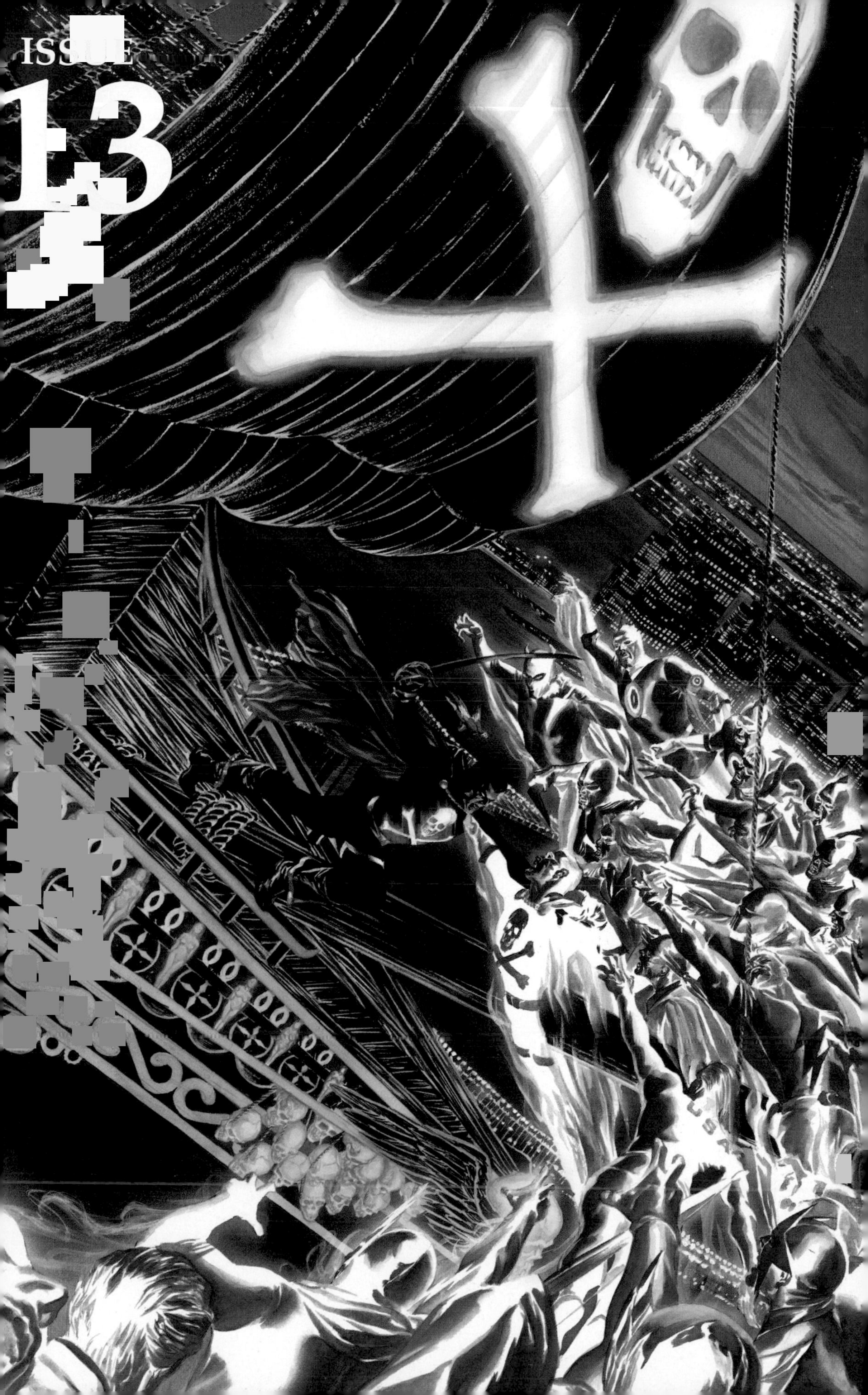
ISSUE
13

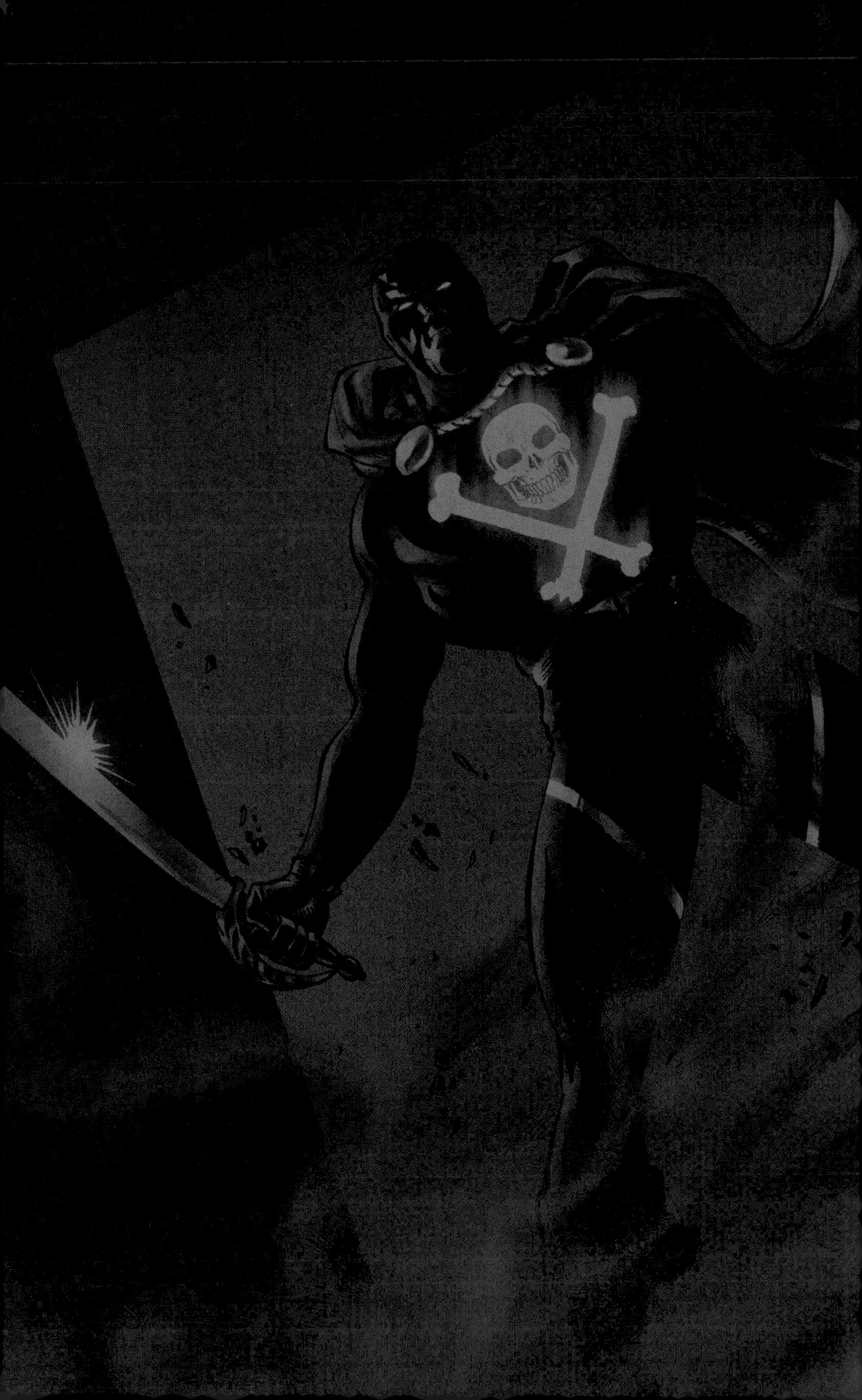

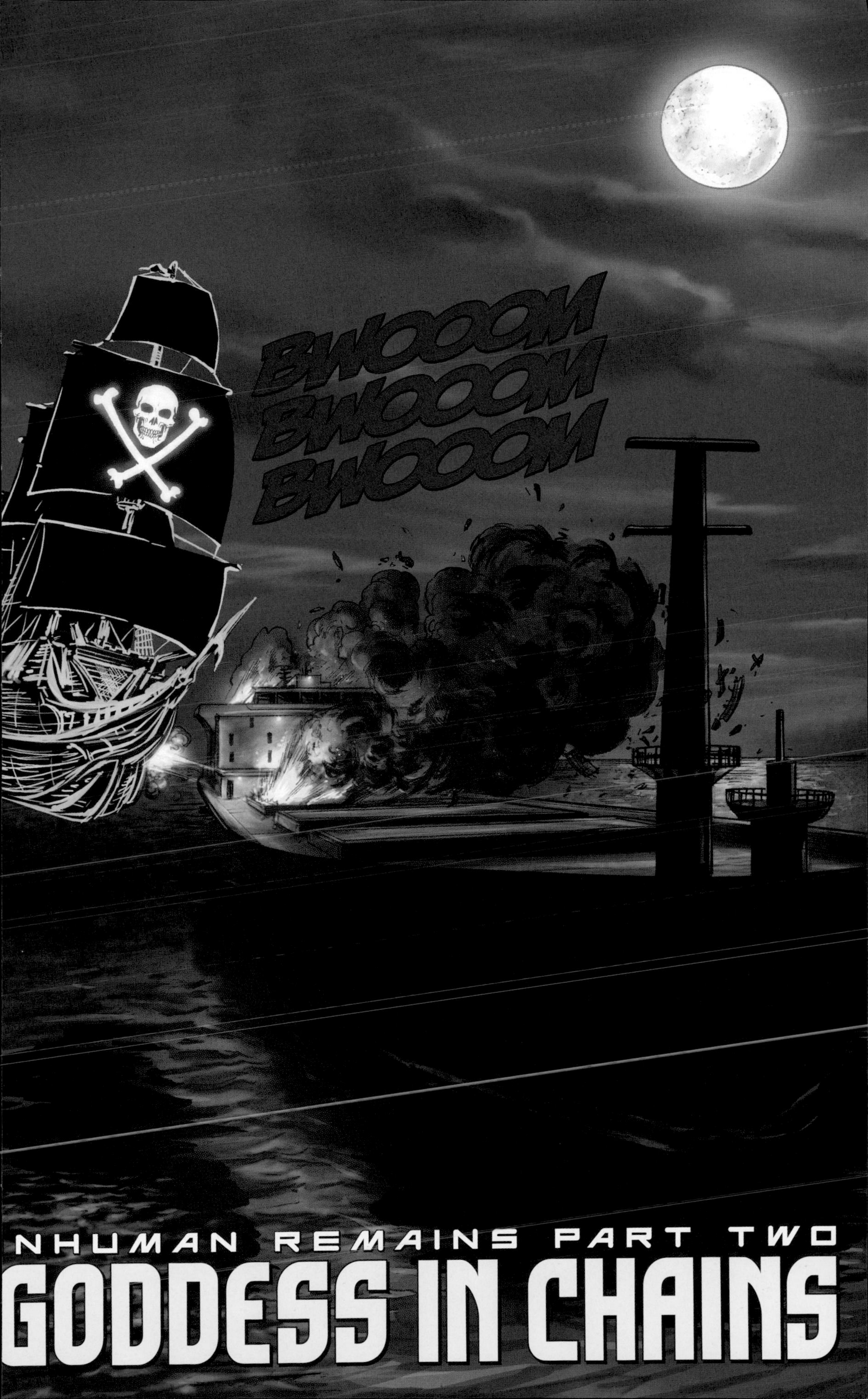
BWOOOM
BWOOOM
BWOOOM
NHUMAN REMAINS PART TWO
GODDESS IN CHAINS

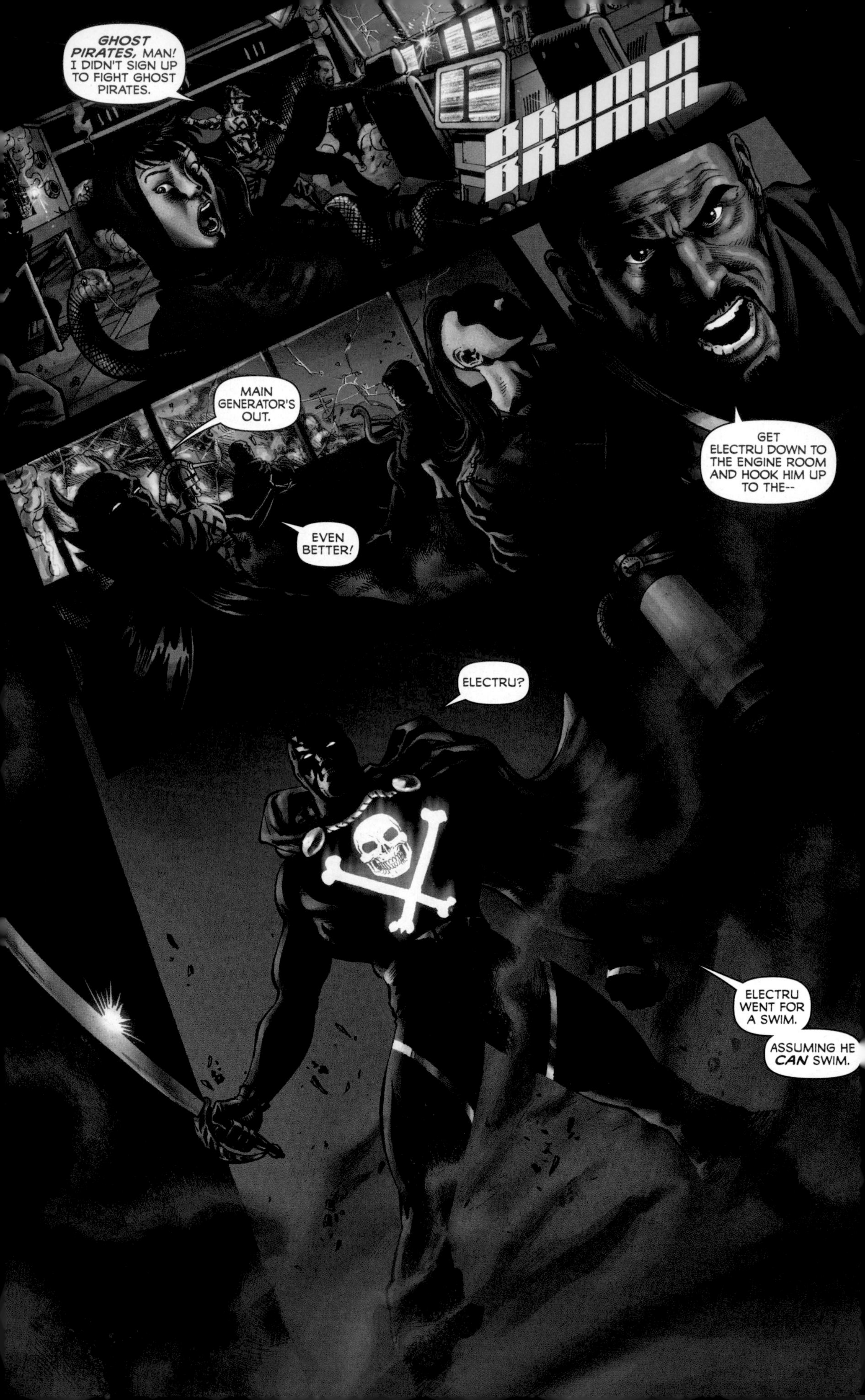
GHOST PIRATES, MAN! I DIDN'T SIGN UP TO FIGHT GHOST PIRATES.
BRUMM BRUMM
MAIN GENERATOR'S OUT.
GET ELECTRU DOWN TO THE ENGINE ROOM AND HOOK HIM UP TO THE--
EVEN BETTER!
ELECTRU?
ELECTRU WENT FOR A SWIM.
ASSUMING HE CAN SWIM.

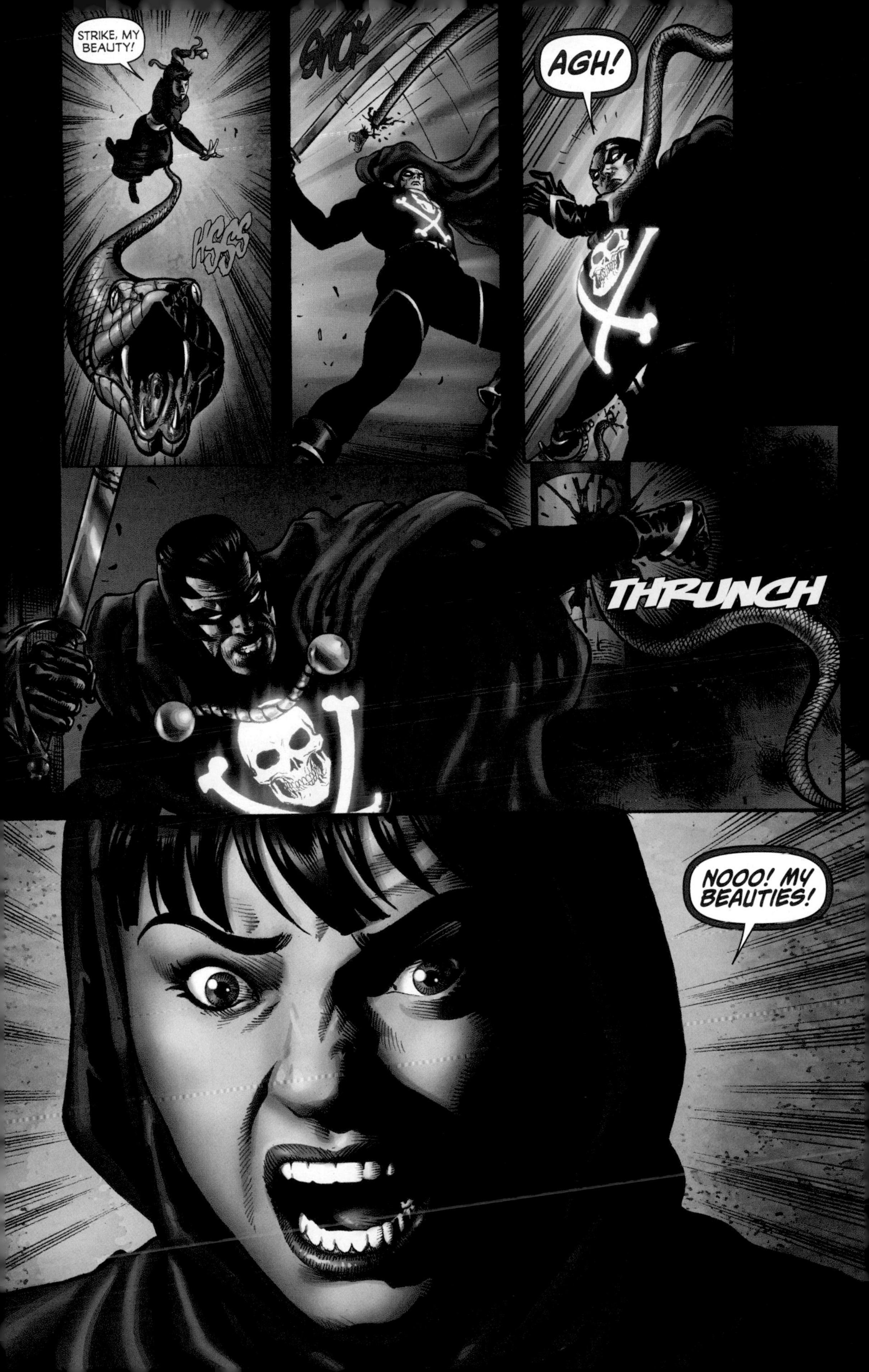
STRIKE, MY BEAUTY!
HSSS
SNICK
AGH!
THRUNCH
NOOO! MY BEAUTIES!

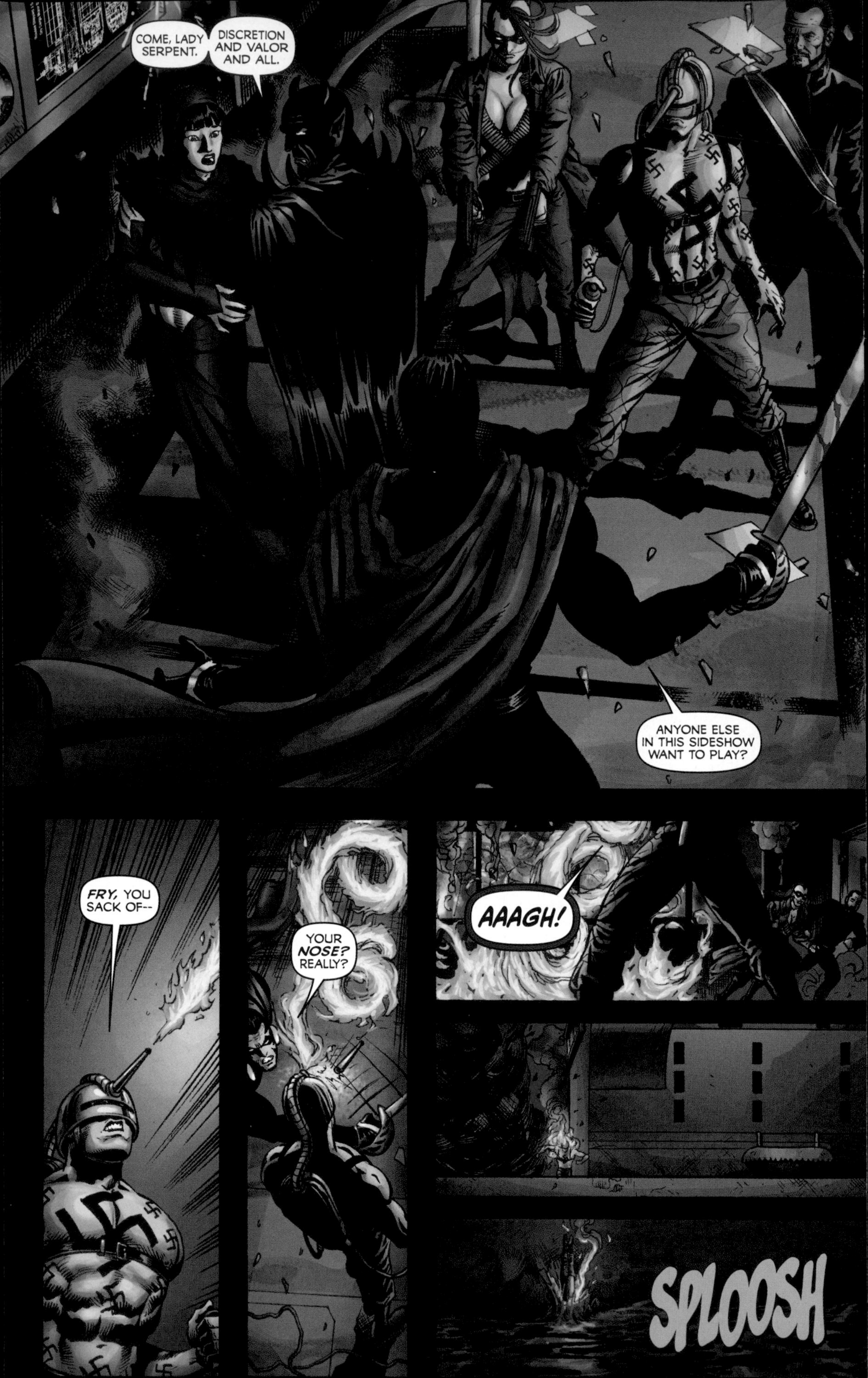
COME, LADY SERPENT.
DISCRETION AND VALOR AND ALL.
ANYONE ELSE IN THIS SIDESHOW WANT TO PLAY?
FRY, YOU SACK OF--
YOUR NOSE? REALLY?
AAAGH!
SPLOOSH

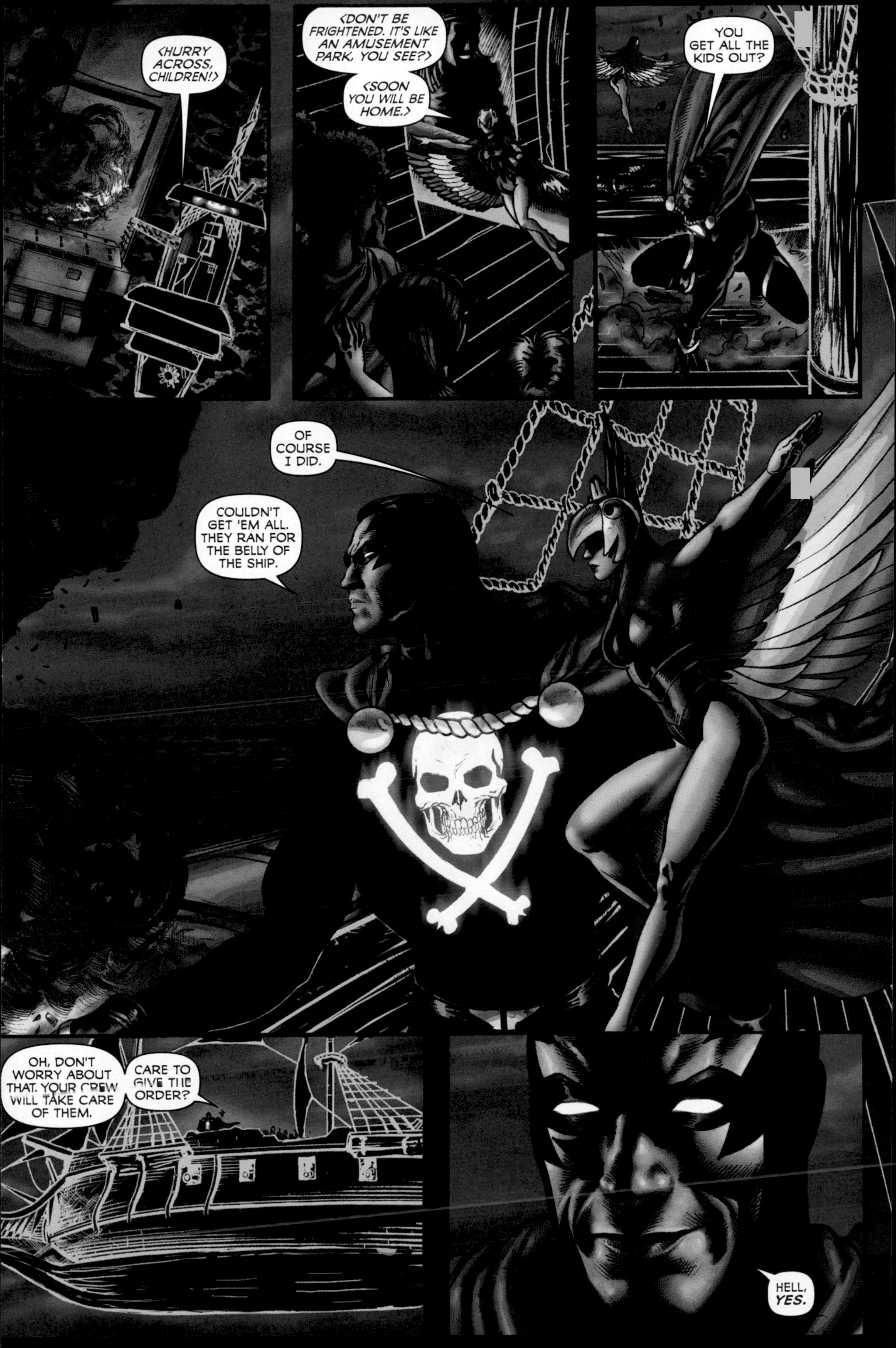

<HURRY ACROSS, CHILDREN!>
<DON'T BE FRIGHTENED. IT'S LIKE AN AMUSEMENT PARK, YOU SEE?>
<SOON YOU WILL BE HOME.>
YOU GET ALL THE KIDS OUT?
OF COURSE I DID.
COULDN'T GET 'EM ALL. THEY RAN FOR THE BELLY OF THE SHIP.
OH, DON'T WORRY ABOUT THAT. YOUR CREW WILL TAKE CARE OF THEM.
CARE TO GIVE THE ORDER?
HELL, YES.

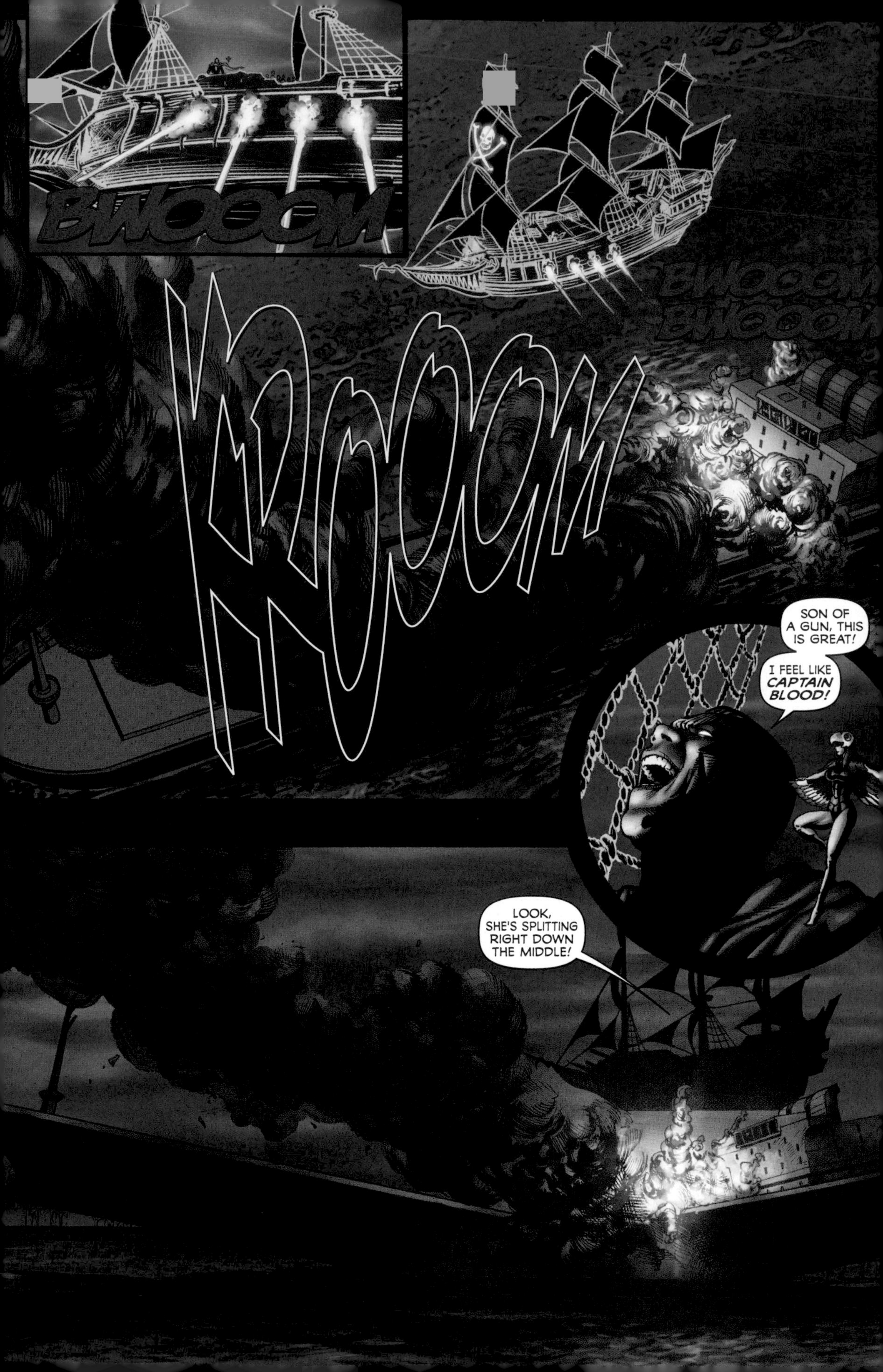
BWOOOM
KROOOM
SON OF A GUN, THIS IS GREAT!
I FEEL LIKE *CAPTAIN BLOOD!*
LOOK, SHE'S SPLITTING RIGHT DOWN THE MIDDLE!

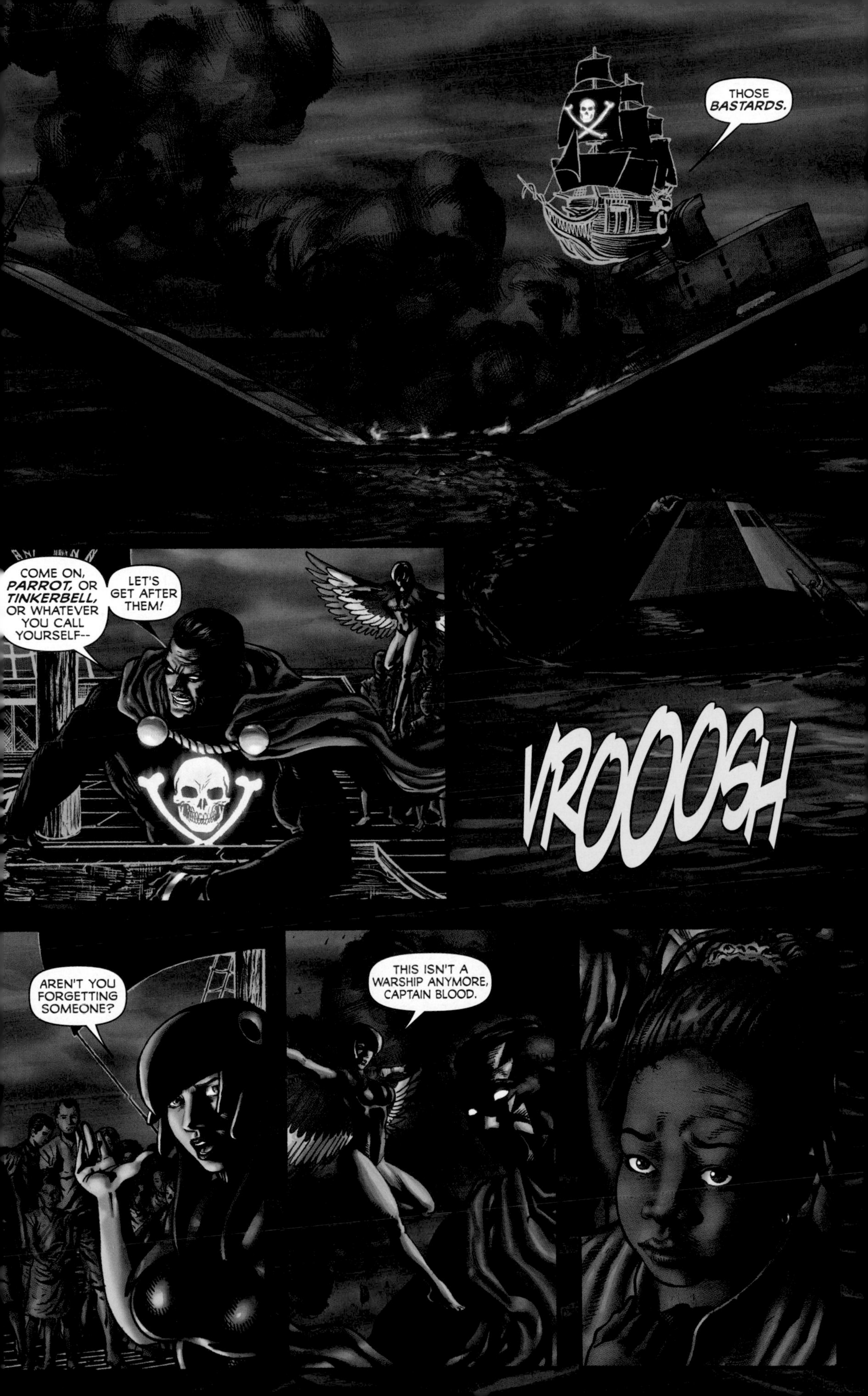
THOSE BASTARDS.
COME ON, PARROT, OR TINKERBELL, OR WHATEVER YOU CALL YOURSELF--
LET'S GET AFTER THEM!
VROOOSH
AREN'T YOU FORGETTING SOMEONE?
THIS ISN'T A WARSHIP ANYMORE, CAPTAIN BLOOD.

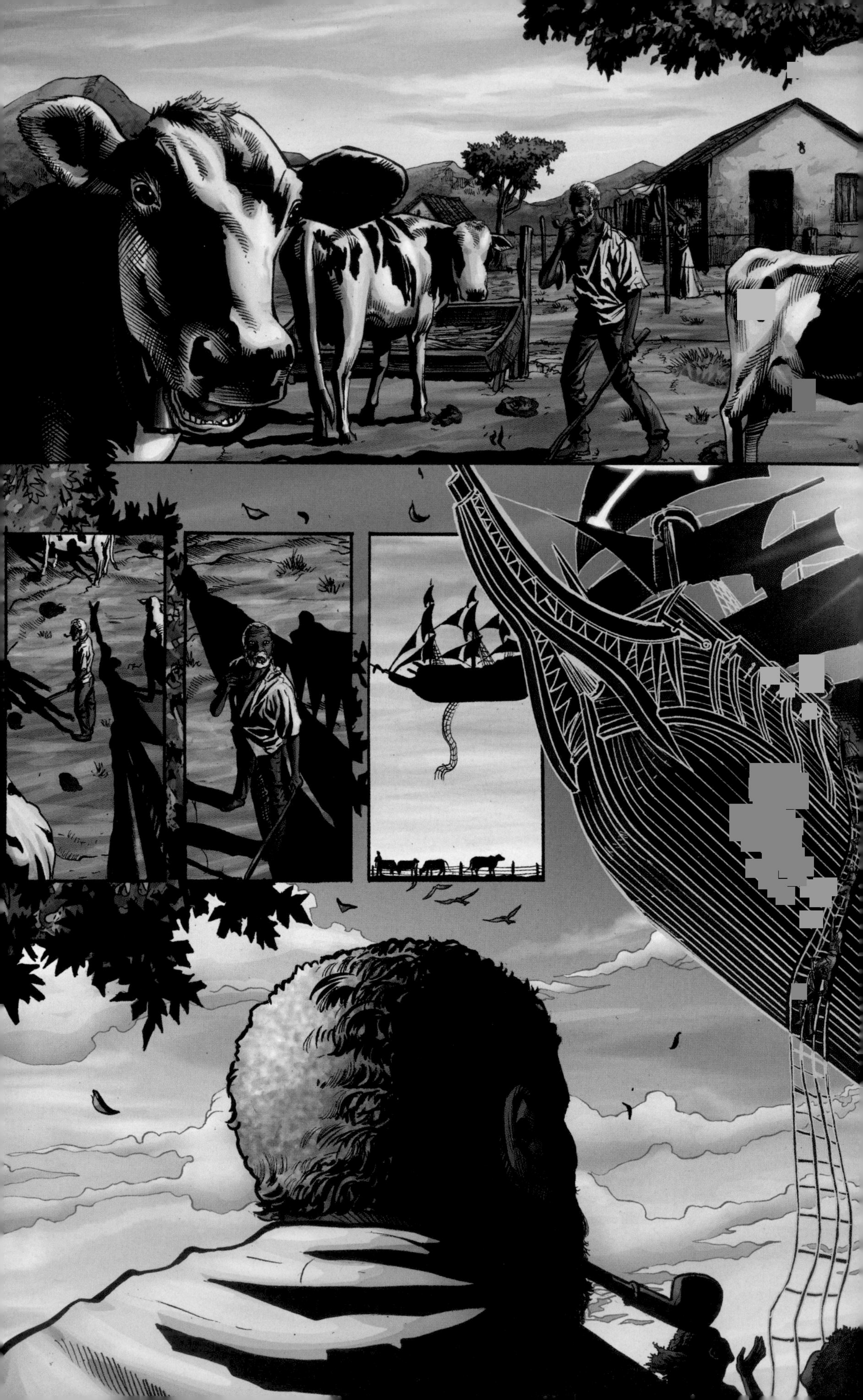

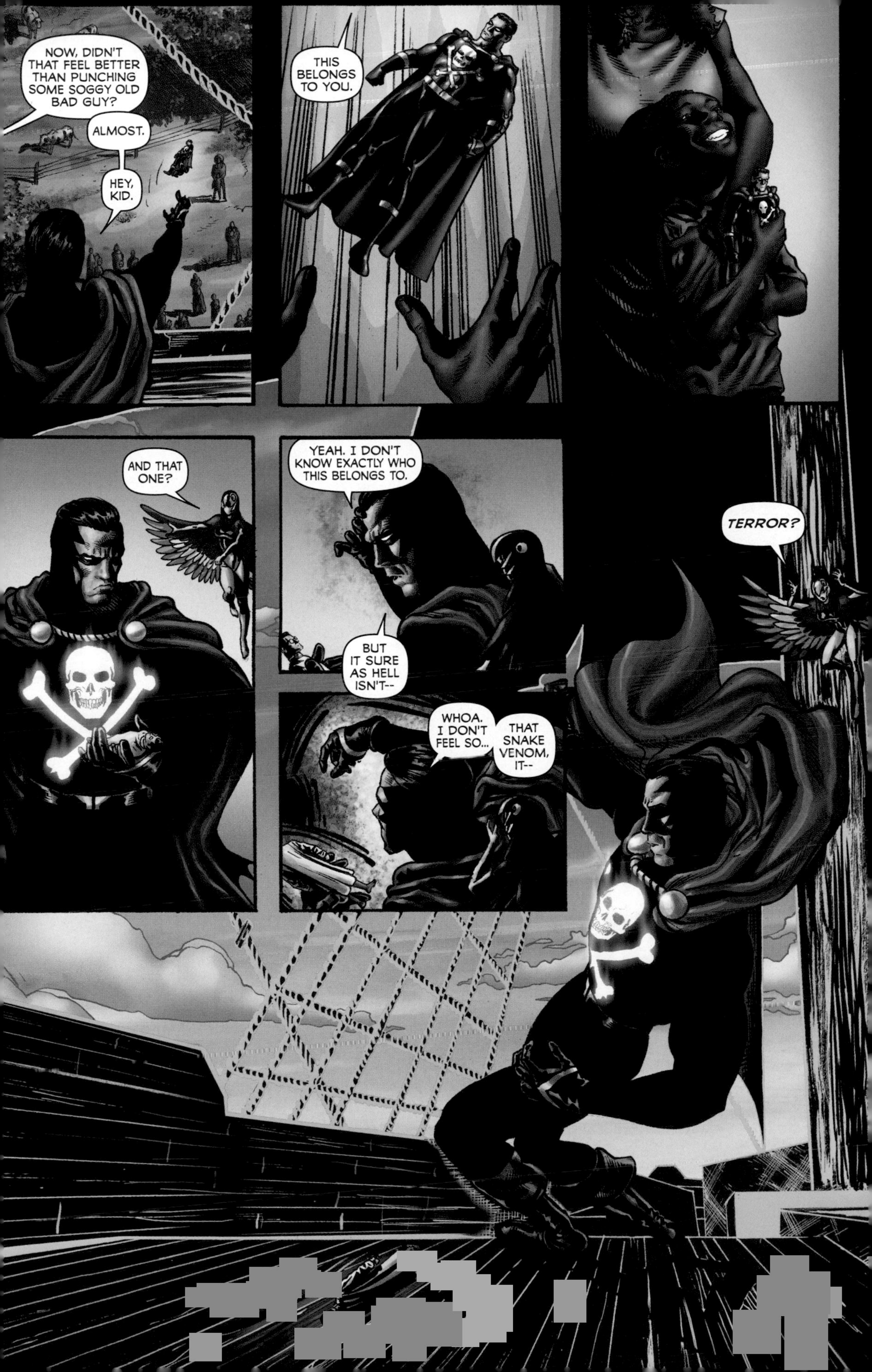
NOW, DIDN'T THAT FEEL BETTER THAN PUNCHING SOME SOGGY OLD BAD GUY?
ALMOST.
HEY, KID.
THIS BELONGS TO YOU.
AND THAT ONE?
YEAH. I DON'T KNOW EXACTLY WHO THIS BELONGS TO.
BUT IT SURE AS HELL ISN'T--
WHOA. I DON'T FEEL SO...
THAT SNAKE VENOM, IT--
TERROR?

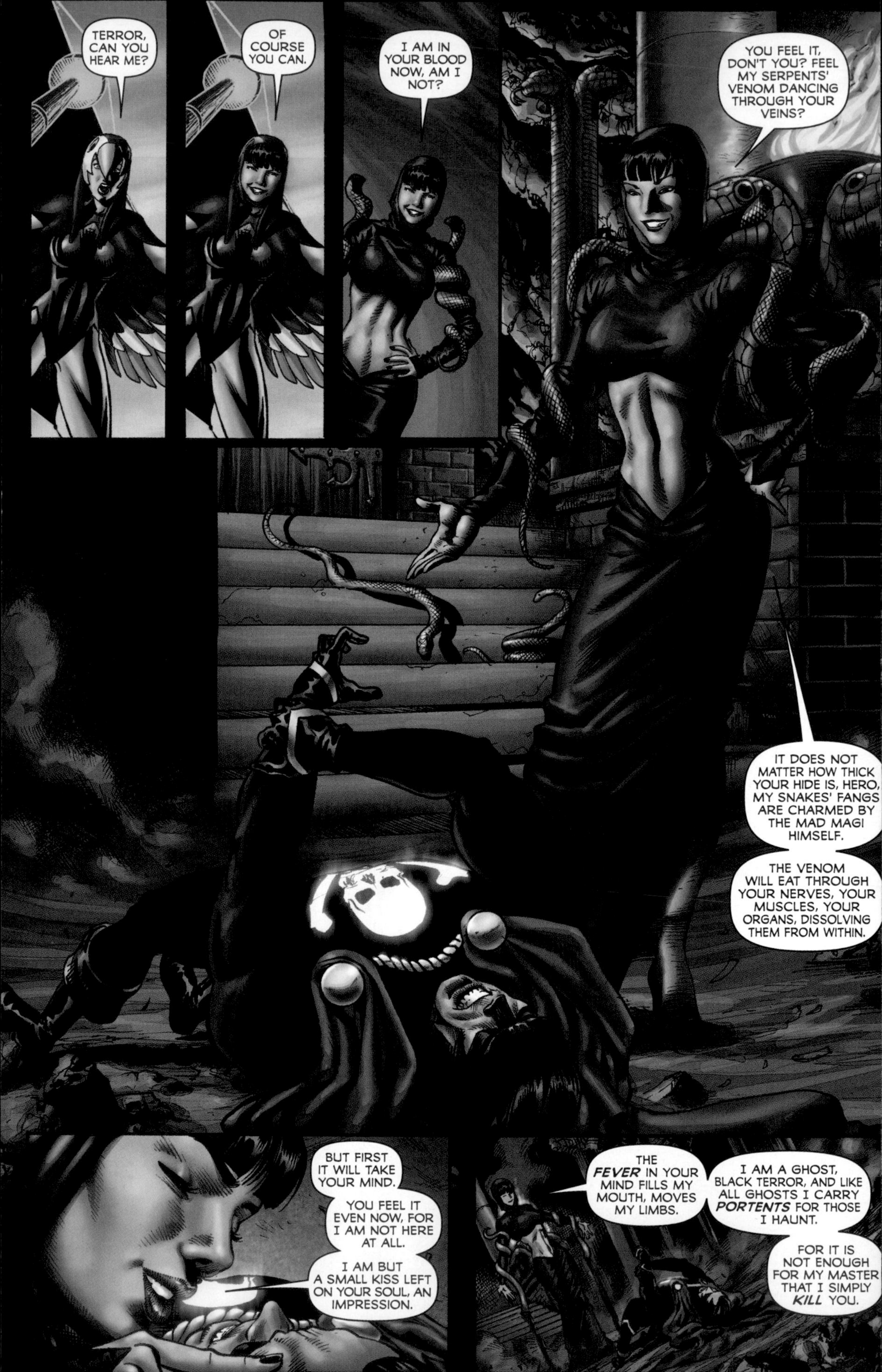

TERROR, CAN YOU HEAR ME?
OF COURSE YOU CAN.
I AM IN YOUR BLOOD NOW, AM I NOT?
YOU FEEL IT, DON'T YOU? FEEL MY SERPENTS' VENOM DANCING THROUGH YOUR VEINS?
IT DOES NOT MATTER HOW THICK YOUR HIDE IS, HERO, MY SNAKES' FANGS ARE CHARMED BY THE MAD MAGI HIMSELF.
THE VENOM WILL EAT THROUGH YOUR NERVES, YOUR MUSCLES, YOUR ORGANS, DISSOLVING THEM FROM WITHIN.
BUT FIRST IT WILL TAKE YOUR MIND.
YOU FEEL IT EVEN NOW, FOR I AM NOT HERE AT ALL.
I AM BUT A SMALL KISS LEFT ON YOUR SOUL, AN IMPRESSION.
THE FEVER IN YOUR MIND FILLS MY MOUTH, MOVES MY LIMBS.
I AM A GHOST, BLACK TERROR, AND LIKE ALL GHOSTS I CARRY PORTENTS FOR THOSE I HAUNT.
FOR IT IS NOT ENOUGH FOR MY MASTER THAT I SIMPLY KILL YOU.

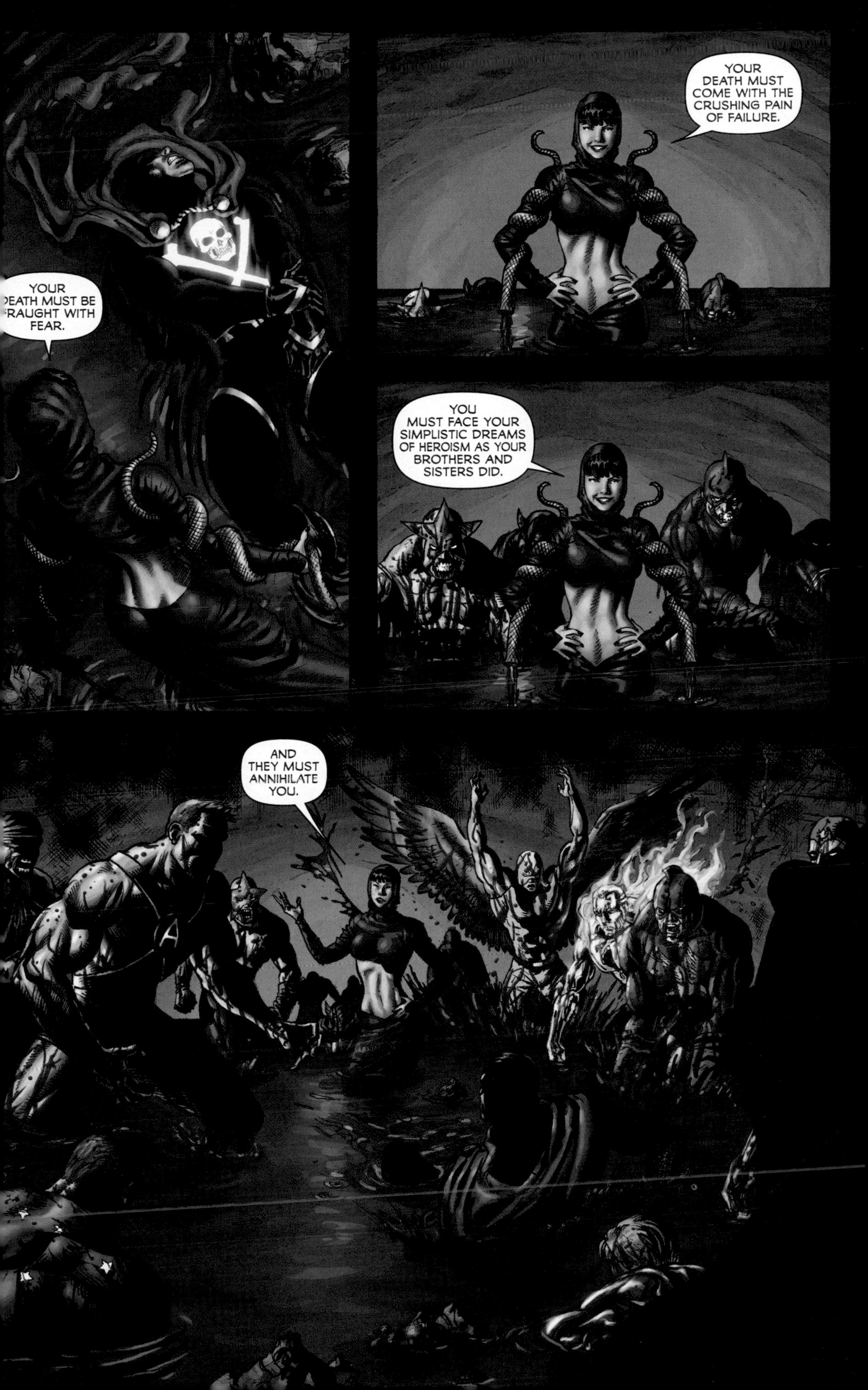
YOUR DEATH MUST BE FRAUGHT WITH FEAR.
YOUR DEATH MUST COME WITH THE CRUSHING PAIN OF FAILURE.
YOU MUST FACE YOUR SIMPLISTIC DREAMS OF HEROISM AS YOUR BROTHERS AND SISTERS DID.
AND THEY MUST ANNIHILATE YOU.

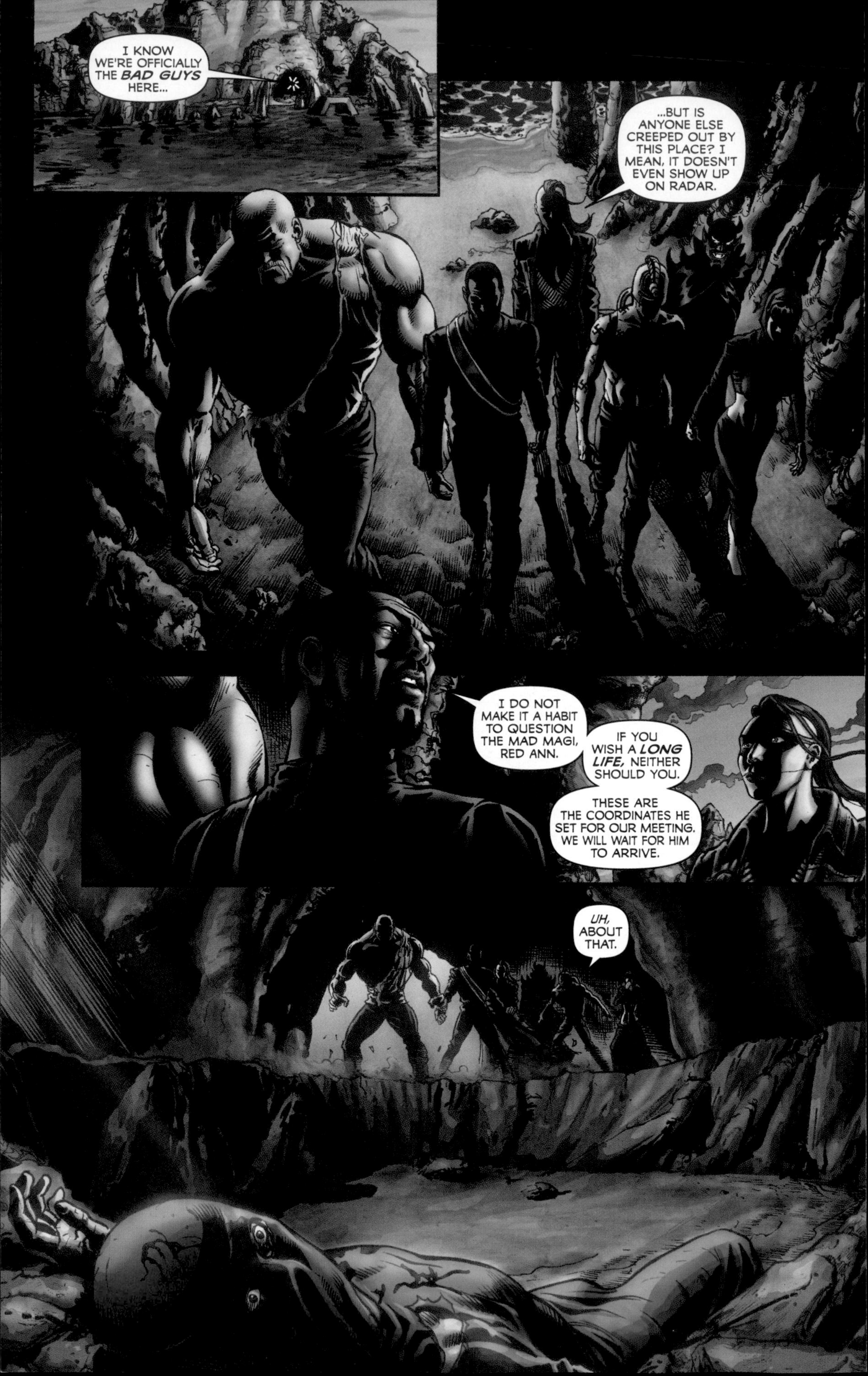
I KNOW WE'RE OFFICIALLY THE *BAD GUYS* HERE...
...BUT IS ANYONE ELSE CREEPED OUT BY THIS PLACE? I MEAN, IT DOESN'T EVEN SHOW UP ON RADAR.
I DO NOT MAKE IT A HABIT TO QUESTION THE MAD MAGI, RED ANN.
IF YOU WISH A *LONG LIFE,* NEITHER SHOULD YOU.
THESE ARE THE COORDINATES HE SET FOR OUR MEETING. WE WILL WAIT FOR HIM TO ARRIVE.
UH, ABOUT THAT.

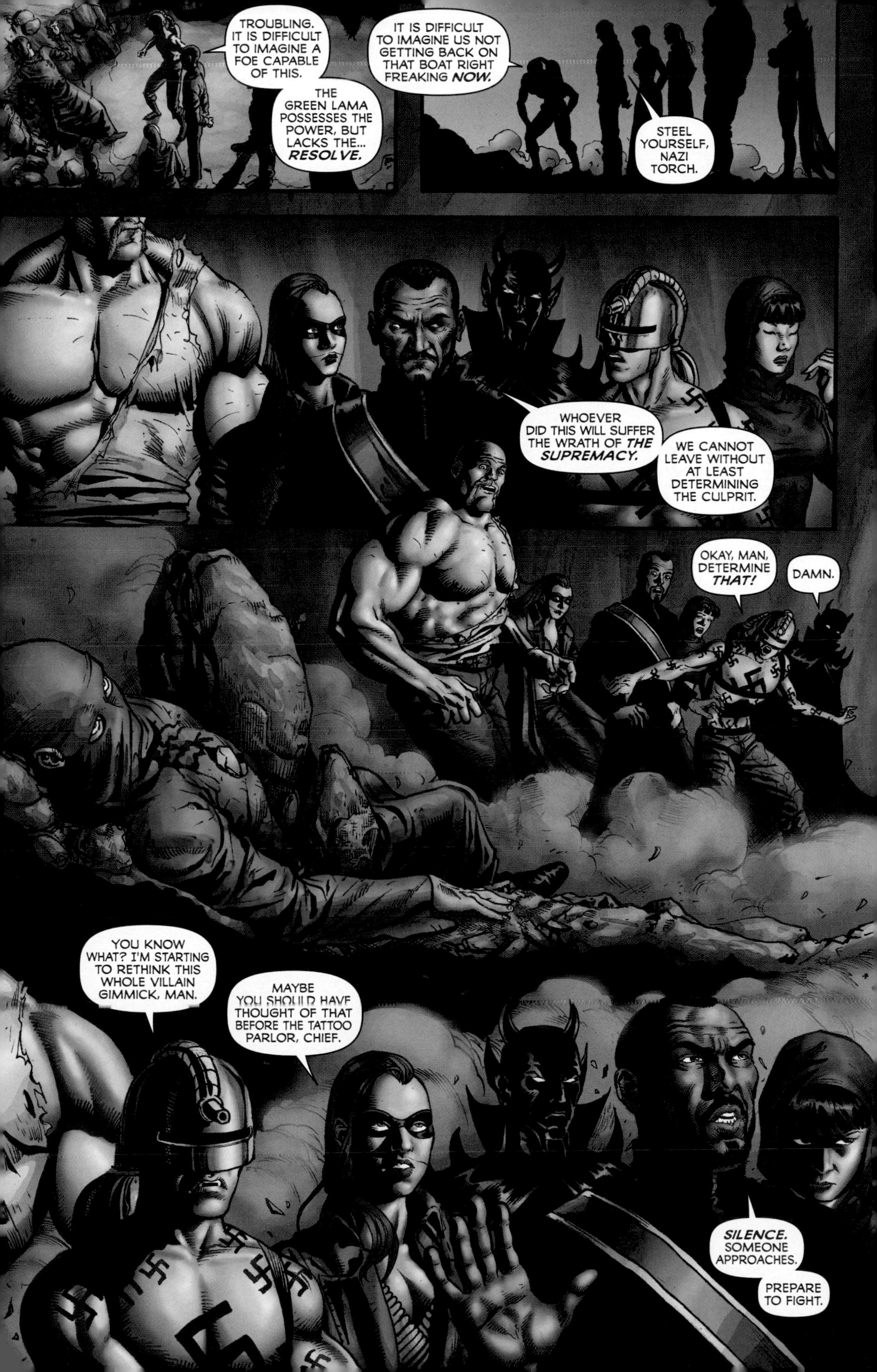
TROUBLING. IT IS DIFFICULT TO IMAGINE A FOE CAPABLE OF THIS.
THE GREEN LAMA POSSESSES THE POWER, BUT LACKS THE... RESOLVE.
IT IS DIFFICULT TO IMAGINE US NOT GETTING BACK ON THAT BOAT RIGHT FREAKING NOW.
STEEL YOURSELF, NAZI TORCH.
WHOEVER DID THIS WILL SUFFER THE WRATH OF THE SUPREMACY.
WE CANNOT LEAVE WITHOUT AT LEAST DETERMINING THE CULPRIT.
OKAY, MAN, DETERMINE THAT!
DAMN.
YOU KNOW WHAT? I'M STARTING TO RETHINK THIS WHOLE VILLAIN GIMMICK, MAN.
MAYBE YOU SHOULD HAVE THOUGHT OF THAT BEFORE THE TATTOO PARLOR, CHIEF.
SILENCE. SOMEONE APPROACHES.
PREPARE TO FIGHT.

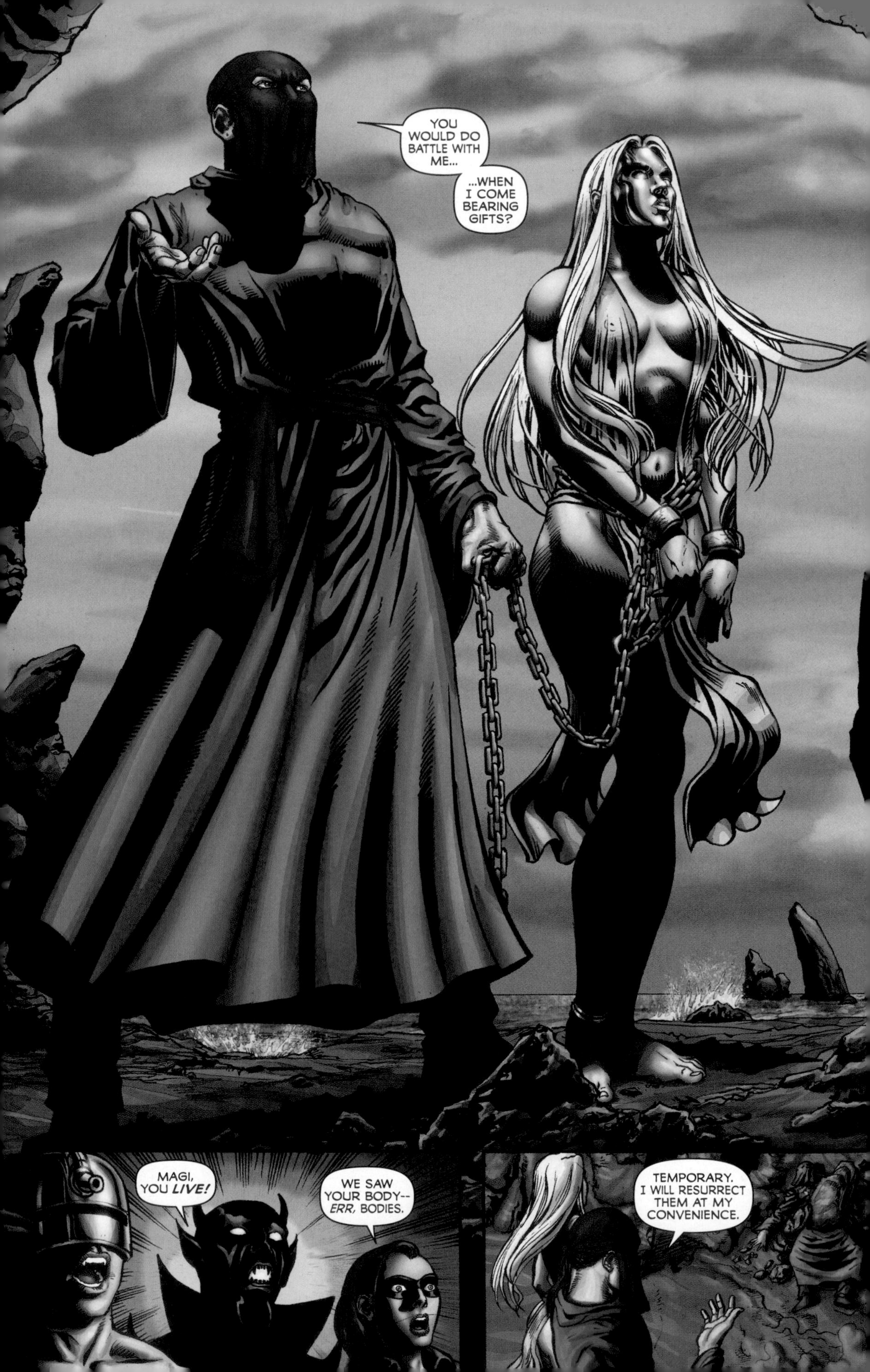
YOU WOULD DO BATTLE WITH ME...
...WHEN I COME BEARING GIFTS?
MAGI, YOU *LIVE!*
WE SAW YOUR BODY-- *ERR,* BODIES.
TEMPORARY. I WILL RESURRECT THEM AT MY CONVENIENCE.

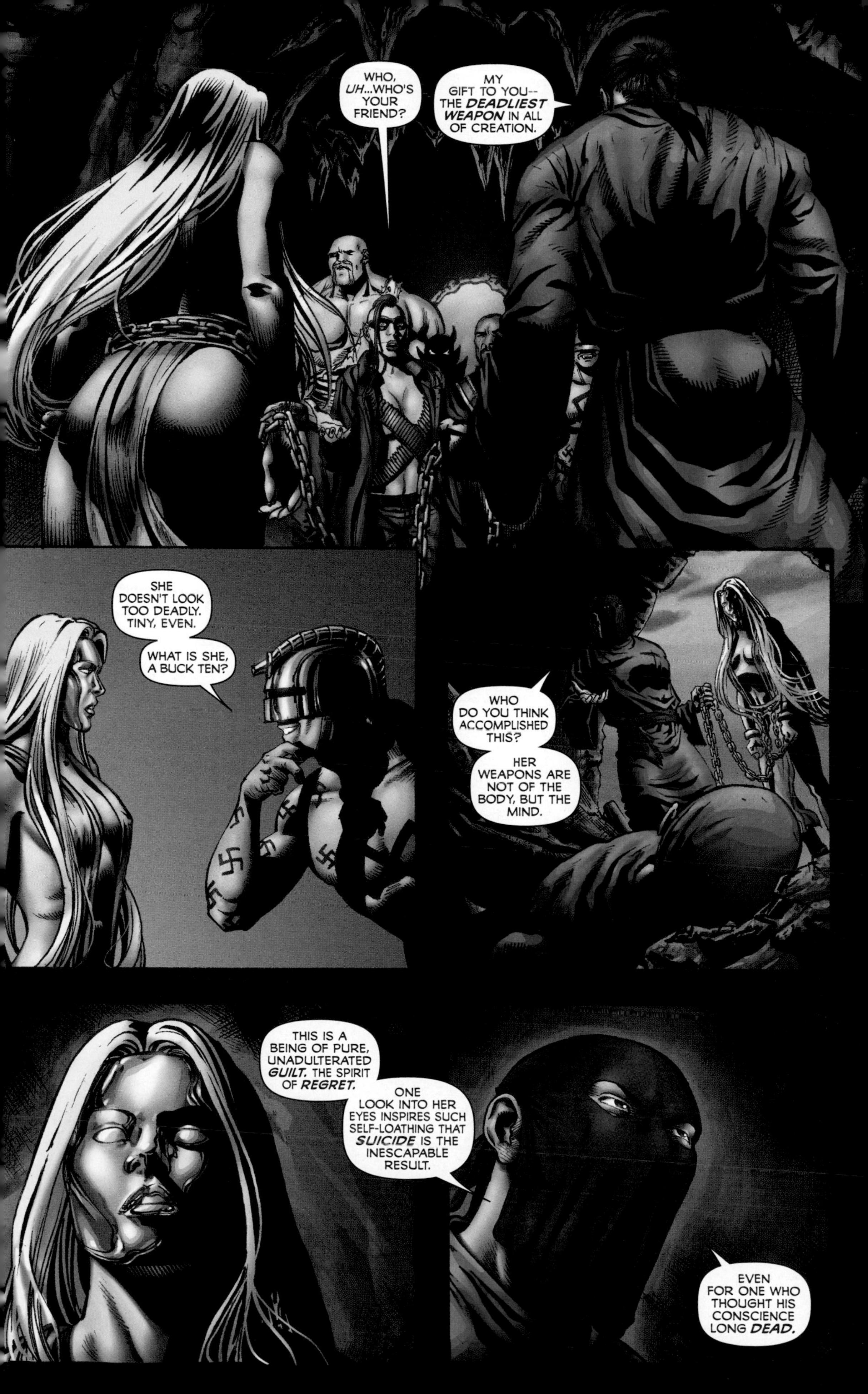

WHO, UH...WHO'S YOUR FRIEND?
MY GIFT TO YOU-- THE DEADLIEST WEAPON IN ALL OF CREATION.
SHE DOESN'T LOOK TOO DEADLY. TINY, EVEN.
WHAT IS SHE, A BUCK TEN?
WHO DO YOU THINK ACCOMPLISHED THIS?
HER WEAPONS ARE NOT OF THE BODY, BUT THE MIND.
THIS IS A BEING OF PURE, UNADULTERATED GUILT. THE SPIRIT OF REGRET.
ONE LOOK INTO HER EYES INSPIRES SUCH SELF-LOATHING THAT SUICIDE IS THE INESCAPABLE RESULT.
EVEN FOR ONE WHO THOUGHT HIS CONSCIENCE LONG DEAD.

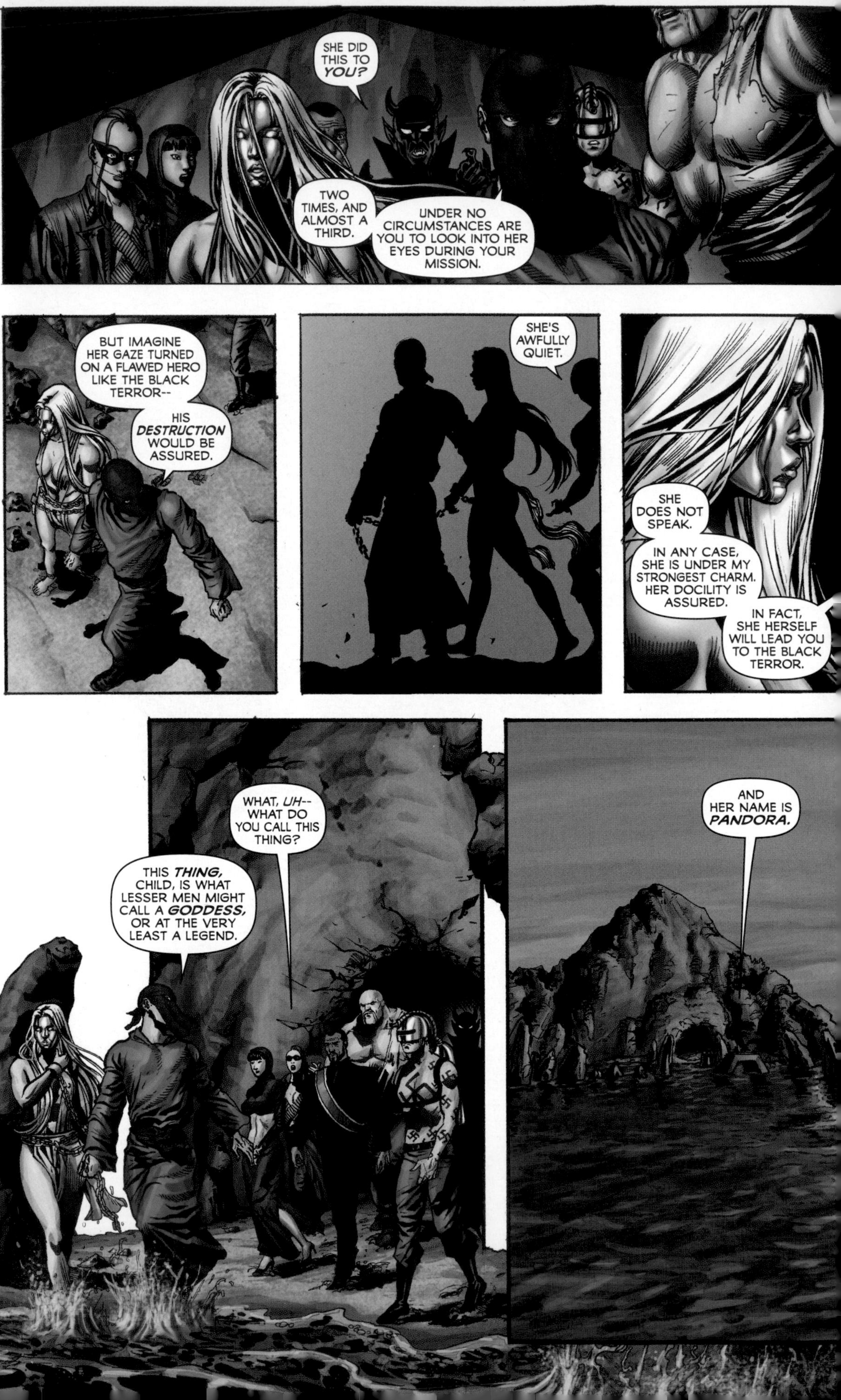
SHE DID THIS TO YOU?
TWO TIMES, AND ALMOST A THIRD.
UNDER NO CIRCUMSTANCES ARE YOU TO LOOK INTO HER EYES DURING YOUR MISSION.
BUT IMAGINE HER GAZE TURNED ON A FLAWED HERO LIKE THE BLACK TERROR--
HIS DESTRUCTION WOULD BE ASSURED.
SHE'S AWFULLY QUIET.
SHE DOES NOT SPEAK.
IN ANY CASE, SHE IS UNDER MY STRONGEST CHARM. HER DOCILITY IS ASSURED.
IN FACT, SHE HERSELF WILL LEAD YOU TO THE BLACK TERROR.
WHAT, UH-- WHAT DO YOU CALL THIS THING?
THIS THING, CHILD, IS WHAT LESSER MEN MIGHT CALL A GODDESS, OR AT THE VERY LEAST A LEGEND.
AND HER NAME IS PANDORA.

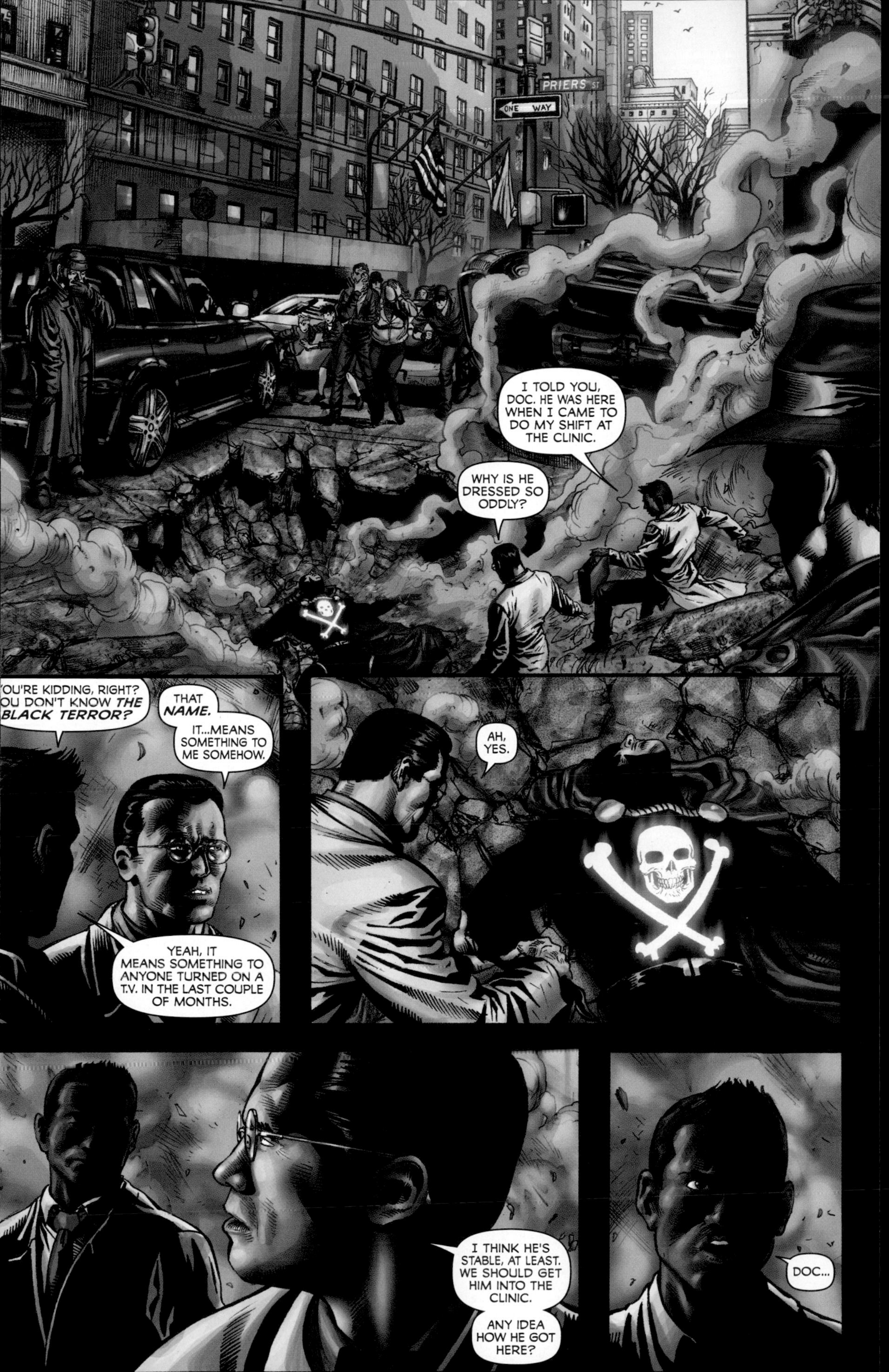
PRIERS ST
ONE WAY
I TOLD YOU, DOC. HE WAS HERE WHEN I CAME TO DO MY SHIFT AT THE CLINIC.
WHY IS HE DRESSED SO ODDLY?
YOU'RE KIDDING, RIGHT? YOU DON'T KNOW *THE BLACK TERROR?*
THAT ***NAME.***
IT...MEANS SOMETHING TO ME SOMEHOW.
YEAH, IT MEANS SOMETHING TO ANYONE TURNED ON A T.V. IN THE LAST COUPLE OF MONTHS.
AH, YES.
I THINK HE'S STABLE, AT LEAST. WE SHOULD GET HIM INTO THE CLINIC.
ANY IDEA HOW HE GOT HERE?
DOC...

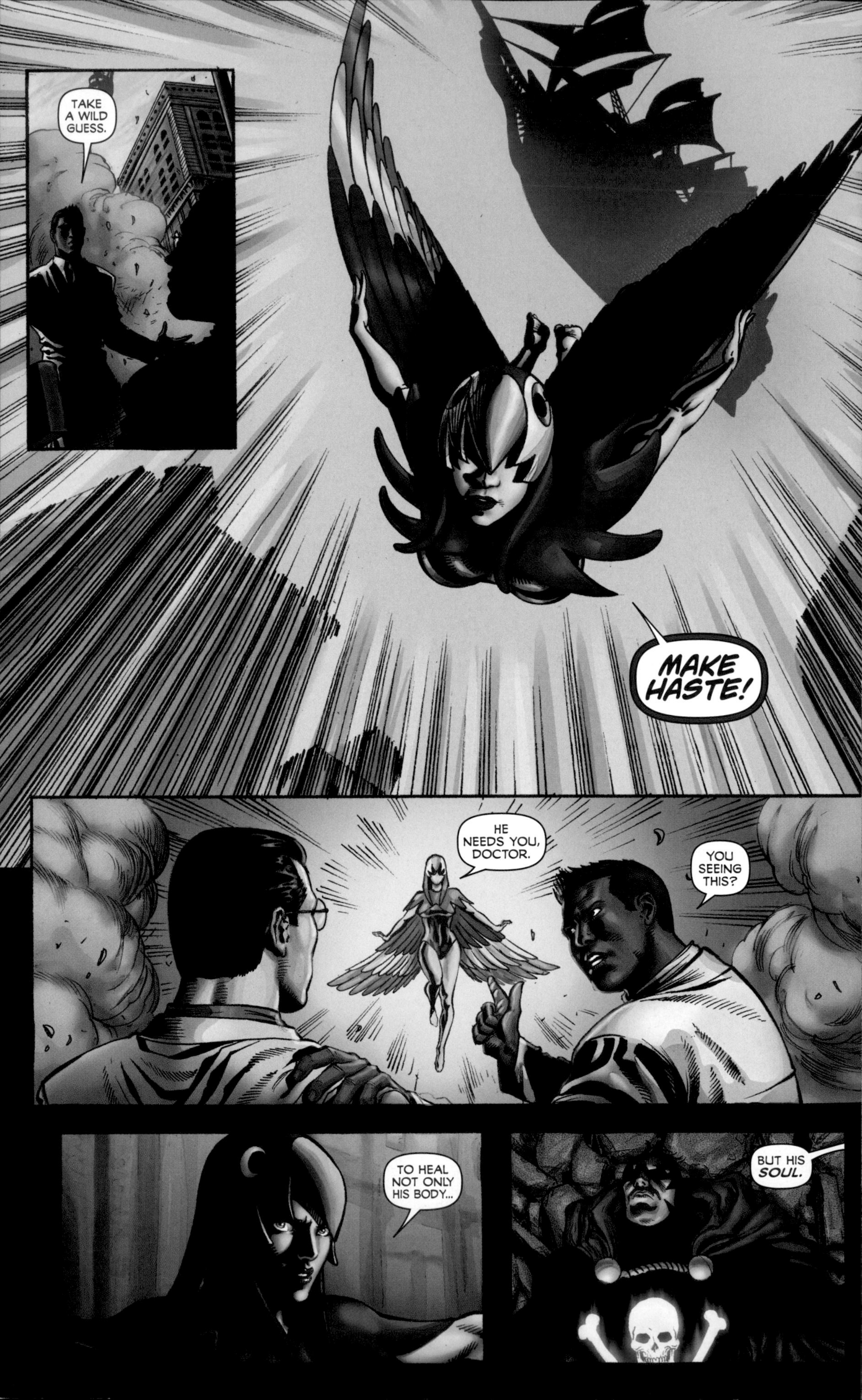
TAKE A WILD GUESS.
MAKE HASTE!
HE NEEDS YOU, DOCTOR.
YOU SEEING THIS?
TO HEAL NOT ONLY HIS BODY...
BUT HIS SOUL.

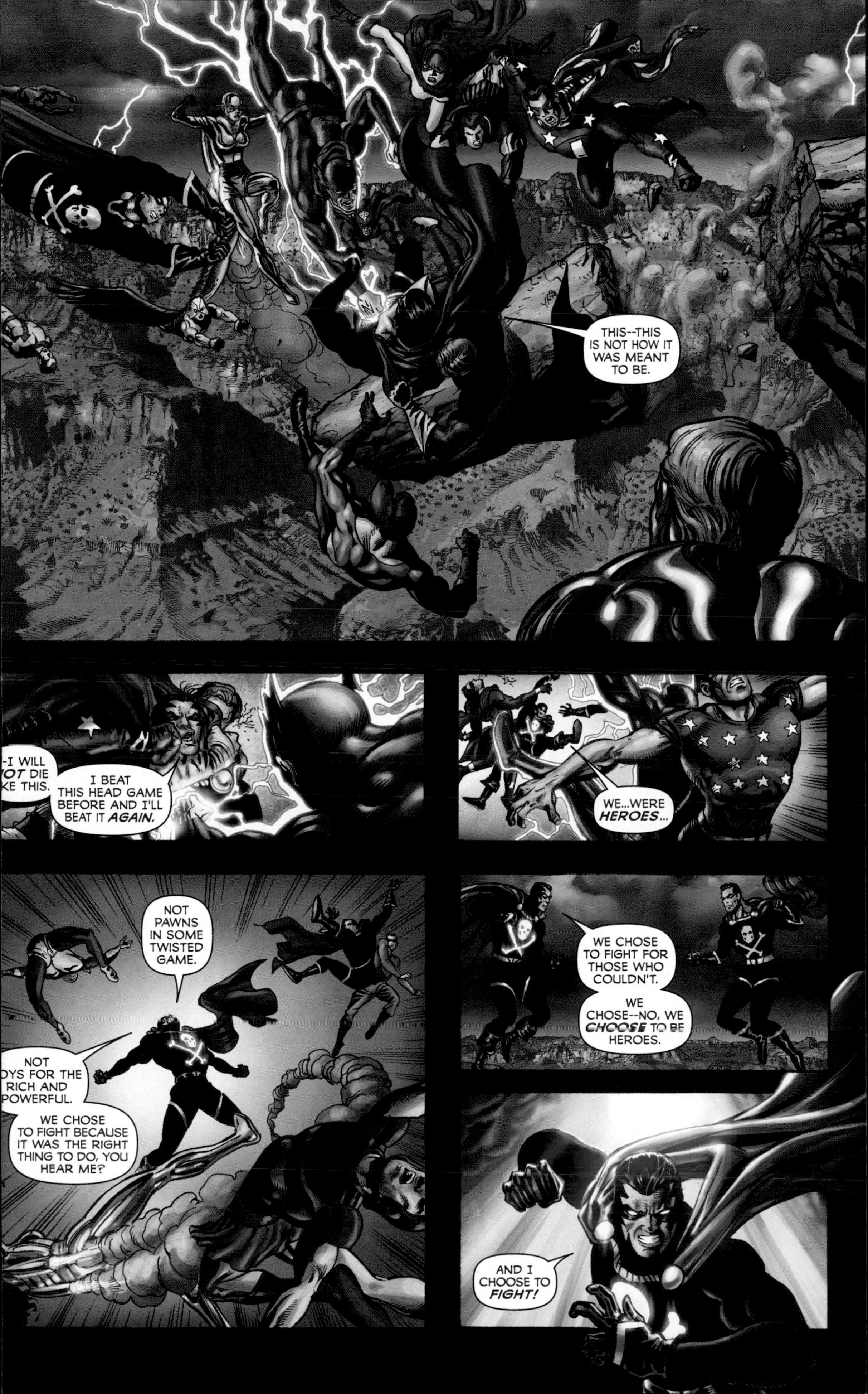

THIS--THIS IS NOT HOW IT WAS MEANT TO BE.
-I WILL *OT* DIE KE THIS.
I BEAT THIS HEAD GAME BEFORE AND I'LL BEAT IT *AGAIN.*
WE...WERE *HEROES*...
NOT PAWNS IN SOME TWISTED GAME.
NOT OYS FOR THE RICH AND POWERFUL.
WE CHOSE TO FIGHT BECAUSE IT WAS THE RIGHT THING TO DO, YOU HEAR ME?
WE CHOSE TO FIGHT FOR THOSE WHO COULDN'T.
WE CHOSE--NO, WE *CHOOSE* TO BE HEROES.
AND I CHOOSE TO *FIGHT!*

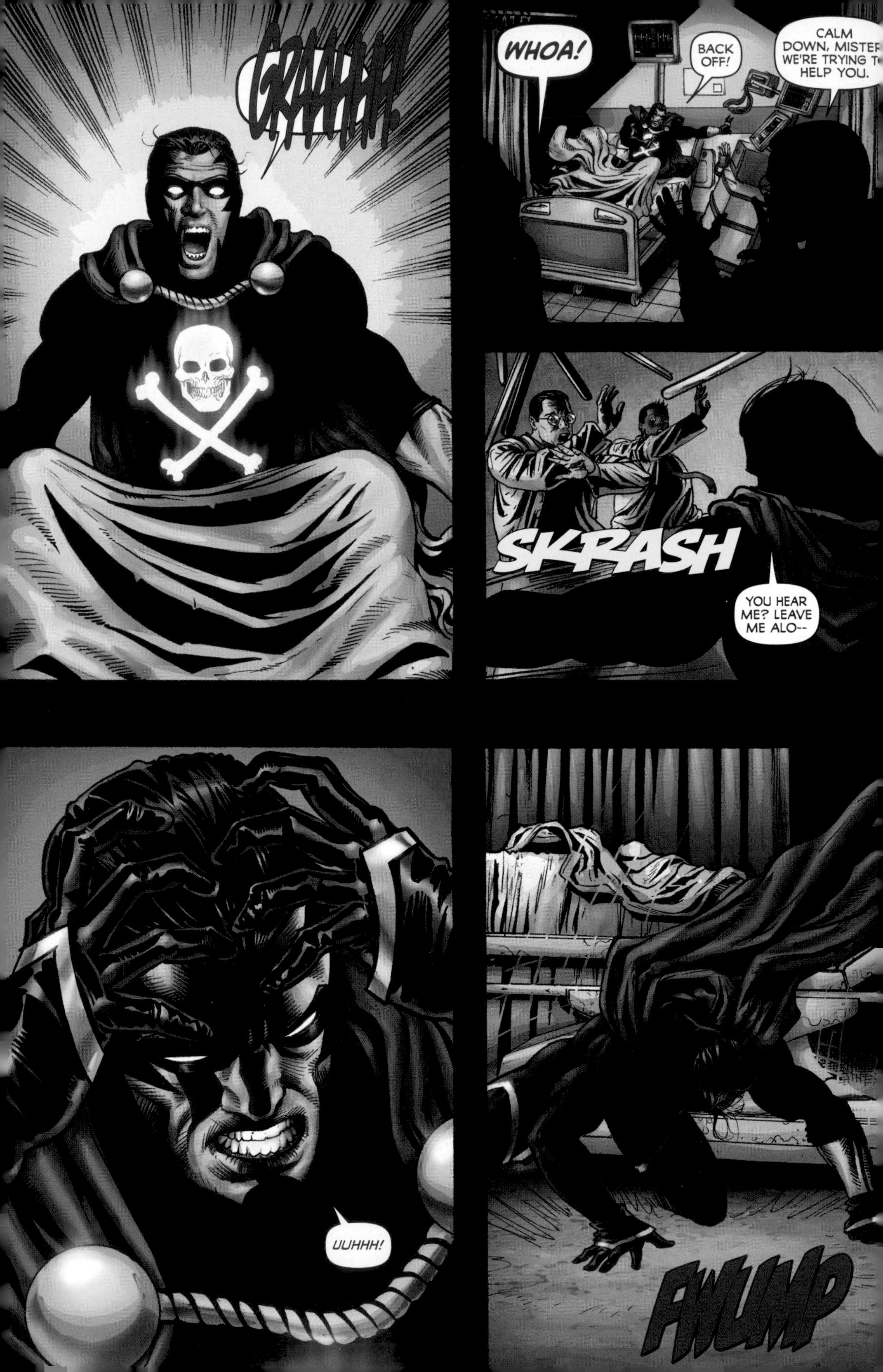
GRAAHH!
WHOA!
BACK OFF!
CALM DOWN, MISTER WE'RE TRYING T HELP YOU.
SKRASH
YOU HEAR ME? LEAVE ME ALO--
UUHHH!
FWUMP

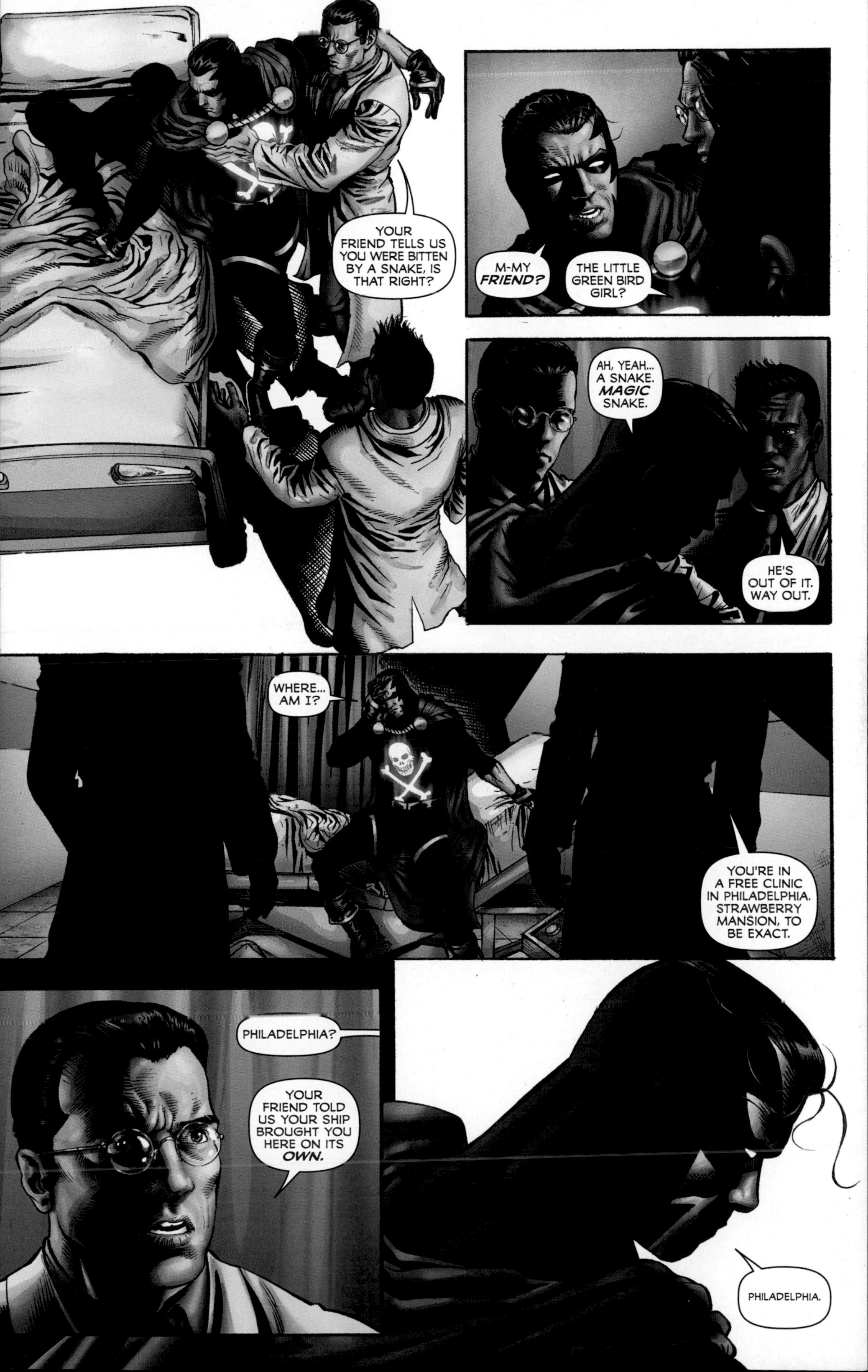
YOUR FRIEND TELLS US YOU WERE BITTEN BY A SNAKE, IS THAT RIGHT?
M-MY *FRIEND?*
THE LITTLE GREEN BIRD GIRL?
AH, YEAH... A SNAKE. *MAGIC* SNAKE.
HE'S OUT OF IT. WAY OUT.
WHERE... AM I?
YOU'RE IN A FREE CLINIC IN PHILADELPHIA. STRAWBERRY MANSION, TO BE EXACT.
PHILADELPHIA?
YOUR FRIEND TOLD US YOUR SHIP BROUGHT YOU HERE ON ITS *OWN.*
PHILADELPHIA.

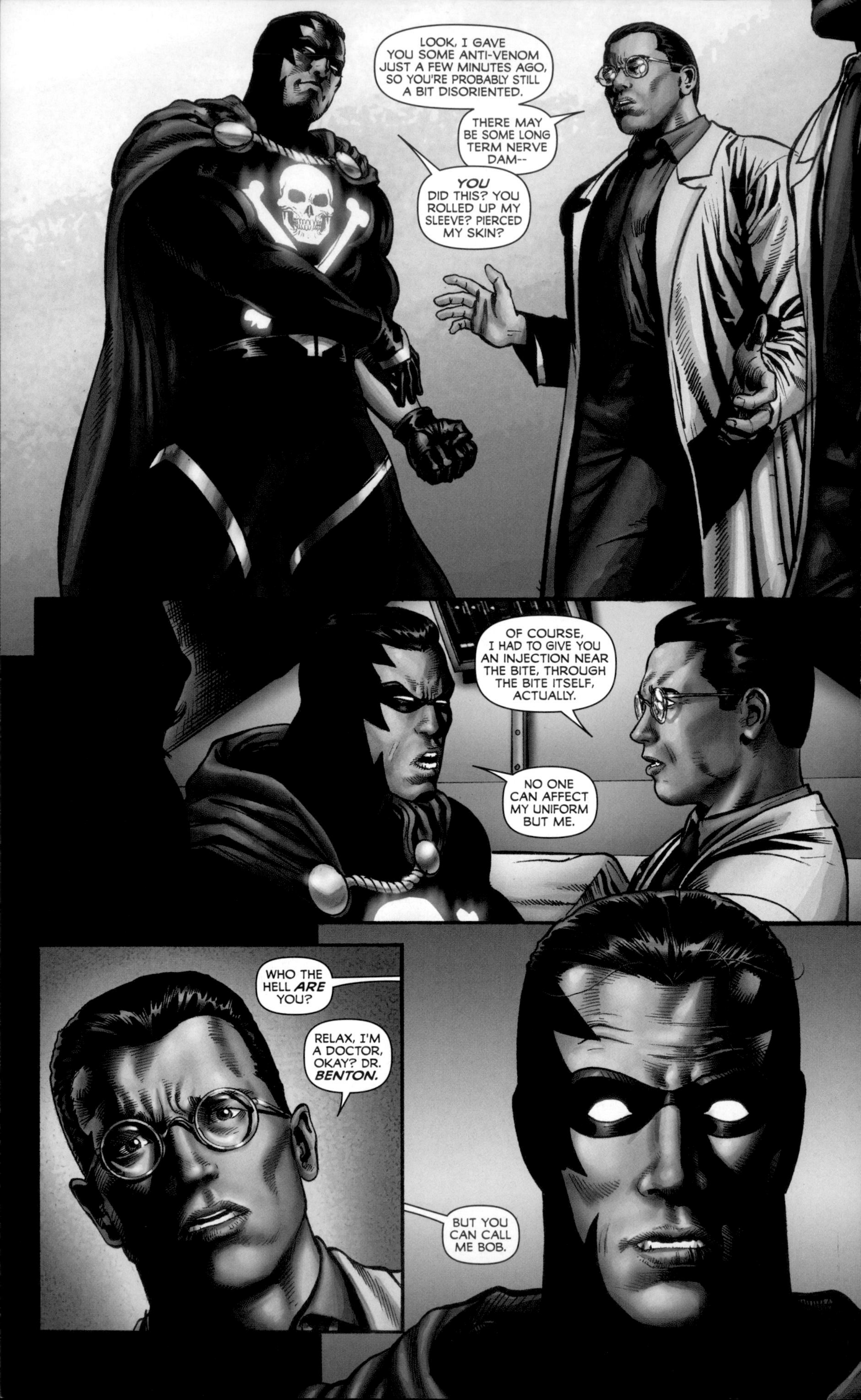
LOOK, I GAVE YOU SOME ANTI-VENOM JUST A FEW MINUTES AGO, SO YOU'RE PROBABLY STILL A BIT DISORIENTED.
THERE MAY BE SOME LONG TERM NERVE DAM--
YOU DID THIS? YOU ROLLED UP MY SLEEVE? PIERCED MY SKIN?
OF COURSE, I HAD TO GIVE YOU AN INJECTION NEAR THE BITE, THROUGH THE BITE ITSELF, ACTUALLY.
NO ONE CAN AFFECT MY UNIFORM BUT ME.
WHO THE HELL *ARE* YOU?
RELAX, I'M A DOCTOR, OKAY? DR. *BENTON.*
BUT YOU CAN CALL ME BOB.

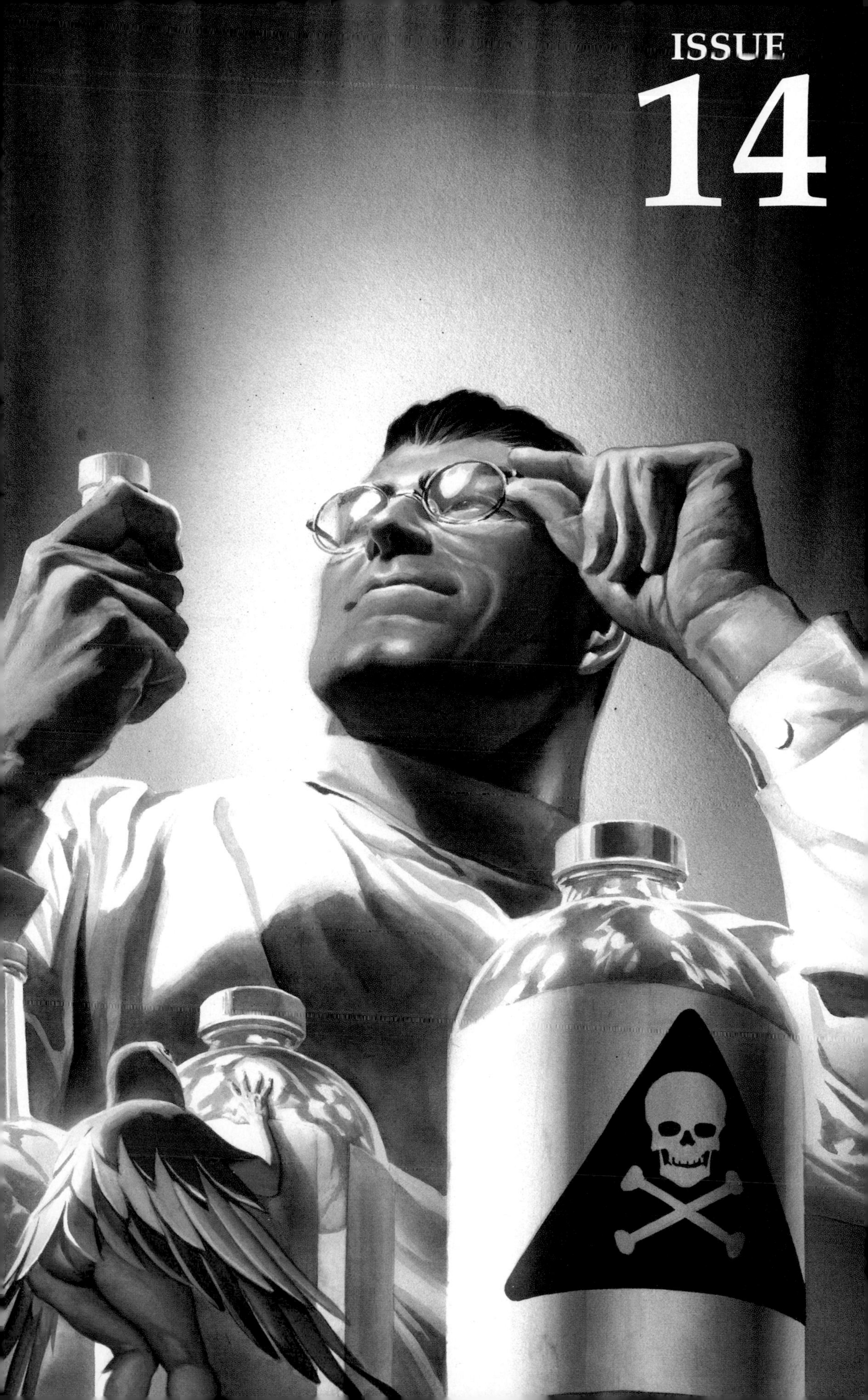
ISSUE
14

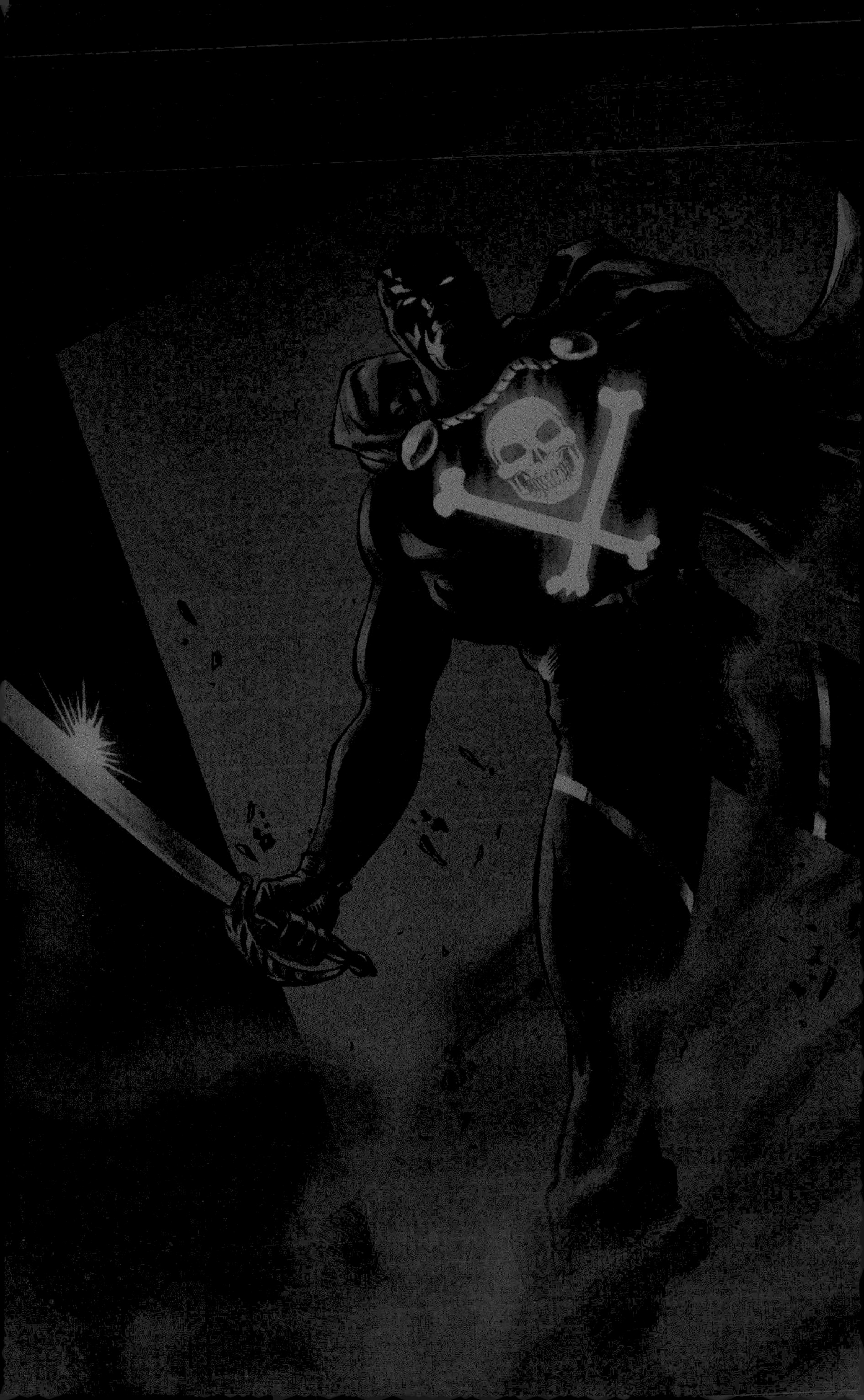

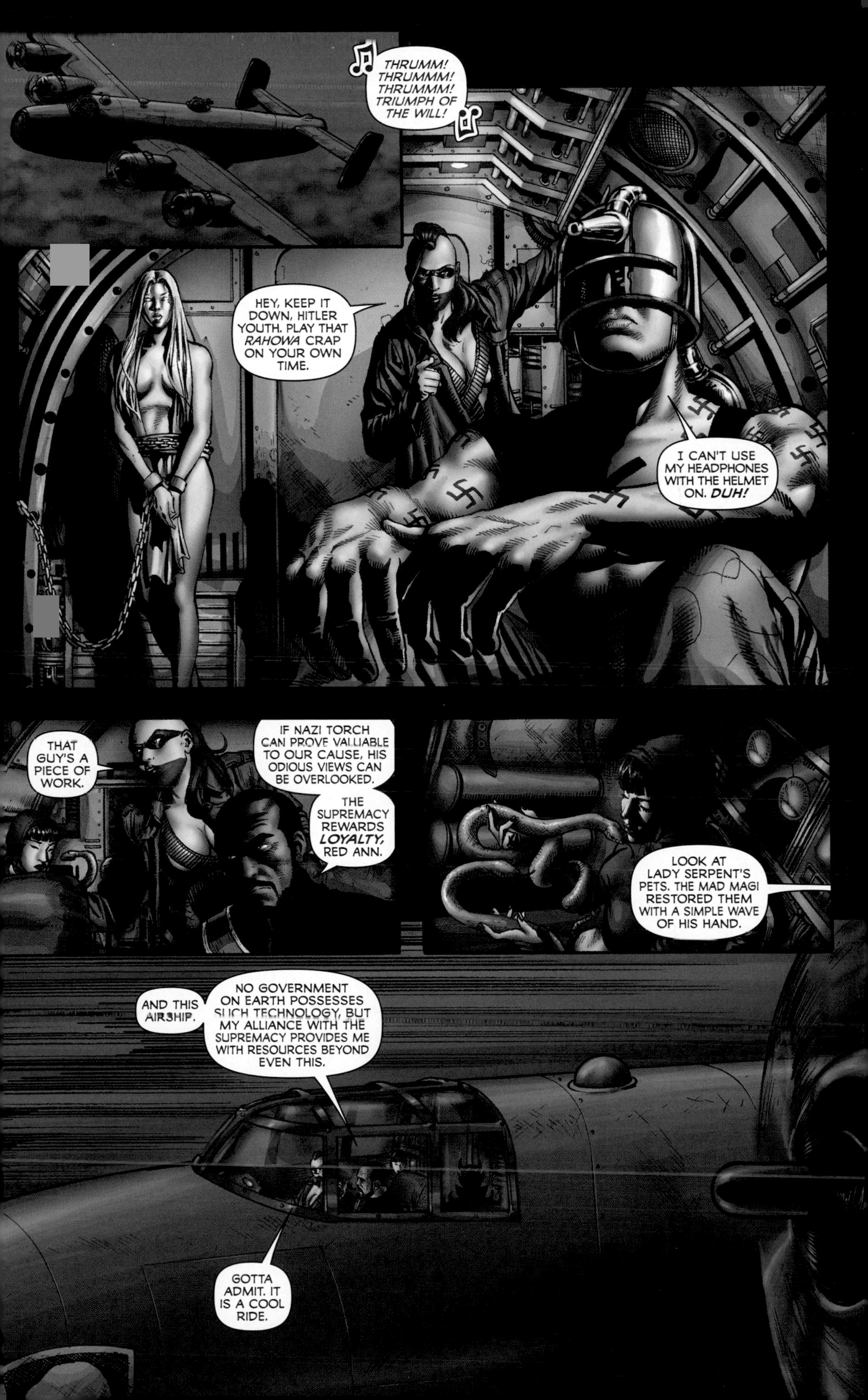
THRUMM! THRUMMM! THRUMMM! TRIUMPH OF THE WILL!
HEY, KEEP IT DOWN, HITLER YOUTH. PLAY THAT *RAHOWA* CRAP ON YOUR OWN TIME.
I CAN'T USE MY HEADPHONES WITH THE HELMET ON. ***DUH!***
THAT GUY'S A PIECE OF WORK.
IF NAZI TORCH CAN PROVE VALUABLE TO OUR CAUSE, HIS ODIOUS VIEWS CAN BE OVERLOOKED.
THE SUPREMACY REWARDS ***LOYALTY,*** RED ANN.
LOOK AT LADY SERPENT'S PETS. THE MAD MAGI RESTORED THEM WITH A SIMPLE WAVE OF HIS HAND.
AND THIS AIRSHIP.
NO GOVERNMENT ON EARTH POSSESSES SUCH TECHNOLOGY, BUT MY ALLIANCE WITH THE SUPREMACY PROVIDES ME WITH RESOURCES BEYOND EVEN THIS.
GOTTA ADMIT. IT IS A COOL RIDE.

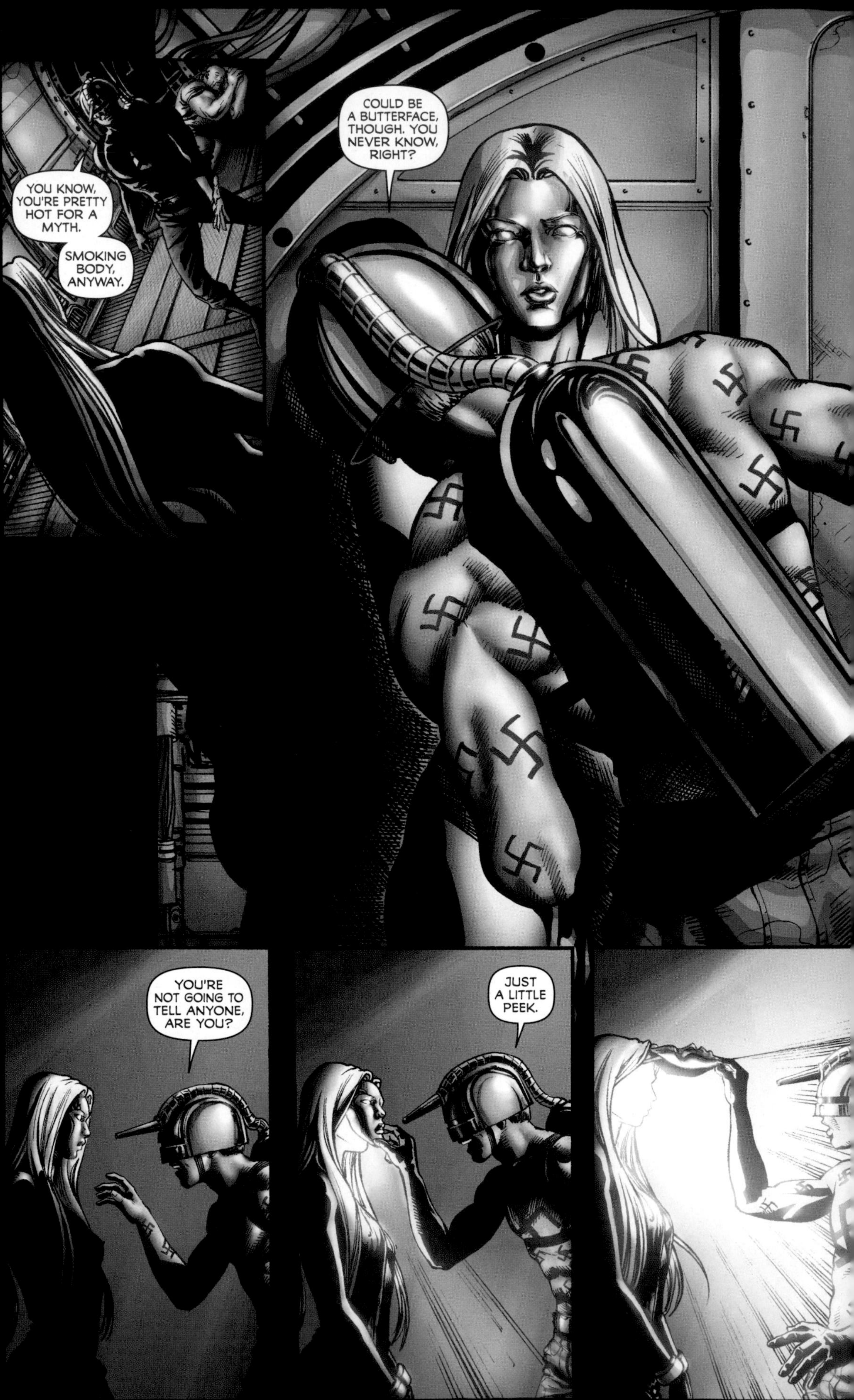
YOU KNOW, YOU'RE PRETTY HOT FOR A MYTH.
SMOKING BODY, ANYWAY.
COULD BE A BUTTERFACE, THOUGH. YOU NEVER KNOW, RIGHT?
YOU'RE NOT GOING TO TELL ANYONE, ARE YOU?
JUST A LITTLE PEEK.

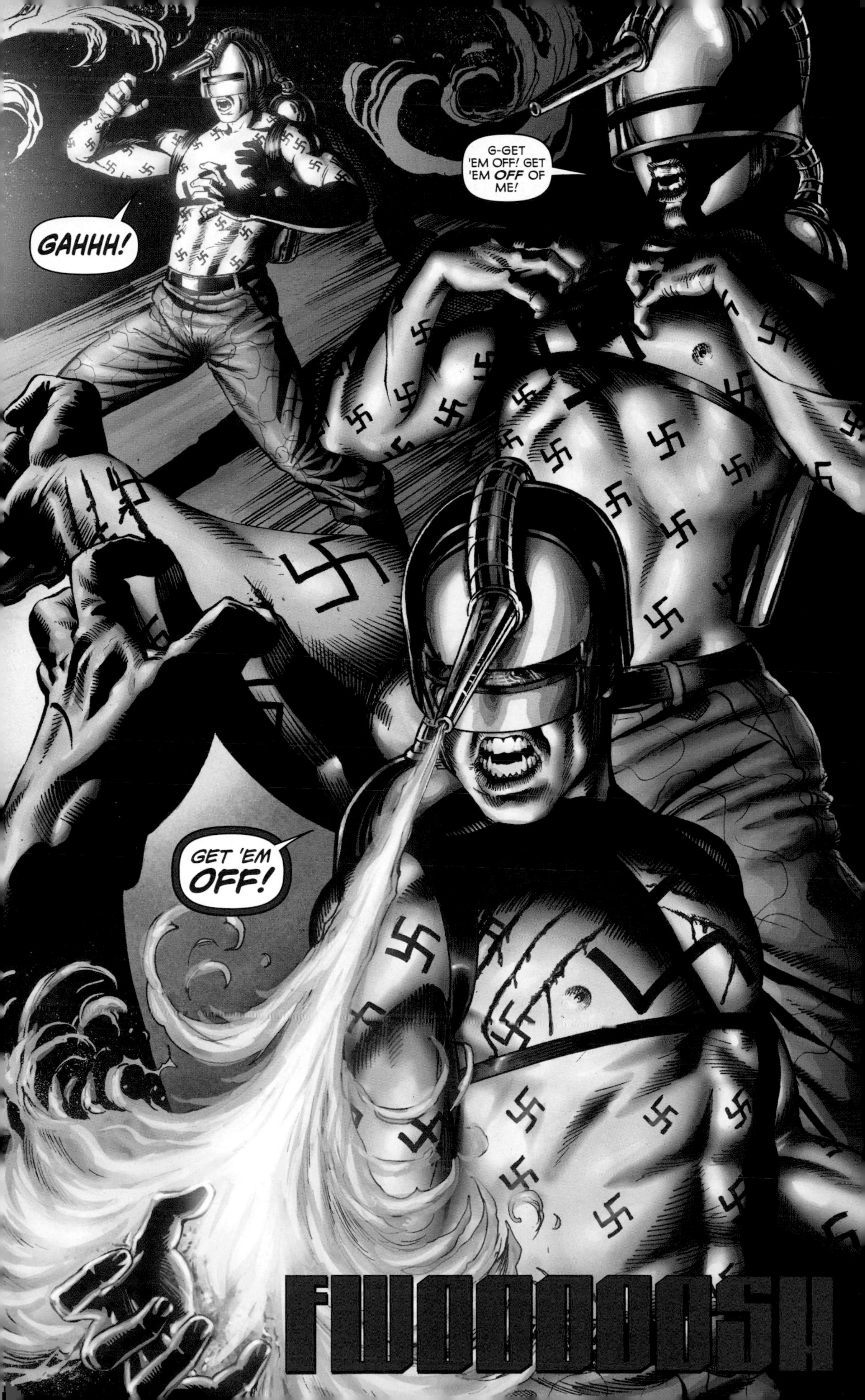
G-GET 'EM OFF! GET 'EM OFF OF ME!
GAHHH!
GET 'EM OFF!
FWOOOOSH

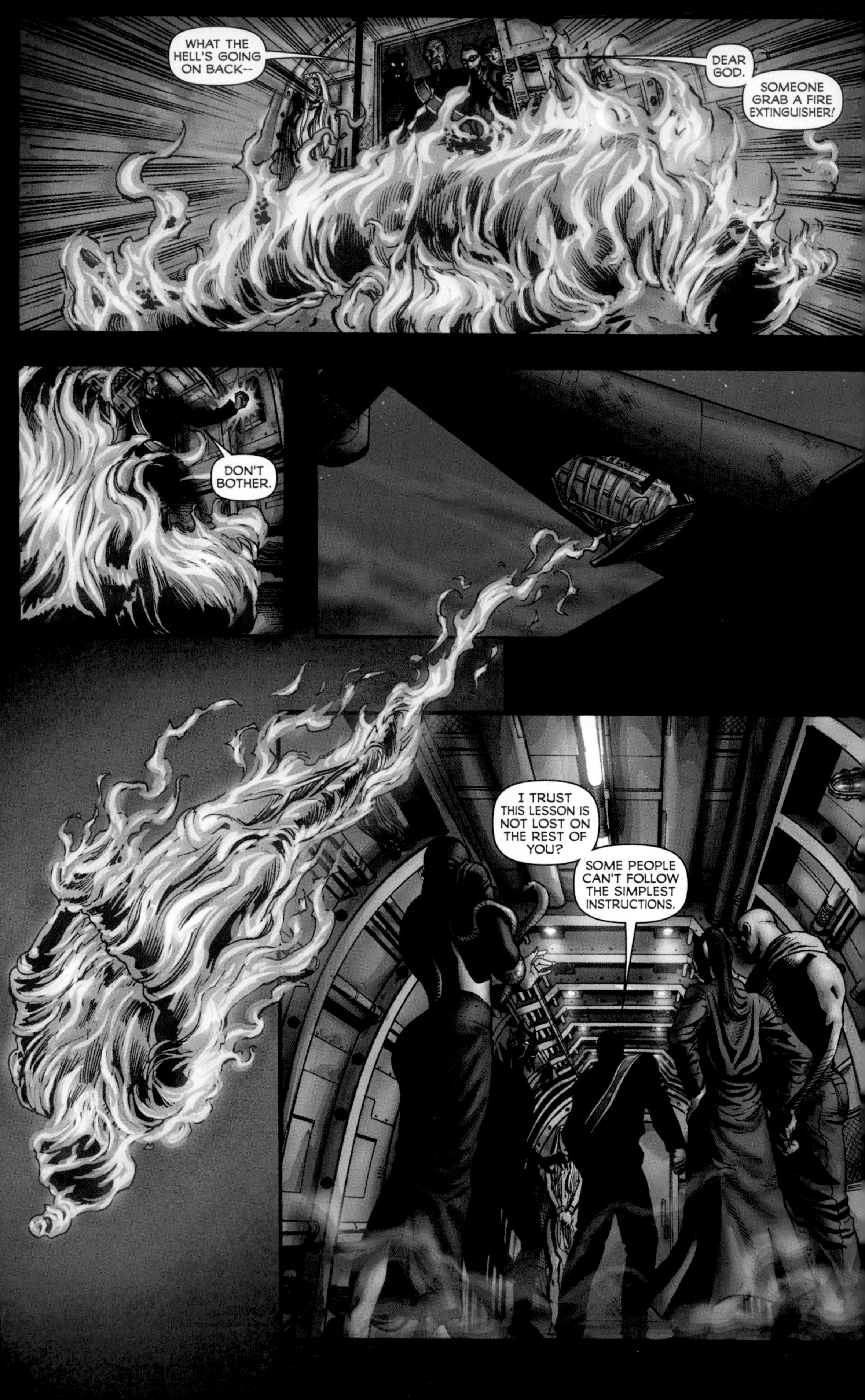
WHAT THE HELL'S GOING ON BACK--
DEAR GOD.
SOMEONE GRAB A FIRE EXTINGUISHER!
DON'T BOTHER.
I TRUST THIS LESSON IS NOT LOST ON THE REST OF YOU?
SOME PEOPLE CAN'T FOLLOW THE SIMPLEST INSTRUCTIONS.

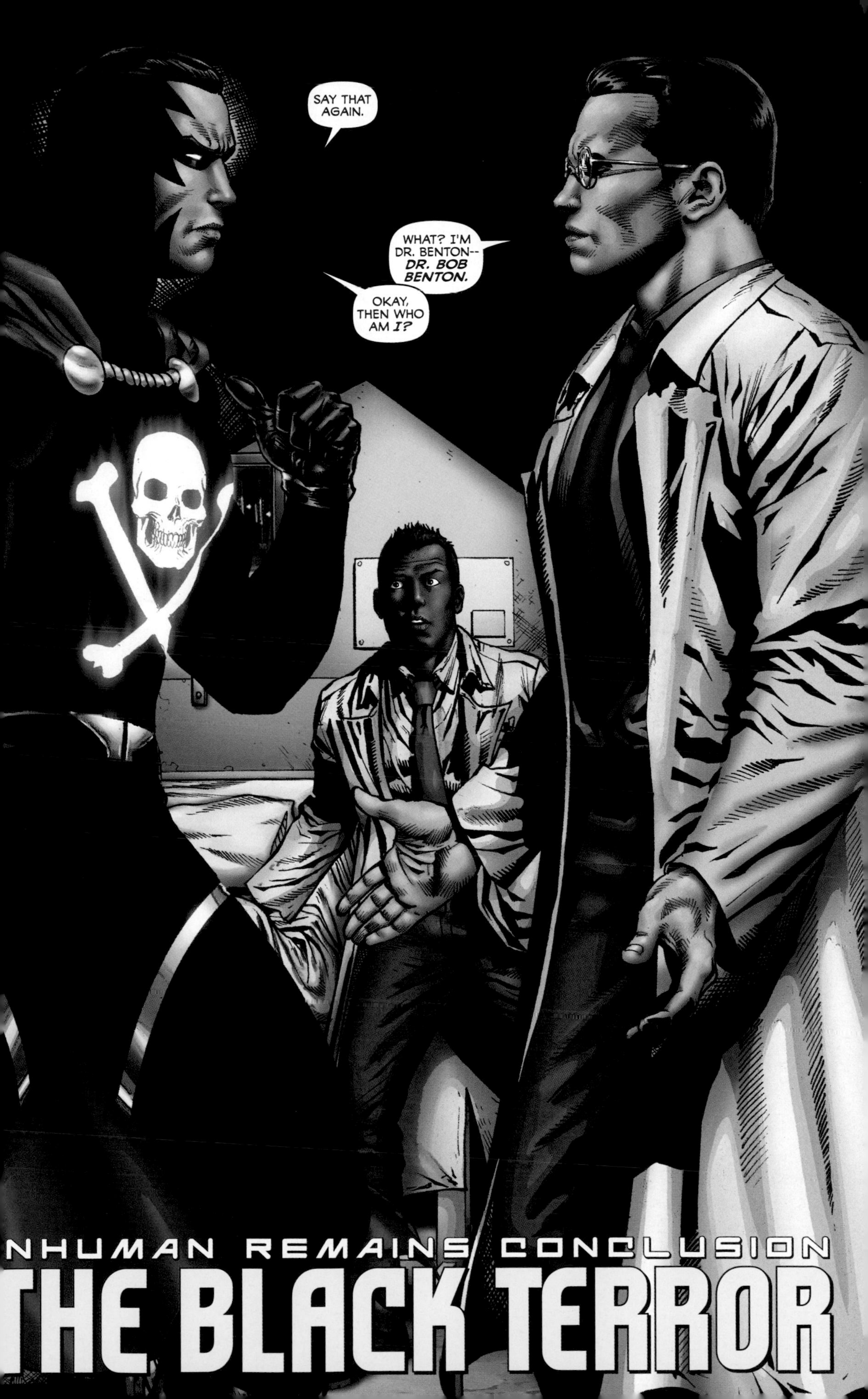
SAY THAT AGAIN.
WHAT? I'M DR. BENTON-- DR. BOB BENTON.
OKAY, THEN WHO AM I?
NHUMAN REMAINS CONCLUSION
THE BLACK TERROR

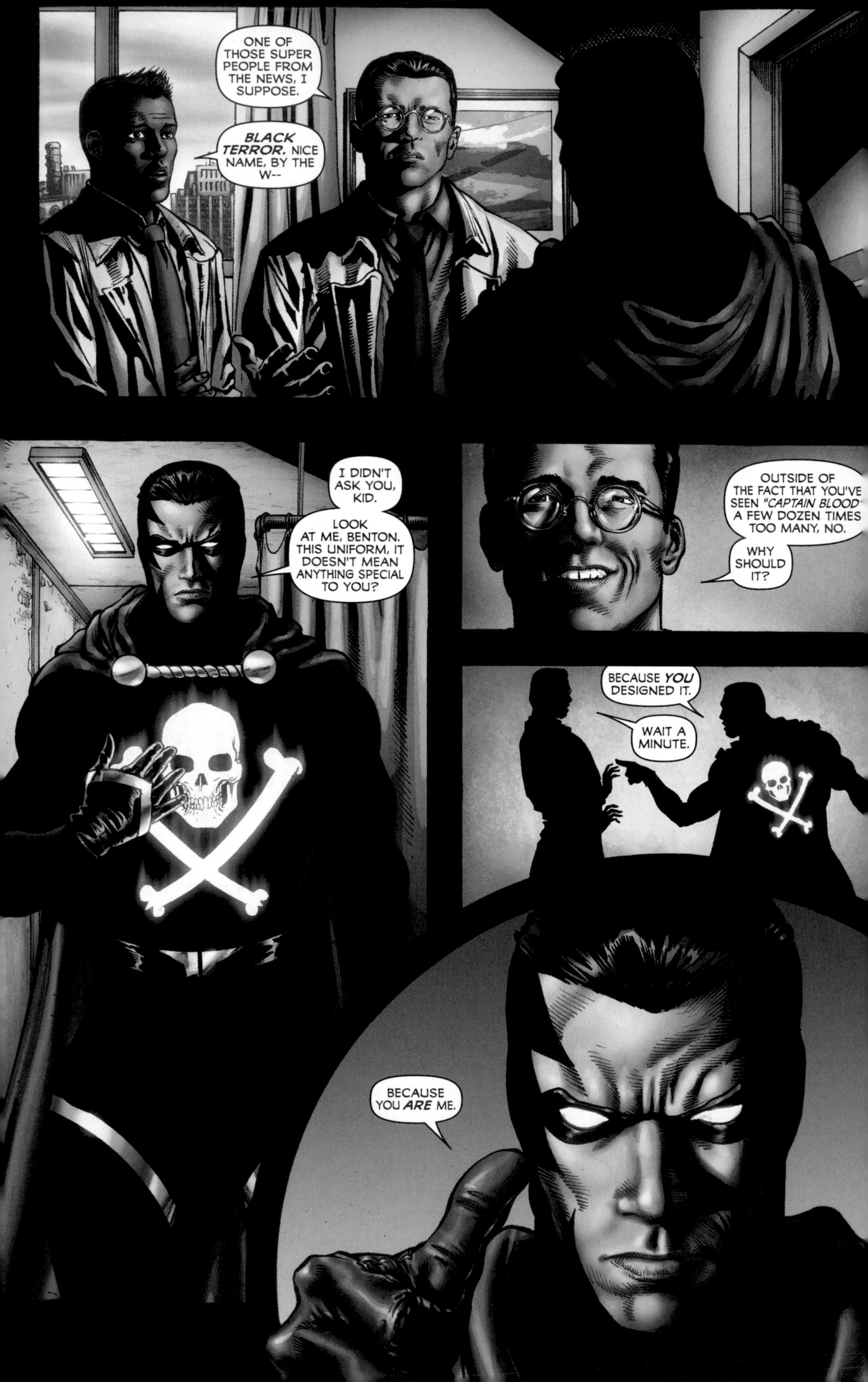
ONE OF THOSE SUPER PEOPLE FROM THE NEWS, I SUPPOSE.
BLACK TERROR. NICE NAME, BY THE W--
I DIDN'T ASK YOU, KID.
LOOK AT ME, BENTON. THIS UNIFORM, IT DOESN'T MEAN ANYTHING SPECIAL TO YOU?
OUTSIDE OF THE FACT THAT YOU'VE SEEN "CAPTAIN BLOOD" A FEW DOZEN TIMES TOO MANY, NO.
WHY SHOULD IT?
BECAUSE YOU DESIGNED IT.
WAIT A MINUTE.
BECAUSE YOU ARE ME.

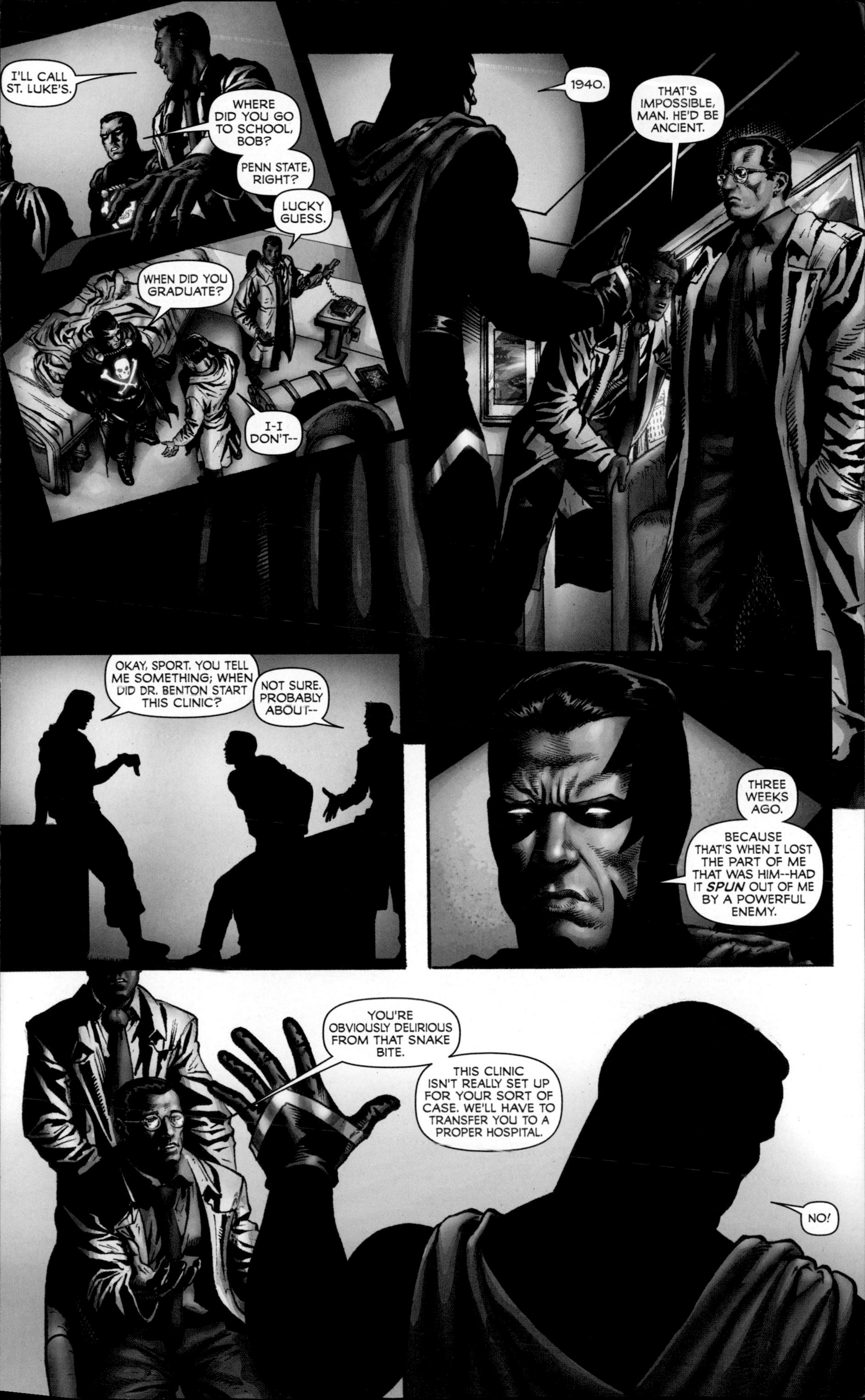
I'LL CALL ST. LUKE'S.
WHERE DID YOU GO TO SCHOOL, BOB?
PENN STATE, RIGHT?
LUCKY GUESS.
WHEN DID YOU GRADUATE?
I-I DON'T--
1940.
THAT'S IMPOSSIBLE, MAN. HE'D BE ANCIENT.
OKAY, SPORT. YOU TELL ME SOMETHING; WHEN DID DR. BENTON START THIS CLINIC?
NOT SURE. PROBABLY ABOUT--
THREE WEEKS AGO.
BECAUSE THAT'S WHEN I LOST THE PART OF ME THAT WAS HIM--HAD IT SPUN OUT OF ME BY A POWERFUL ENEMY.
YOU'RE OBVIOUSLY DELIRIOUS FROM THAT SNAKE BITE.
THIS CLINIC ISN'T REALLY SET UP FOR YOUR SORT OF CASE. WE'LL HAVE TO TRANSFER YOU TO A PROPER HOSPITAL.
NO!

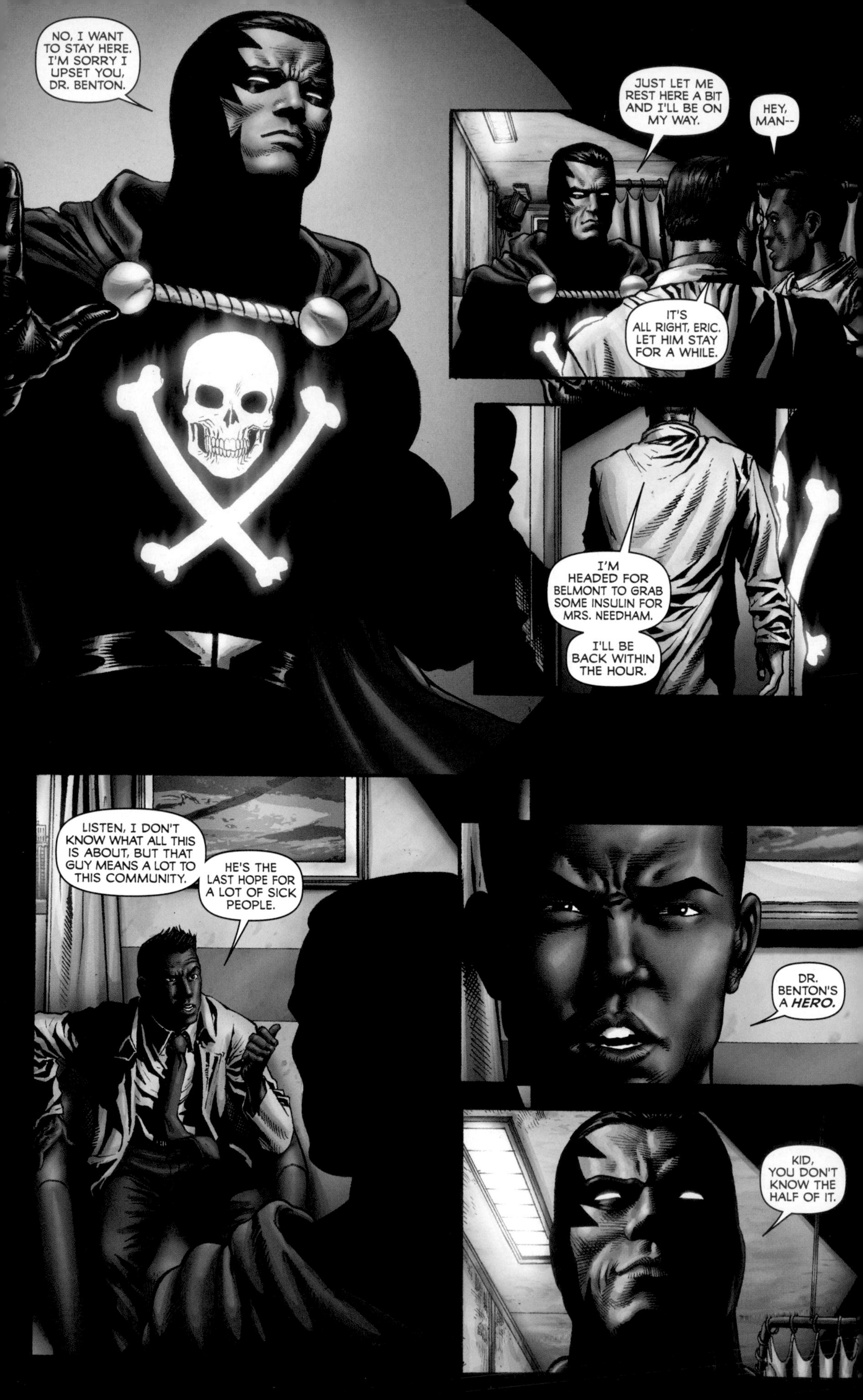
NO, I WANT TO STAY HERE. I'M SORRY I UPSET YOU, DR. BENTON.
JUST LET ME REST HERE A BIT AND I'LL BE ON MY WAY.
HEY, MAN--
IT'S ALL RIGHT, ERIC. LET HIM STAY FOR A WHILE.
I'M HEADED FOR BELMONT TO GRAB SOME INSULIN FOR MRS. NEEDHAM.
I'LL BE BACK WITHIN THE HOUR.
LISTEN, I DON'T KNOW WHAT ALL THIS IS ABOUT, BUT THAT GUY MEANS A LOT TO THIS COMMUNITY.
HE'S THE LAST HOPE FOR A LOT OF SICK PEOPLE.
DR. BENTON'S A *HERO.*
KID, YOU DON'T KNOW THE HALF OF IT.

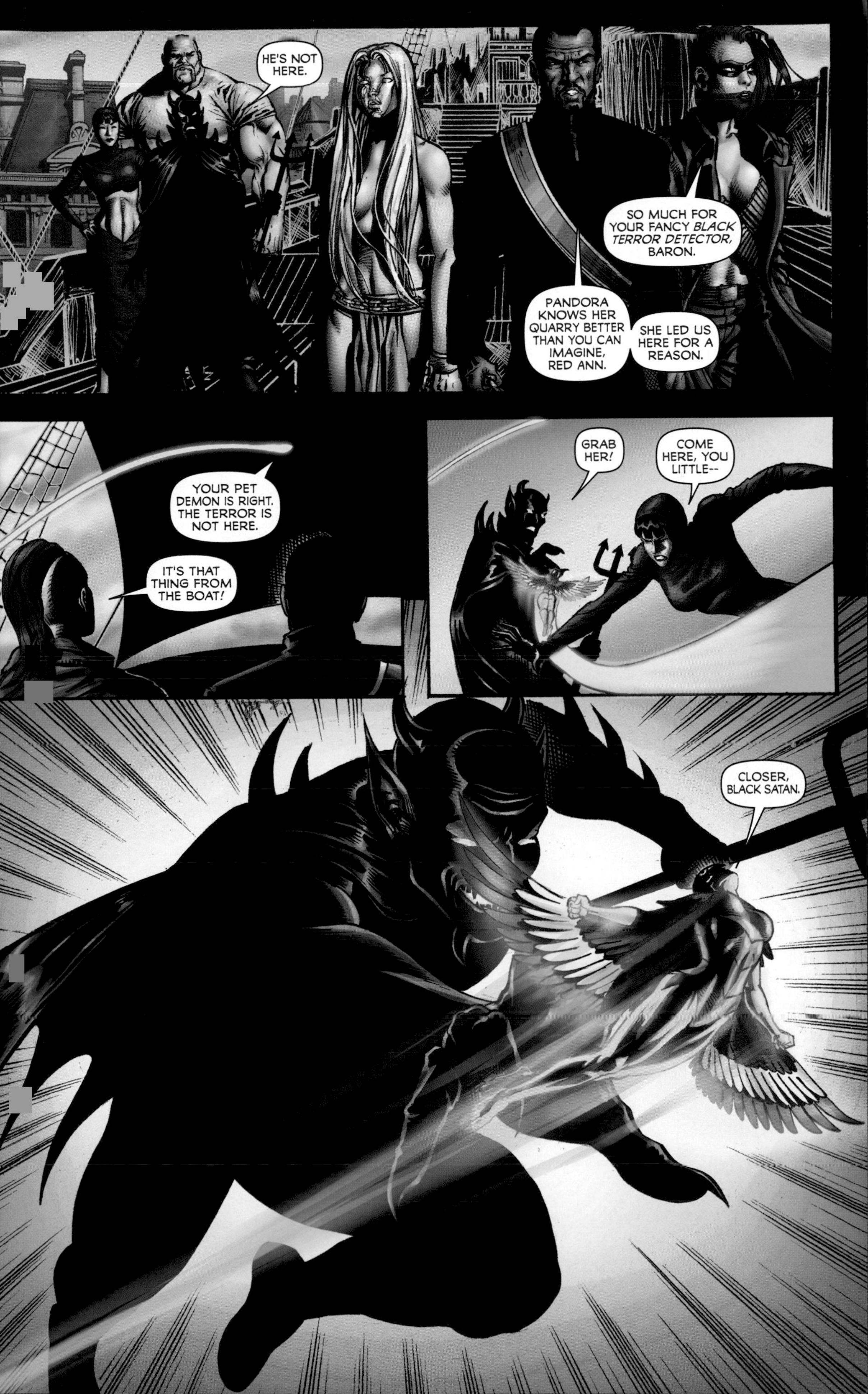
HE'S NOT HERE.
SO MUCH FOR YOUR FANCY *BLACK TERROR DETECTOR,* BARON.
PANDORA KNOWS HER QUARRY BETTER THAN YOU CAN IMAGINE, RED ANN.
SHE LED US HERE FOR A REASON.
YOUR PET DEMON IS RIGHT. THE TERROR IS NOT HERE.
IT'S THAT THING FROM THE BOAT!
GRAB HER!
COME HERE, YOU LITTLE--
CLOSER, BLACK SATAN.

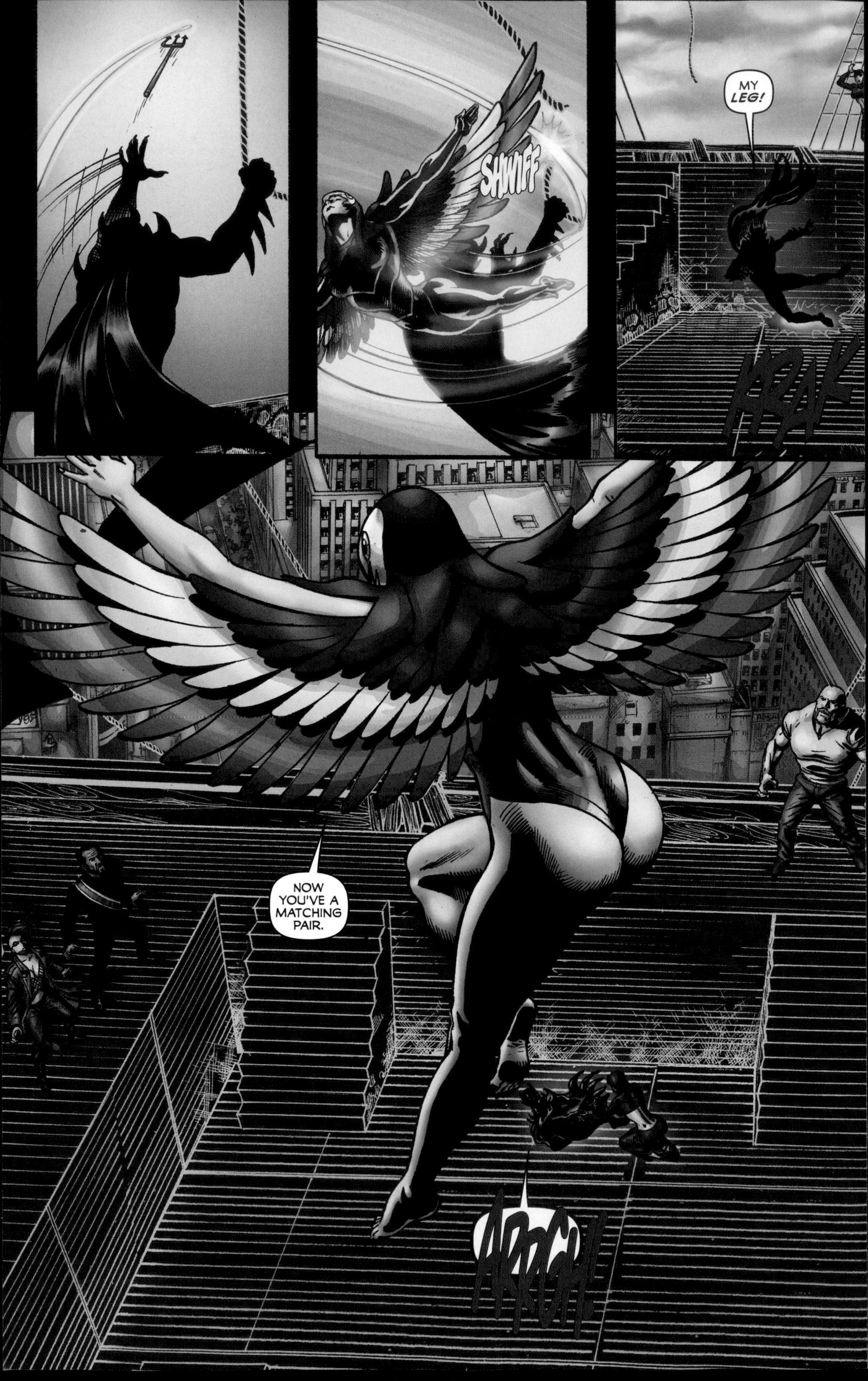
SHWIFF
MY LEG!
KRAK
NOW YOU'VE A MATCHING PAIR.
ARRGH!

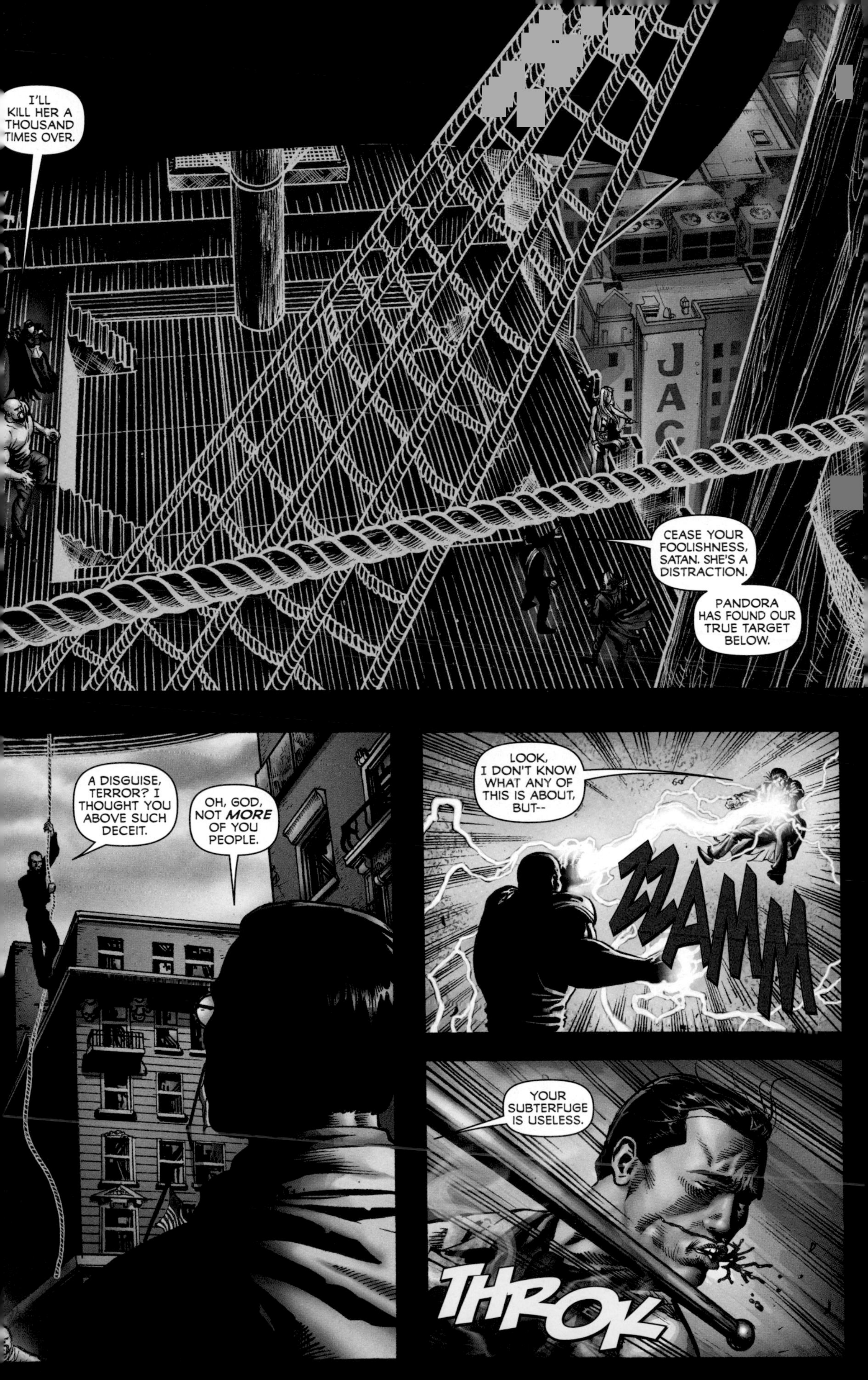
I'LL KILL HER A THOUSAND TIMES OVER.
CEASE YOUR FOOLISHNESS, SATAN. SHE'S A DISTRACTION.
PANDORA HAS FOUND OUR TRUE TARGET BELOW.
JAC
A DISGUISE, TERROR? I THOUGHT YOU ABOVE SUCH DECEIT.
OH, GOD, NOT *MORE* OF YOU PEOPLE.
LOOK, I DON'T KNOW WHAT ANY OF THIS IS ABOUT, BUT--
ZZAMM
YOUR SUBTERFUGE IS USELESS.
THROK

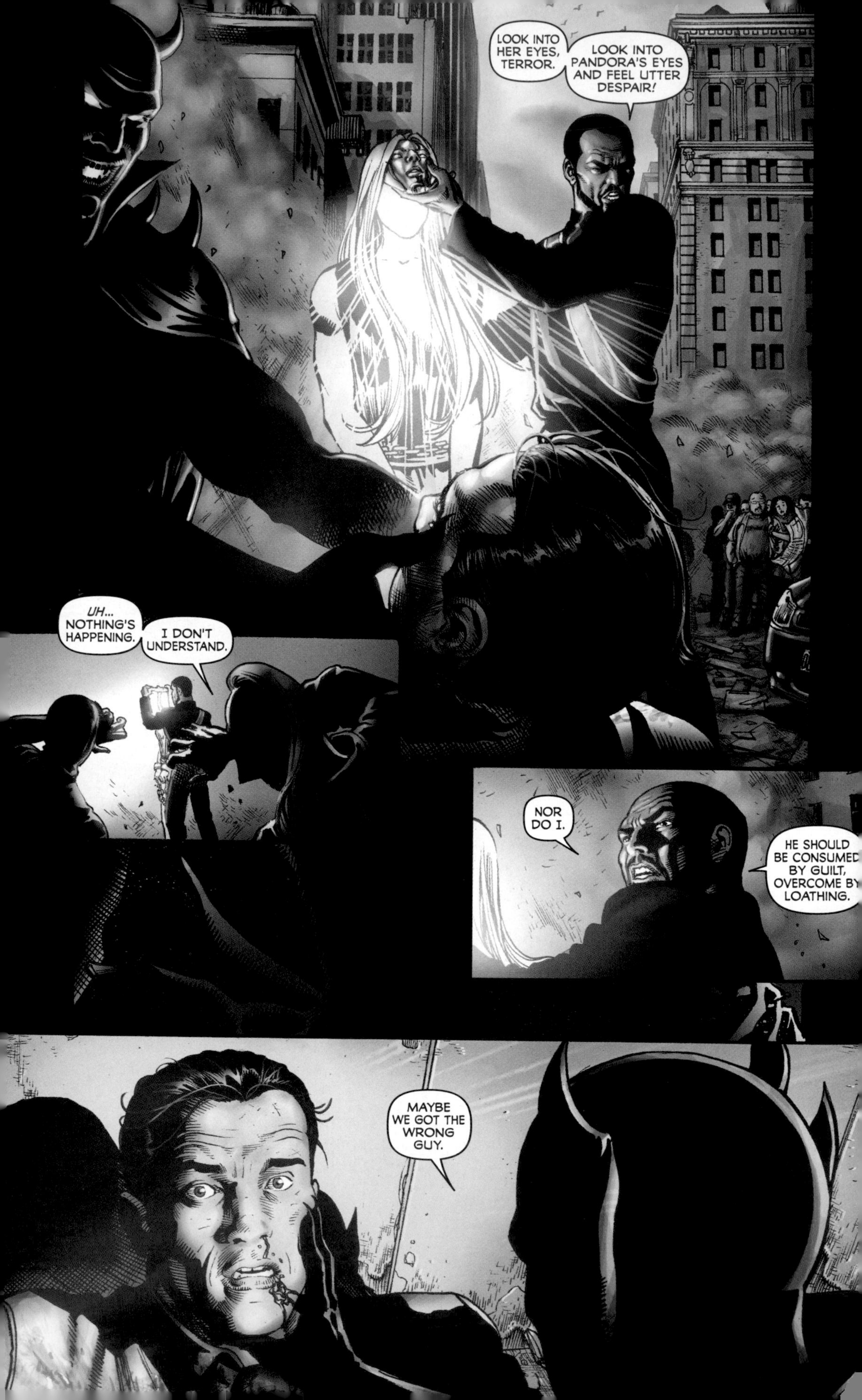
LOOK INTO HER EYES, TERROR.
LOOK INTO PANDORA'S EYES AND FEEL UTTER DESPAIR!
UH... NOTHING'S HAPPENING.
I DON'T UNDERSTAND.
NOR DO I.
HE SHOULD BE CONSUMED BY GUILT, OVERCOME BY LOATHING.
MAYBE WE GOT THE WRONG GUY.

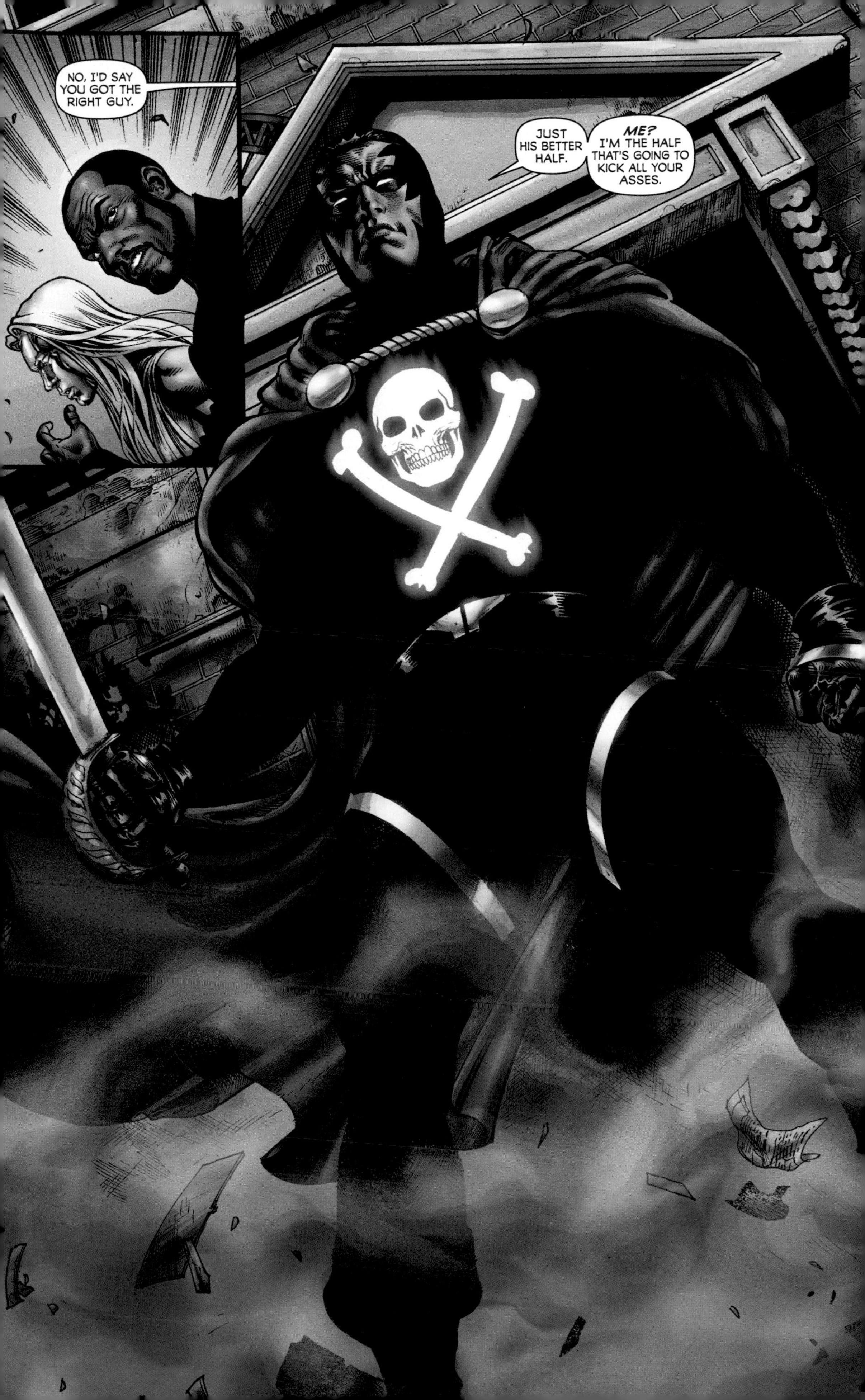
NO, I'D SAY YOU GOT THE RIGHT GUY.
JUST HIS BETTER HALF.
ME? I'M THE HALF THAT'S GOING TO KICK ALL YOUR ASSES.

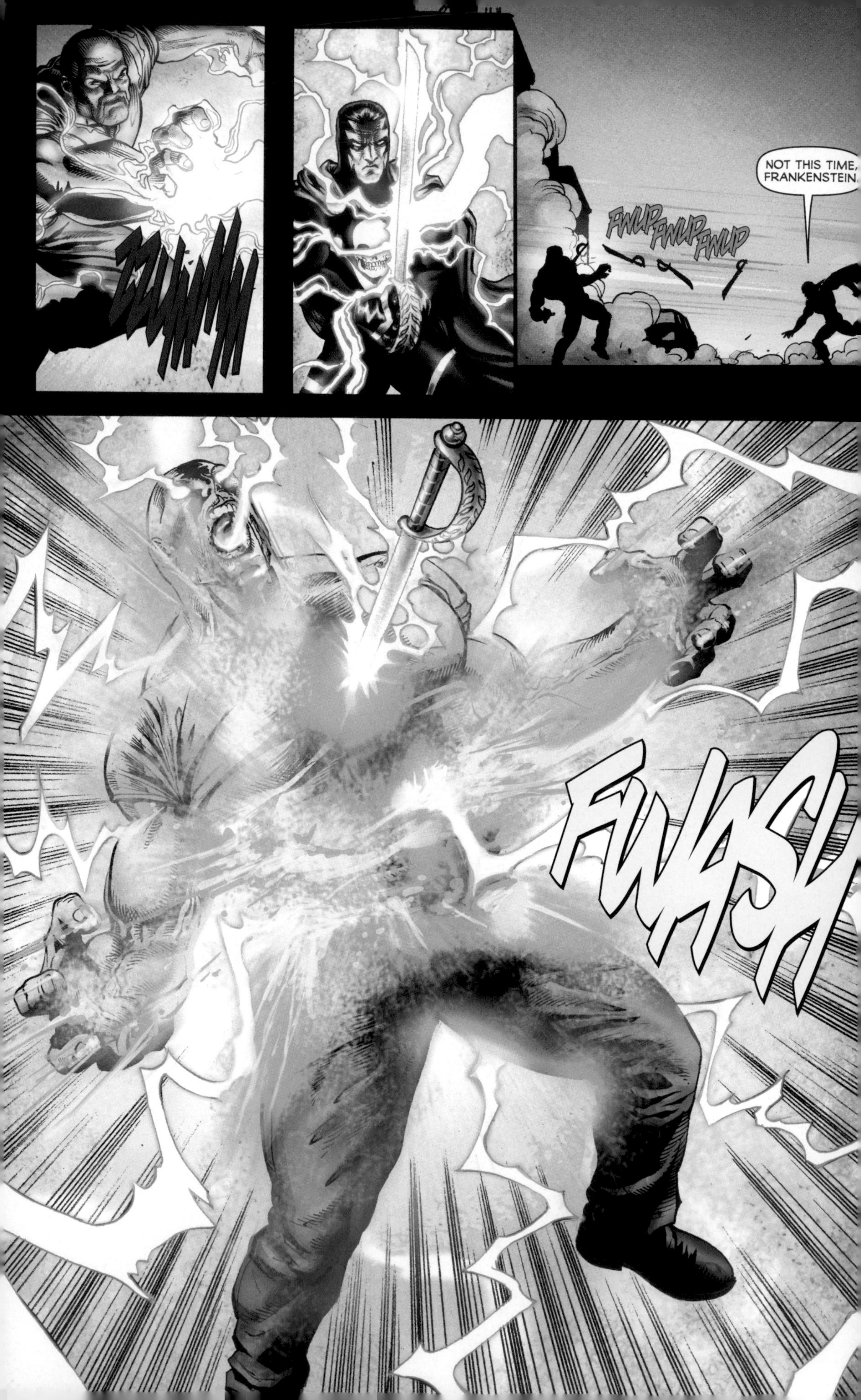
ZZAKKKKK
NOT THIS TIME, FRANKENSTEIN.
FWUP FWUP FWUP
FWASH

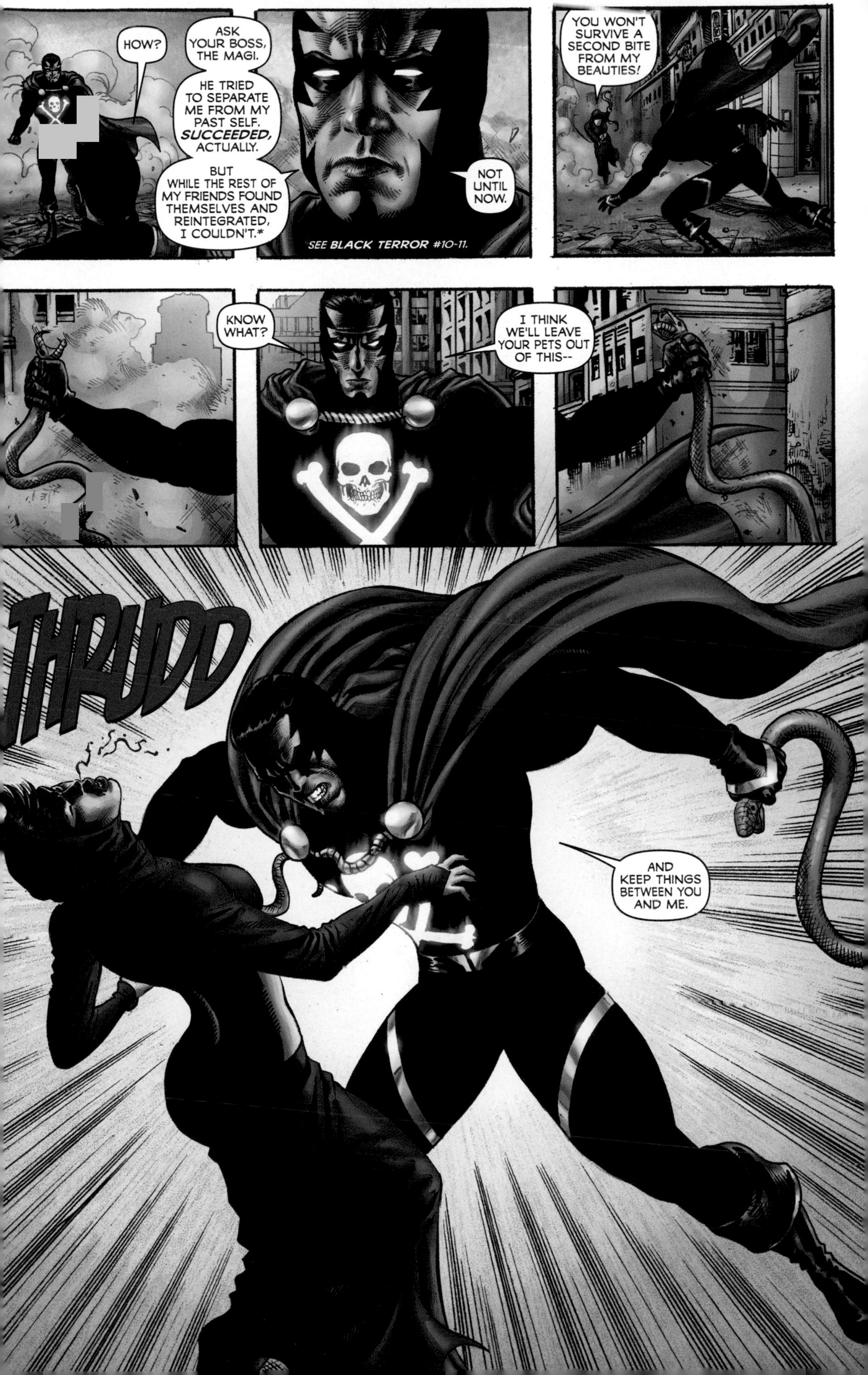
HOW?
ASK YOUR BOSS, THE MAGI.
HE TRIED TO SEPARATE ME FROM MY PAST SELF. SUCCEEDED, ACTUALLY.
BUT WHILE THE REST OF MY FRIENDS FOUND THEMSELVES AND REINTEGRATED, I COULDN'T.*
NOT UNTIL NOW.
*SEE BLACK TERROR #10-11.
YOU WON'T SURVIVE A SECOND BITE FROM MY BEAUTIES!
KNOW WHAT?
I THINK WE'LL LEAVE YOUR PETS OUT OF THIS--
THUDD
AND KEEP THINGS BETWEEN YOU AND ME.

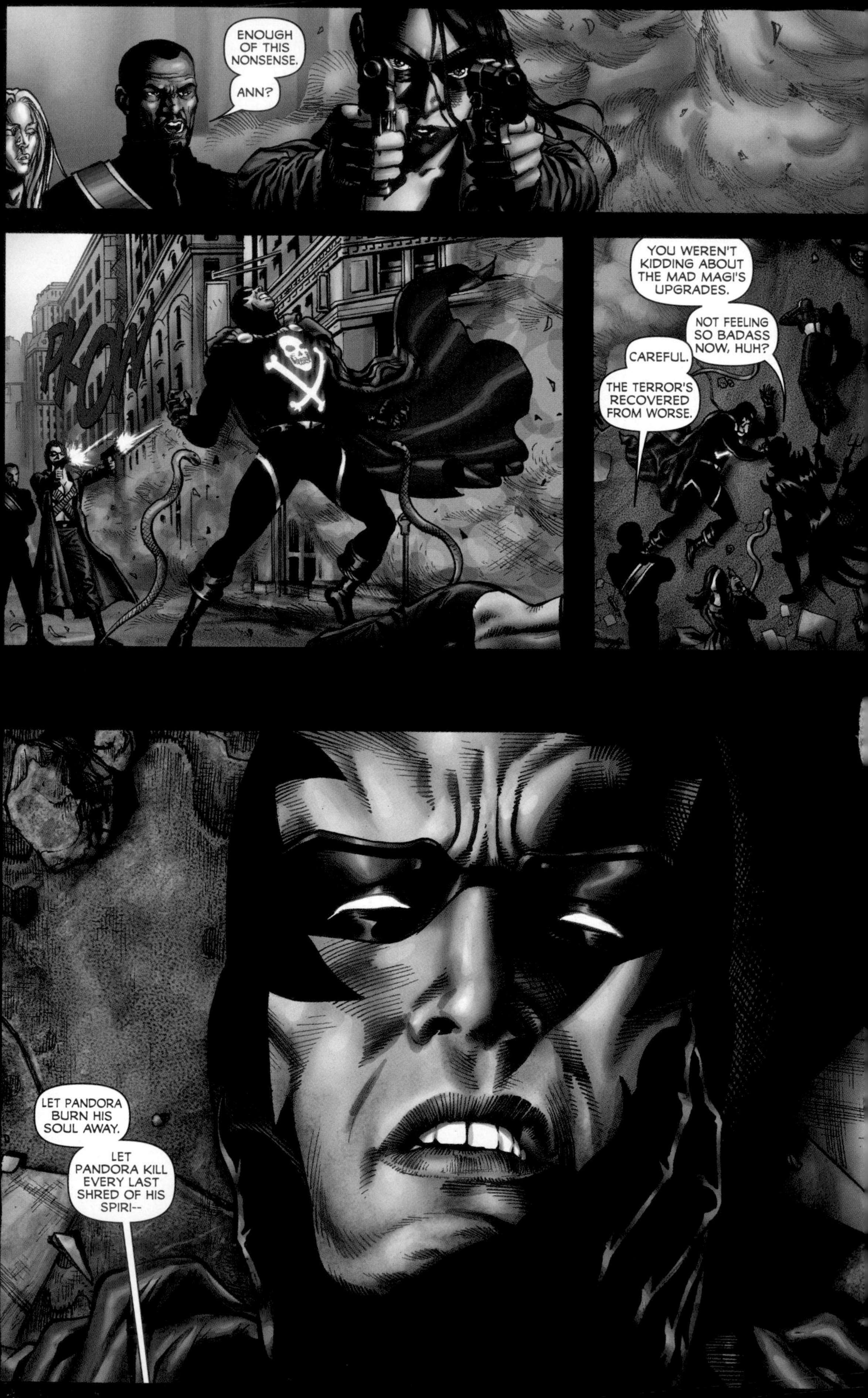
ENOUGH OF THIS NONSENSE.
ANN?
PKOW
YOU WEREN'T KIDDING ABOUT THE MAD MAGI'S UPGRADES.
NOT FEELING SO BADASS NOW, HUH?
CAREFUL.
THE TERROR'S RECOVERED FROM WORSE.
LET PANDORA BURN HIS SOUL AWAY.
LET PANDORA KILL EVERY LAST SHRED OF HIS SPIRI--

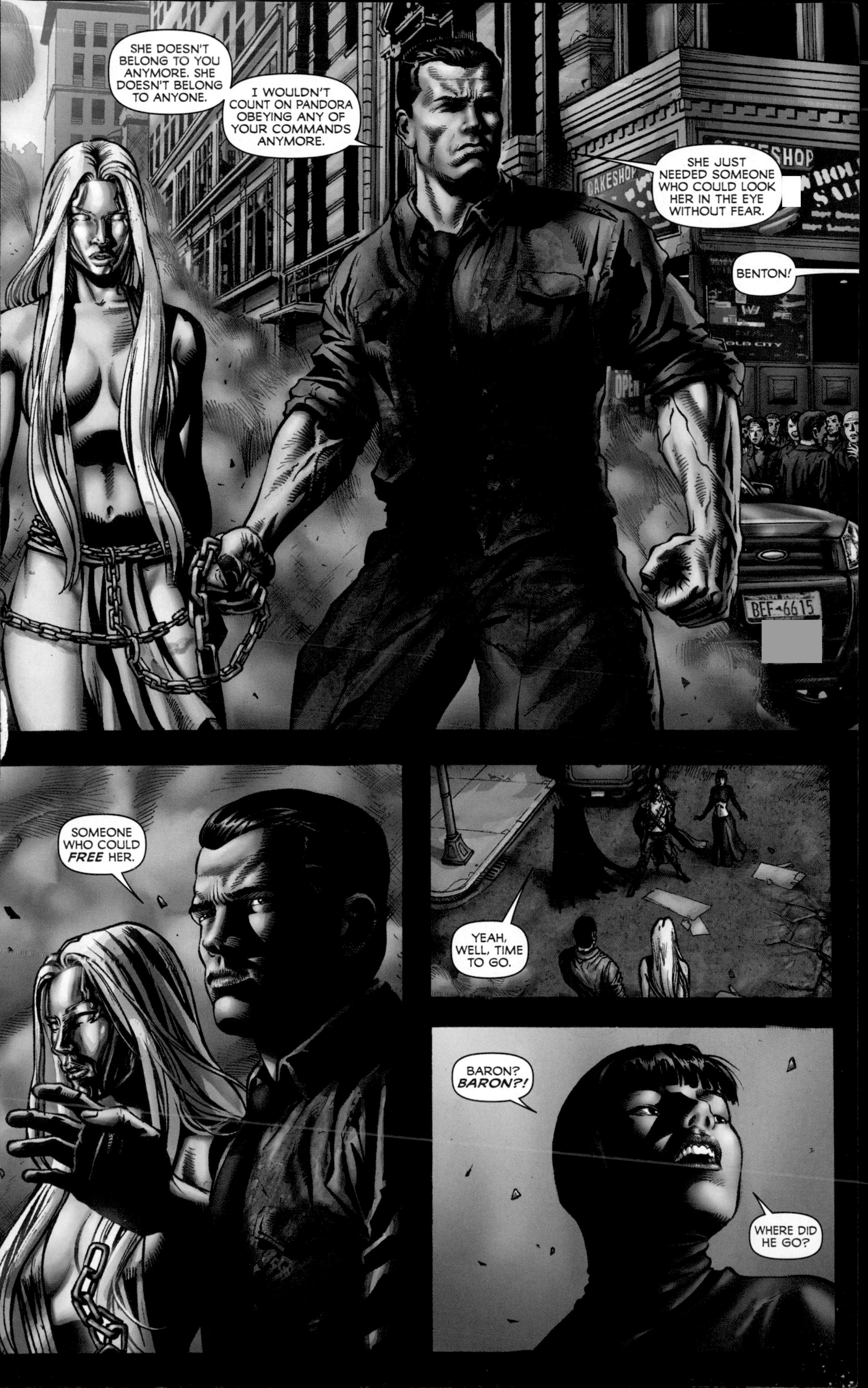
SHE DOESN'T BELONG TO YOU ANYMORE. SHE DOESN'T BELONG TO ANYONE.
I WOULDN'T COUNT ON PANDORA OBEYING ANY OF YOUR COMMANDS ANYMORE.
SHE JUST NEEDED SOMEONE WHO COULD LOOK HER IN THE EYE WITHOUT FEAR.
BENTON!
SOMEONE WHO COULD *FREE* HER.
YEAH, WELL, TIME TO GO.
BARON? ***BARON?!***
WHERE DID HE GO?

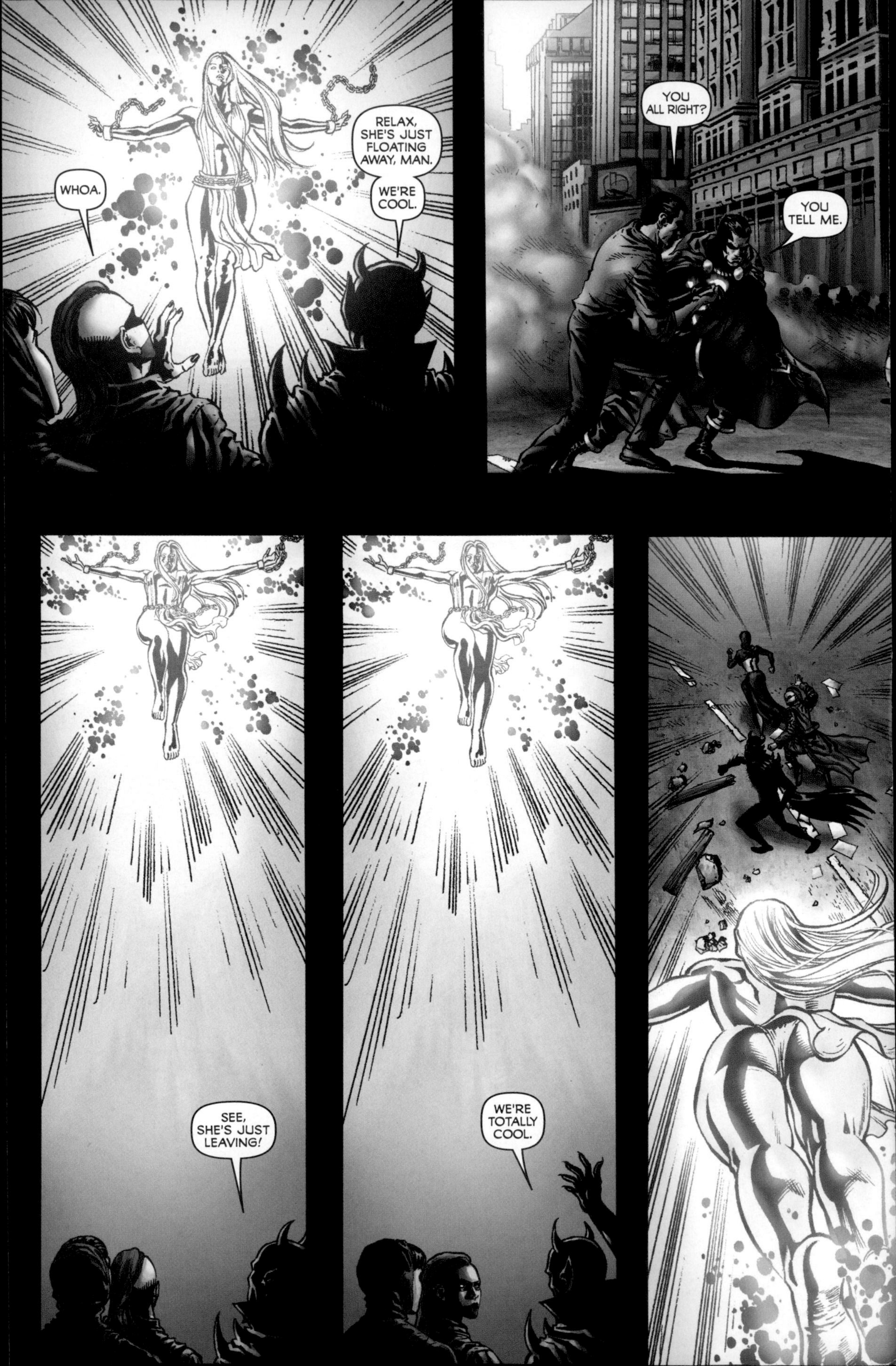
WHOA.
RELAX, SHE'S JUST FLOATING AWAY, MAN.
WE'RE COOL.
YOU ALL RIGHT?
YOU TELL ME.
SEE, SHE'S JUST LEAVING!
WE'RE TOTALLY COOL.

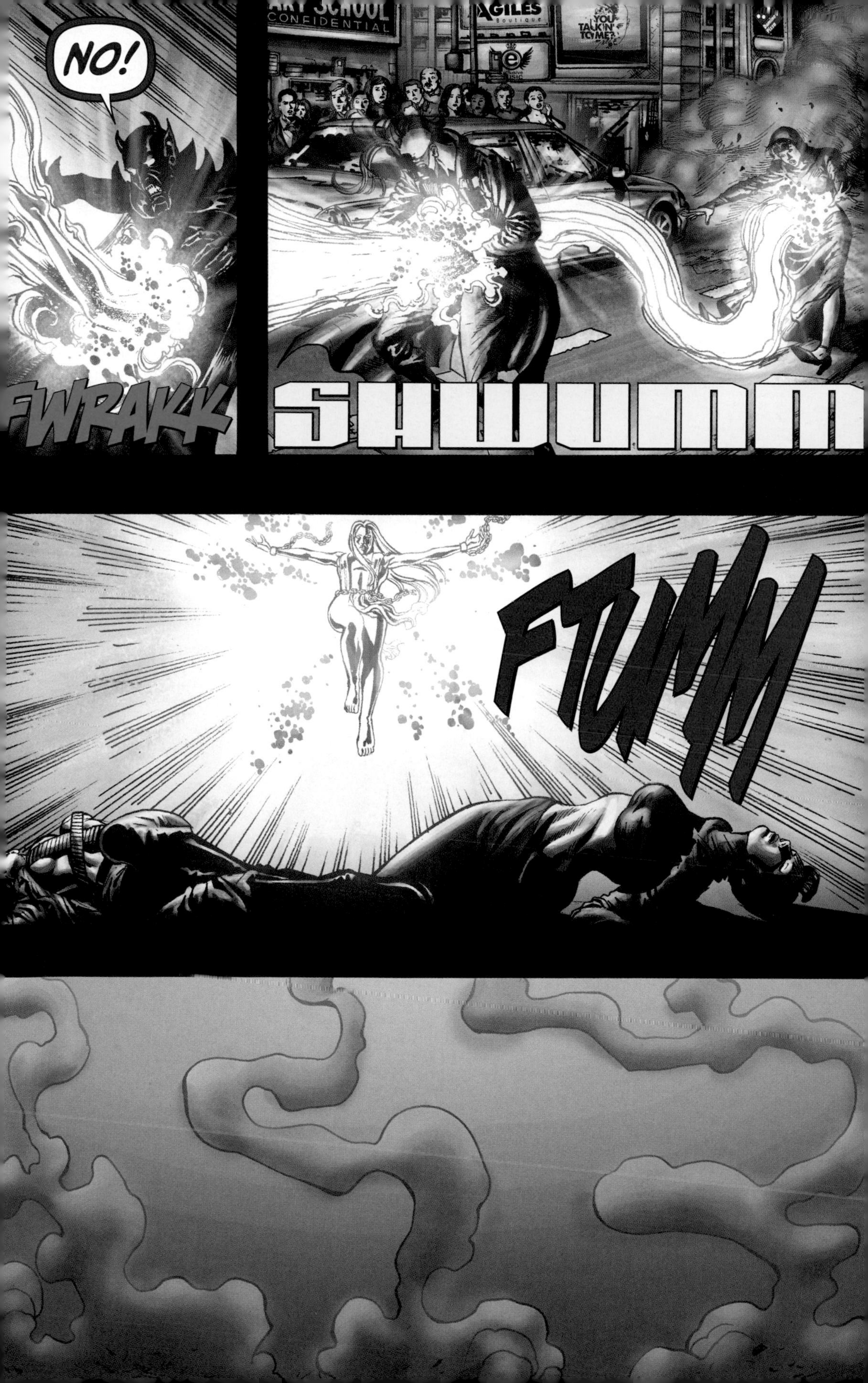
NO!
FWRAKK
ART SCHOOL
CONFIDENTIAL
AGILES
Boutique
YOU TALKIN' TO ME?
SHWUMM
FTUMM

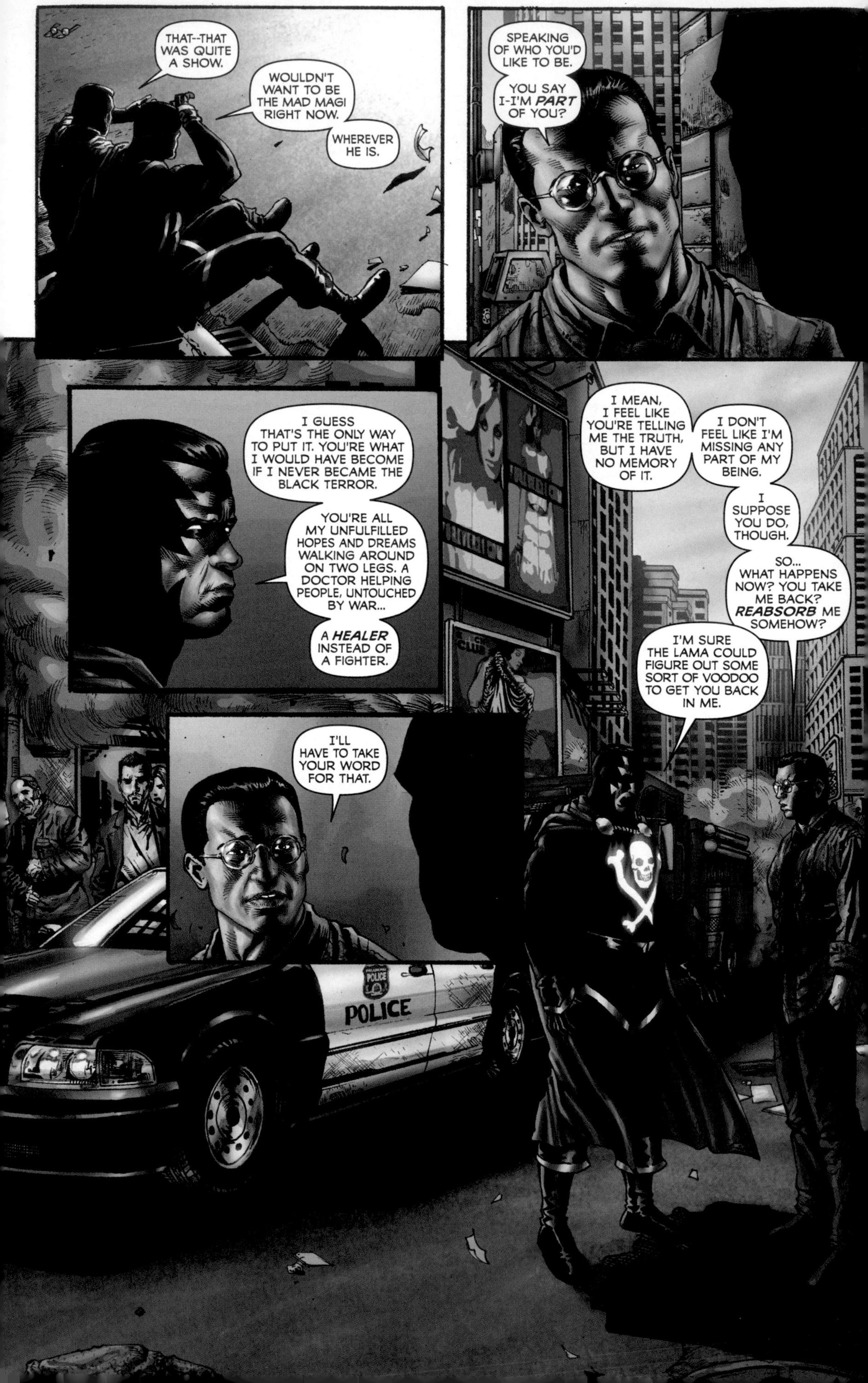
THAT--THAT WAS QUITE A SHOW.
WOULDN'T WANT TO BE THE MAD MAGI RIGHT NOW.
WHEREVER HE IS.
SPEAKING OF WHO YOU'D LIKE TO BE.
YOU SAY I-I'M PART OF YOU?
I GUESS THAT'S THE ONLY WAY TO PUT IT. YOU'RE WHAT I WOULD HAVE BECOME IF I NEVER BECAME THE BLACK TERROR.
YOU'RE ALL MY UNFULFILLED HOPES AND DREAMS WALKING AROUND ON TWO LEGS. A DOCTOR HELPING PEOPLE, UNTOUCHED BY WAR...
A HEALER INSTEAD OF A FIGHTER.
I MEAN, I FEEL LIKE YOU'RE TELLING ME THE TRUTH, BUT I HAVE NO MEMORY OF IT.
I DON'T FEEL LIKE I'M MISSING ANY PART OF MY BEING.
I SUPPOSE YOU DO, THOUGH.
SO... WHAT HAPPENS NOW? YOU TAKE ME BACK? REABSORB ME SOMEHOW?
I'M SURE THE LAMA COULD FIGURE OUT SOME SORT OF VOODOO TO GET YOU BACK IN ME.
I'LL HAVE TO TAKE YOUR WORD FOR THAT.
POLICE

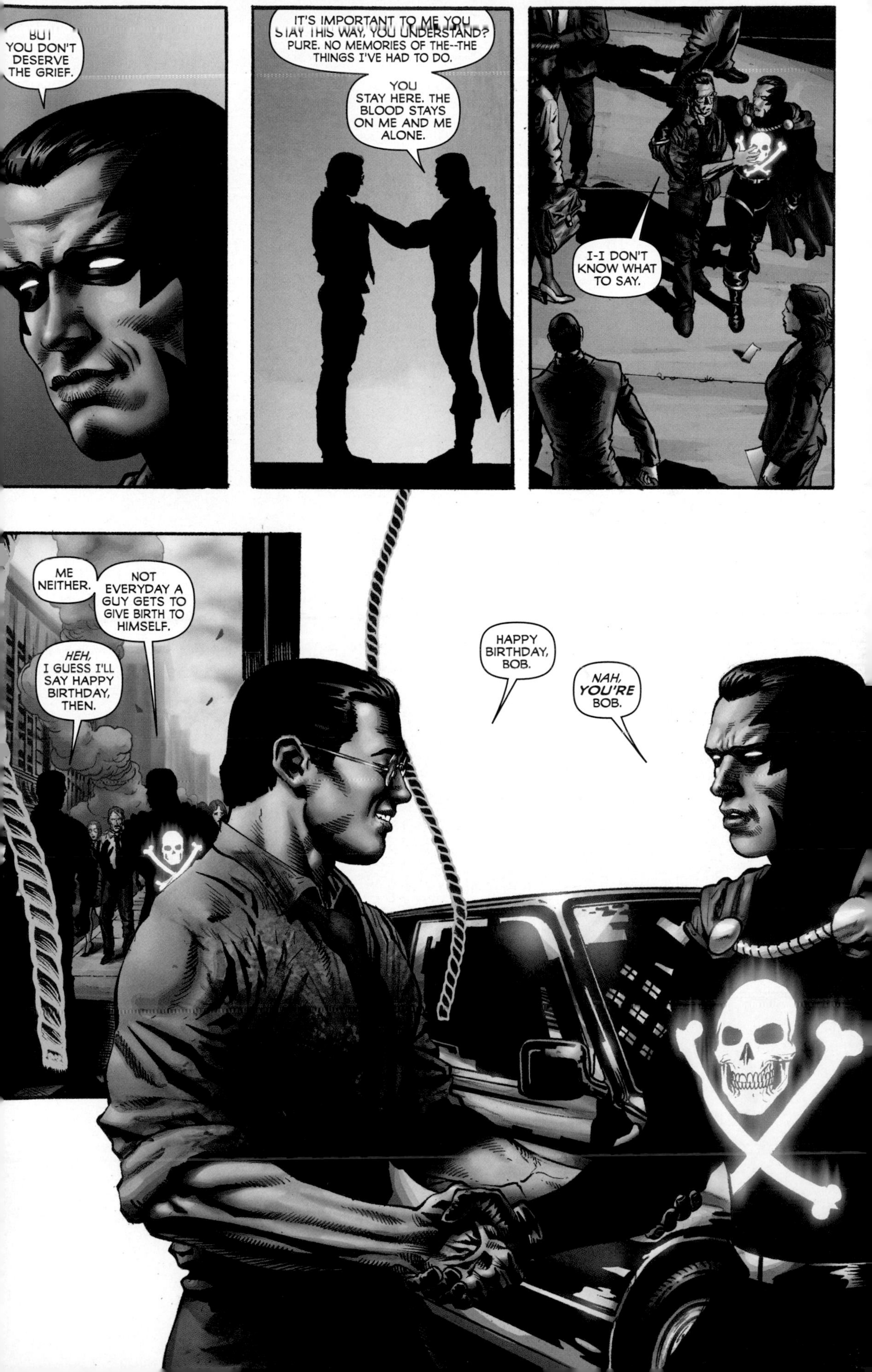
BUT YOU DON'T DESERVE THE GRIEF.
IT'S IMPORTANT TO ME YOU STAY THIS WAY, YOU UNDERSTAND? PURE. NO MEMORIES OF THE--THE THINGS I'VE HAD TO DO.
YOU STAY HERE. THE BLOOD STAYS ON ME AND ME ALONE.
I-I DON'T KNOW WHAT TO SAY.
ME NEITHER.
NOT EVERYDAY A GUY GETS TO GIVE BIRTH TO HIMSELF.
HEH, I GUESS I'LL SAY HAPPY BIRTHDAY, THEN.
HAPPY BIRTHDAY, BOB.
NAH, YOU'RE BOB.

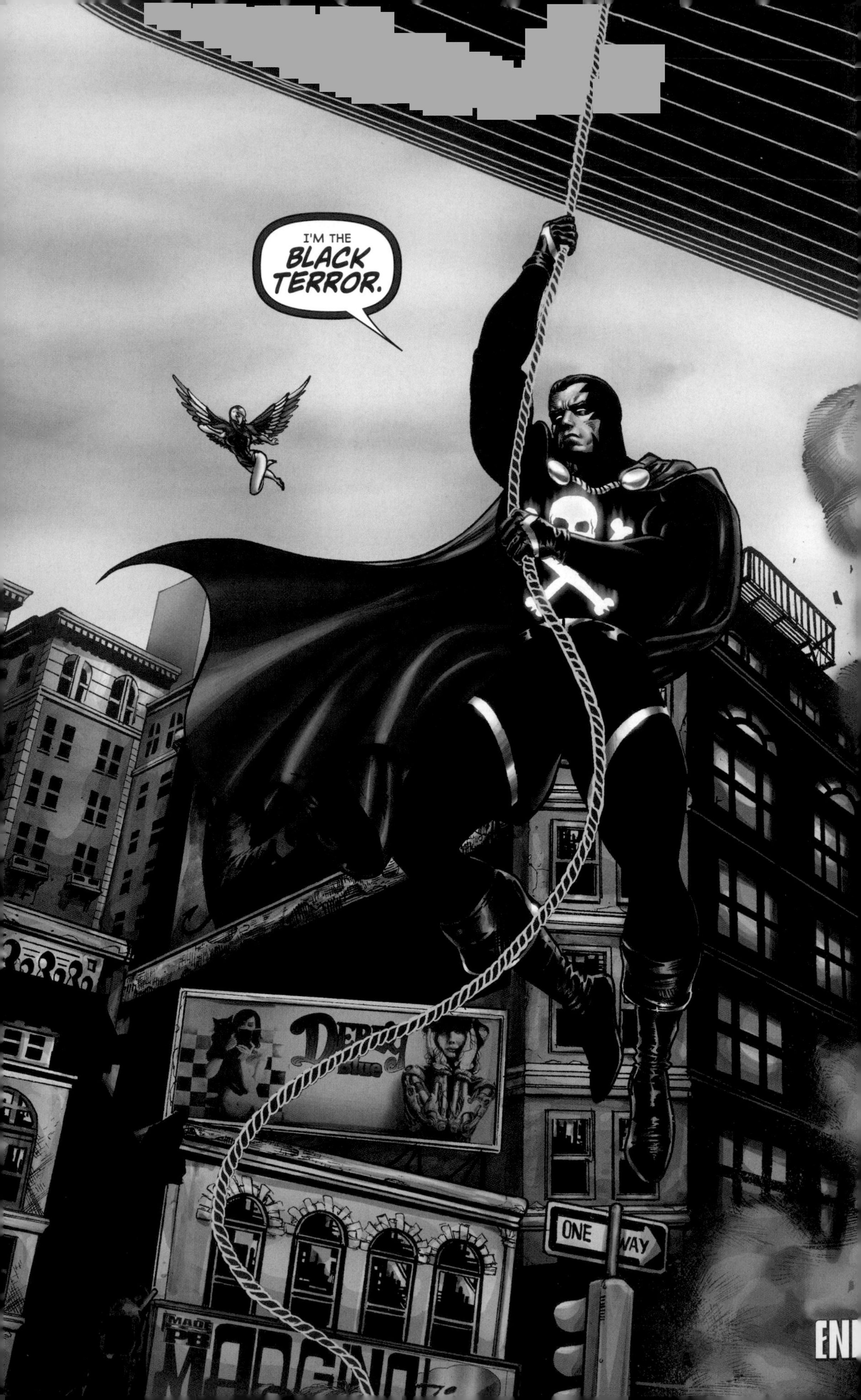
I'M THE BLACK TERROR.
ONE WAY

Cover Gallery

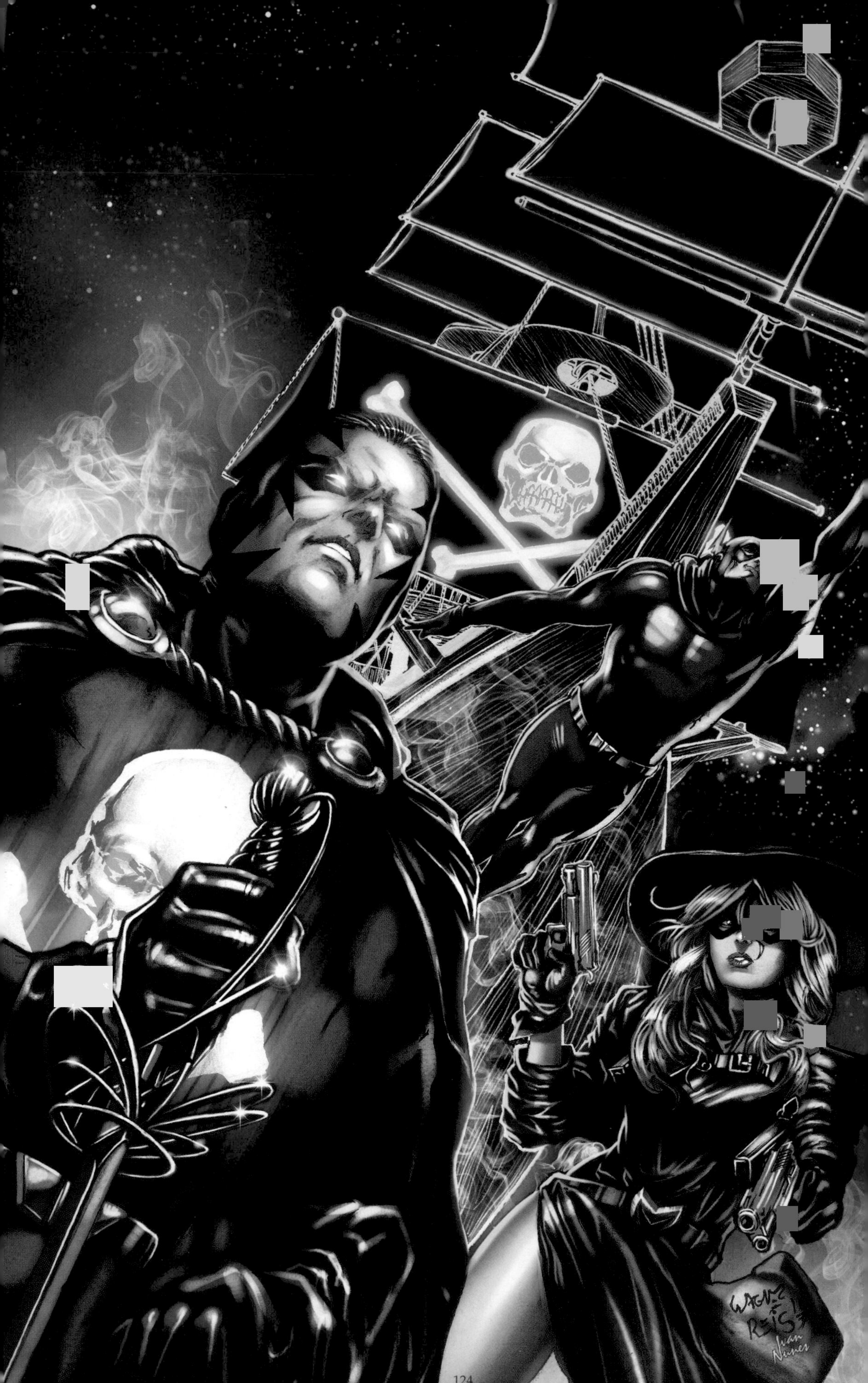

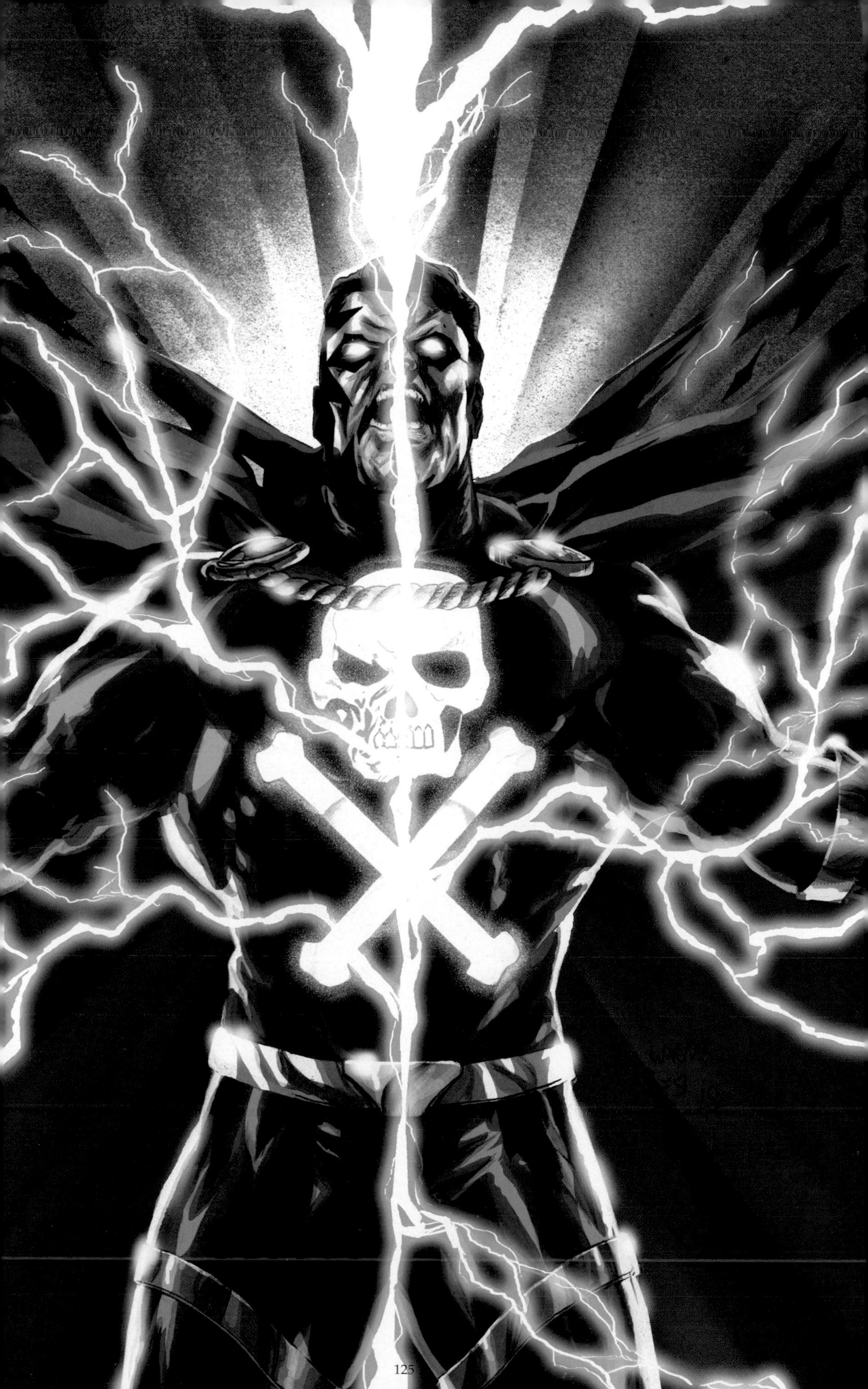

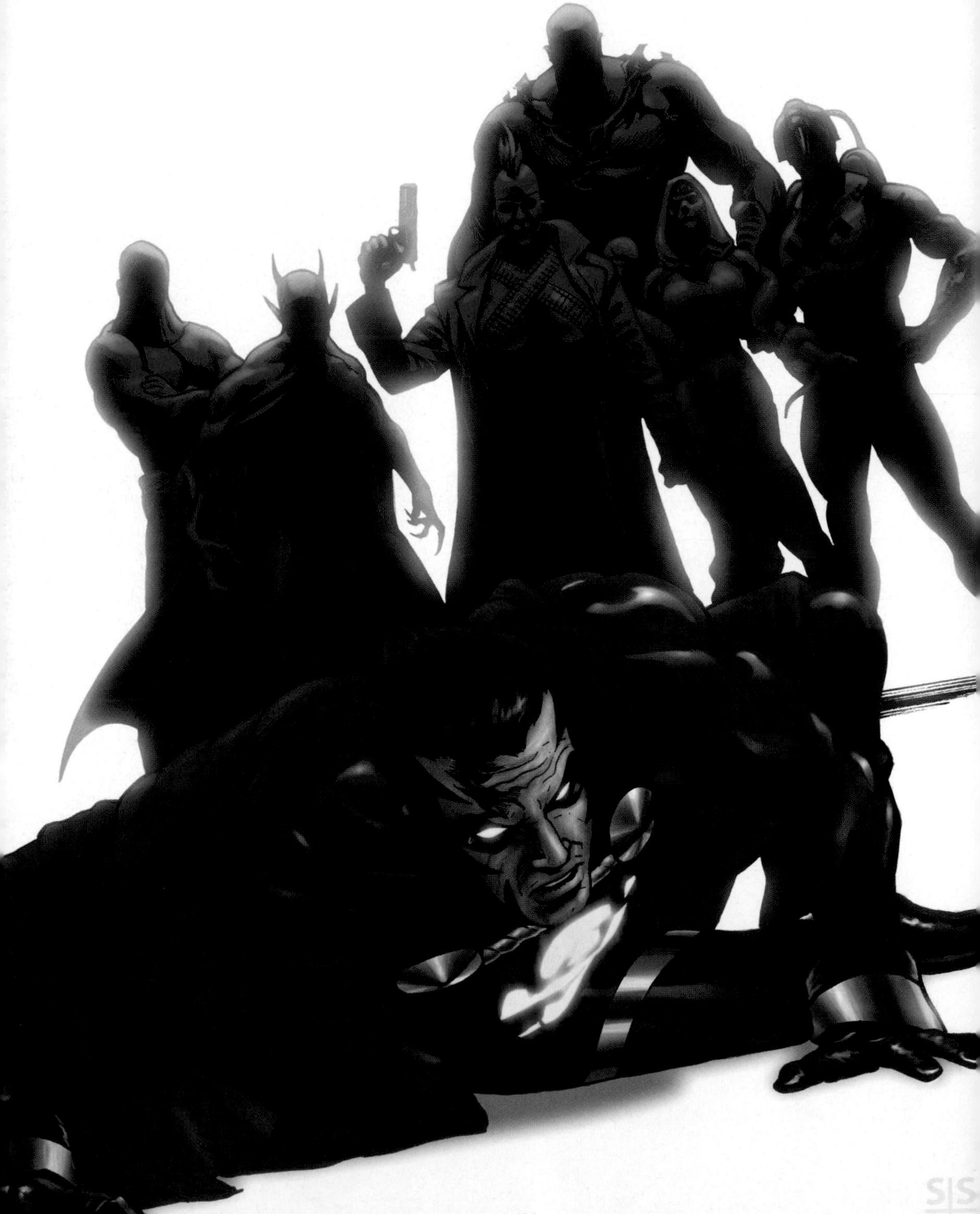

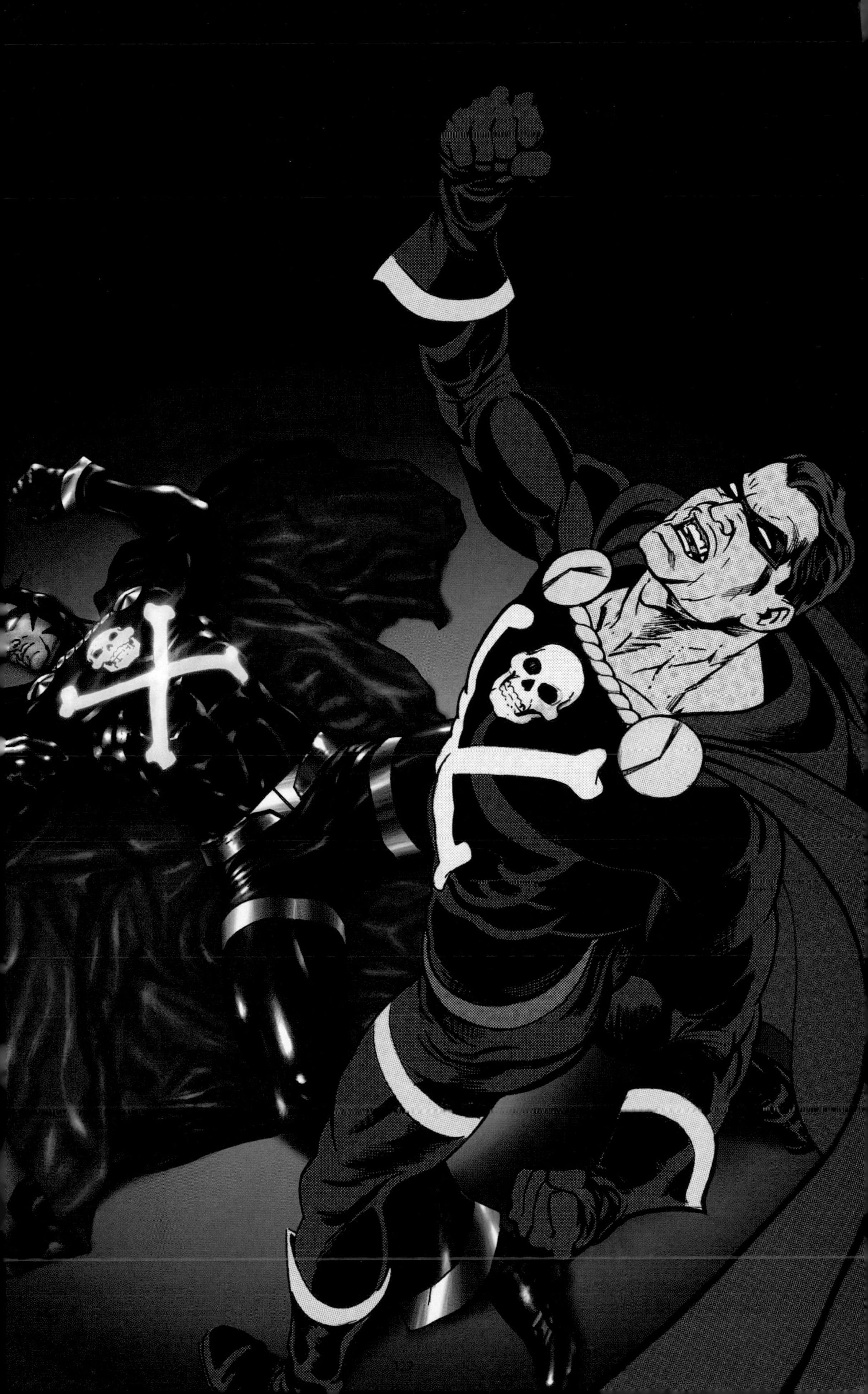

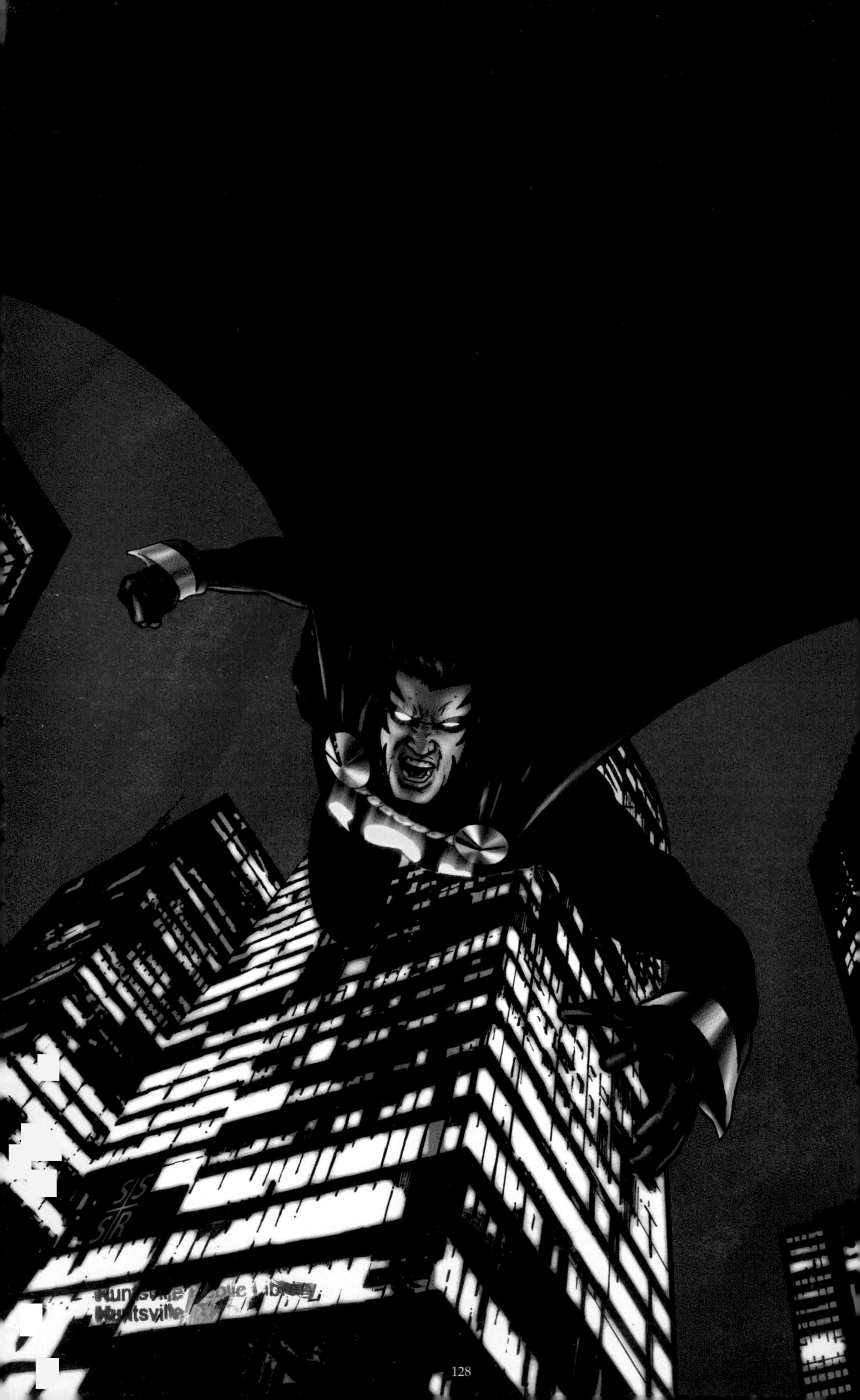